何か言ってみる

暮らしの
英単語
9000

中村秀和
Hidekazu Nakamura

語研

➤「学び心」と「遊び心」を大切に学習しましょう！——

「学び心」とは，知識を深め，新しい言葉に触れる喜びを指します。本書は，日常の生活シーンに密着した常識語からビジネスシーンの基本語彙まで，総項目数9300強の単語・フレーズを，場面別・トピック別に分類した生活密着型単語集です。「学び心」が一層育まれるように，必要に応じて，見出し語の関連語やコロケーション（よく一緒に使われる単語の組み合わせ），用例も楽しみながら学べるよう配慮しました。また，和製語は英語ではどう言うかについてもサポートしました。さらに，発音に注意を要する単語には発音記号を添え，正確な発音をチェックできるようにしました。

「遊び心」とは，楽しみながら学ぶことの重要性を表しています。本書に付属の赤シートを利用して，「英語で何という？」「スペルは？」という発想をベースに"クイズ感覚で楽しみながら英語で言ってみたり，スペルを確認したりできる"ようにしました。赤シートや文字色の工夫が，単語の視覚的な覚えやすさを引き立て，学ぶことが「遊び心」に満ちた冒険に変わることでしょう。

本書があなたの英語学習のパートナーとなり，言葉の奥深さや楽しさを共有できれば幸いです。「学び心」と「遊び心」を大切に，一緒に素敵な英語の旅を楽しみましょう！　そして，新しい言葉の発見やコミュニケーションの喜びを共有しながら，あなたの英語スキルが「学び心」と「遊び心」に満ちたものになることを願っています。

末筆となりましたが，本書の編集担当者である（株）語研の島袋一郎さんに，心より感謝申し上げます。彼の尽力，そしてプロフェッショナリズムと情熱により読者の皆様の手に本書をお届けすることができました。

中村秀和

目 次

👫 1. 人について知る

1. 人体

2. 外見・容姿

3. 感情・情緒

4. 思考・判断・感覚

5. 性格・人柄

6. 一日の行動

7. 人間関係・ライフイベント

🍽 2. 食べる・飲む

1. 飲食のキーワード & フレーズ

2. 食材 & 食料品

3. 料理

14. 学ぶ

15. 仕事をする

【装丁】

神田昇和 (Norikazu KANDA)

1.

人について知る

1. 人体

★からだ

(頭・手・足を含めた) からだ, 肉体, 身体	body [bádi] ＊ build up one's body (からだを鍛える)
上半身	upper body
下半身	lower body
(頭・手・足以外の) 胴体	body ／ trunk [tráŋk]
感覚器官	sense organ ／ sensory organ
頭	head [héd] ＊ turn one's head (振り向く), turn one's head away (顔を背ける), nod one's head (うなずく), shake one's head (首を横に振る), bend one's head (うつむく), incline one's head (首をかしげる), scratch one's head (頭をかく)
後頭部	the back (part) of the head
脳	brain [bréin] ＊ right brain (右脳), clear brain (明晰な頭脳), use one's brain (頭を使う)
大脳	large brain ／ cerebrum [sərí:brəm] ＊ cerebral cortex (大脳皮質), frontal lobe (前頭葉), temporal lobe (側頭葉), parietal lobe (頭頂葉), occipital lobe (後頭葉), gray matter (灰白質), white matter (白質), thalamus (視床), hypothalamus (視床下部), pituitary gland (下垂体)
小脳	cerebellum [sèrəbéləm]

脳幹	brain stem
間脳	interbrain [íntərbrèin]
髪	hair [héər] ＊ arrange [do/dress] one's hair (髪を整える), brush [set] one's hair (髪をブラッシング [セット] する), have [get] one's hair cut short (髪を切って短くしてもらう)
つむじ	hair whorl [hwɔ́:l]
顔, 顔面	face [féis] ＊ round [oval] face (丸い [面長の] 顔), shave off someone's facial hair (顔の毛を剃る)
額 (ひたい)	forehead
眉間 (みけん)	the middle of the forehead ／ between the eyebrows
こめかみ	temple〈通例, 複数形〉
頬 (ほお)	cheek [ʧí:k] ＊ kiss someone's cheek (〜の頬にキスする)
頬骨	cheekbone
あご	jaw [ʤɔ́:]
あご先	chin [ʧín]
首	neck [nék] ＊ bend one's neck (首を曲げる), get a stiff neck (肩 [首] がこる)
襟首, うなじ	the nape of the neck
肩	shoulder [ʃóuldər] ＊ stiff shoulders (肩こり), frozen shoulder (五十肩), massage someone's shoulders (〜の肩をもむ)

目	eye [ái]
	＊ open [shut] *one's* eyes（目を開く［閉じる］），farsightedness（遠視，老眼），nearsightedness（近視），My eyes are aging.（もう老眼だよ）
眼球	eyeball
（眼球の）虹彩（こうさい）	iris [áiəris]
瞳，瞳孔	pupil [pjú:pl]
角膜	cornea [kɔ́:rniə]
網膜	retina [rétənə]
	＊ retinitis（網膜炎），detached retina（網膜剥離）
結膜	conjunctiva [kùndʒʌŋktáivə]
	＊ conjunctivitis [kəndʒàŋktəváitis]（結膜炎）／ pinkeye（流行性結膜炎）
水晶体	a (crystalline) lens
硝子体（しょうしたい）	vitreous [vítriəs] body
涙腺（るいせん）	lachrymal gland
目尻	the outer corner of the eye
	＊ crow's feet（目尻のしわ〔カラスの足跡〕）
まゆ毛	eyebrow [áibràu]
	＊ knit *one's* (eye) brows（= frown〔まゆをひそめる〕）
まつ毛	eyelash
まぶた	eyelid
涙	tear [tíər]
	＊ wipe [dry] *one's* tears（涙を拭く），be easily moved to tears（涙もろい）
目やに	gum [gʌ́m] ／ sleep《口》
	＊ rub sleep out of *one's* eyes（目をこすって目やにをとる）

耳	ear
	＊ clean *one's* ear（耳掃除をする），earpick（耳かき）
耳たぶ	earlobe [íərlòub]
耳の穴	earhole
鼓膜	eardrum ／ tympanic membrane
	＊ have a raptured eardrum（鼓膜が破れる）
三半規管	semicircular canals
耳あか	earwax [íərwæ̀ks]
	＊ remove earwax（耳あかをとる）

鼻	nose [nóuz]
	＊ high-bridged [flat] nose（高い［低い］鼻），pick *one's* nose（鼻の穴をほじる），pinch [hold] *one's* nose（鼻をつまむ）
鼻水	snivel [snívl] ／ snot [snát]《口》
	＊「鼻水が出てるよ」は Your nose is running.《直接的》／ You've got a runny nose.《婉曲的》
鼻水が出る	have a runny nose
鼻筋	the ridge of the nose
鼻毛	nose hair
	＊ pull out *one's* nose hairs（鼻毛を抜く），「鼻毛が出てるよ」は You've got a nose hair sticking out.《直接的》／ You've got something in your nose.《婉曲的》
鼻の穴	nostril [nástrl]
鼻くそ	dried mucus [mjú:kəs] ／ booger [bú:gər]《米》／ bogey [bóugi]《英》
	＊ dig [pick] *one's* nose（鼻をほじる）

鼻腔	nasal cavity [néizl kǽvəti]
いびき（をかく）	snore [snɔ́ːr]

口	mouth [máuθ] ＊rinse one's mouth（口をすすぐ）。keep one's mouth open [closed]（口を開けた［閉じた］ままにしておく），oral（口の），oral cavity（口腔）
唇	lips ＊bite one's lip（唇をかむ），compress one's lips（唇をぎゅっと結ぶ），lip-sync（くちパク）
舌	tongue [tʌ́ŋ] ＊the tip of one's tongue（舌先），put [stick] out one's tongue（舌を出す），bite one's tongue（舌をかむ），tongue twister（早口言葉）
口臭	bad [foul] breath ＊have bad [foul] breath（口臭がする，息が臭い）

歯	teeth [tíːθ] ＊tooth の複数形。gnash [grind] one's teeth（歯ぎしりする）
歯に挟まる	get stuck in the teeth
乳歯	milk [baby] tooth / deciduous tooth
永久歯	permanent tooth
親知らず	wisdom tooth ＊pull out one's wisdom tooth（親知らずを抜く）
前歯	front tooth
出っ歯	protruding tooth / buck tooth

奥歯	back tooth / molar
《重なっている》八重歯	double tooth
《斜めに出た》八重歯	oblique [əblíːk] tooth
犬歯	cuspid [kʌ́spid] / canine [kéinain] tooth
義歯	false [fɔ́ːls] tooth
入れ歯	denture [dénʧər]
歯冠	crown [kráun]
歯茎	gum [gʌ́m] 《通例，複数形 -s [gʌ́mz]》
プラーク，歯垢（しこう）	plaque [plǽk]
虫歯	tooth decay [- dikèi] / bad tooth ＊cavity（虫歯の穴），have two cavities（虫歯が２本ある），have one's cavity filled（虫歯を詰めてもらう），I had my bad tooth pulled out.（虫歯を抜いてもらいました），prevent tooth decay（虫歯を防ぐ）
歯ぎしり	teeth grinding [tíːθ gràindiŋ] ＊grind one's teeth（歯ぎしりする）

のど	throat [θróut]
のどぼとけ	Adam's apple
唾液，つば	saliva [səláivə] / spittle [spítl]
つばを吐く	spit
よだれ（をたらす）	drool [drúːl]

痰 (たん)	phlegm [flém] ／ sputum [spú:təm] ＊get phlegm in one's throat（痰がのどにからむ）, spit out phlegm（痰を吐く）
扁桃腺	tonsils [tánslz]
声帯	the vocal cords
声	voice
咽頭	pharynx [færiŋks]
喉頭	larynx [læriŋks]
口蓋垂，のどひこ	uvula [jú:vjələ]
息	breath [bréθ] ／ breathing [brí:ðiŋ] ＊breath は呼吸する空気息, 呼気, breathing は呼吸（動作として）を指す。
あくび（をする）	yawn [jɔ́:n] ＊yawn in a meeting（会議であくびをする）, with a yawn（あくびしながら）
脇の下	armpit ／ pit 〈米〉 ＊shave [pluck] one's armpits（脇の下の毛を剃る [抜く]）
脇毛	armpit hair ／ underarm hair
ワキガ，腋臭 (えきしゅう)	body odor 〈米〉 ／ body odour 〈英〉
腕	arm ＊肩から手首まで。 forearm（ひじから手首まで）, upper arm（二の腕）, cross one's arms（腕を組む）, stretch [bend] one's arms（両腕を伸ばす [曲げる]）, biceps brachii [báiseps bráki]（上腕二頭筋）, triceps brachii（上腕三頭筋）

肘	elbow [élbou] ＊bend an [one's ／ the] elbow（ひじを曲げる）, put one's elbows on the table（テーブルに両肘をつく）
手	hand ＊hold one's hand（～の手を握る）, clap one's hands（拍手する）, wash one's hands（手を洗う，お手洗いに行く）, wipe one's hands on a towel（タオルで両手を拭く）, dominant hand（利き手）
手首	wrist [ríst]
右利き（の人）	right-handed person ／ righty ＊Are you right- or left-handed?（利き手はどちらですか）
左利き（の人）	left-handed person ／ lefty ／ southpaw 〈米〉
手の甲	the back of the hand
手のひら	palm [pá:m] ＊put [place] one's palms together（手のひらを合わせる）, face one's palms inward [outward]（手のひらを内側 [外側] に向ける）
手相	the lines in one's palm ＊have one's palm read（手相を見てもらう）, palmistry [palm reading]（手相占い）, head line（頭脳線）, heart line（感情線）, fate line（運命線）, life line（生命線）
握りこぶし	clenched fist ＊clench one's fist（拳を握る）
指	finger ＊sprain[spréin] one's finger（突き指をする）

親指	thumb [θʌ́m]
人差し指	forefinger / index finger
中指	middle finger
薬指	ring finger
小指	little finger / pinkie 《米》
指関節	knuckle [nʌ́kl]
（手の）爪	fingernail
胸	chest ＊pectoralis major [pèktərǽləs méidʒər]（大胸筋）
乳房	breast [brést]
乳首	nipple [nípl]
みぞおち	the pit of the stomach / the solar plexus [pléksəs]
背中	back
腹	abdomen [ǽbdəmən] / belly [béli] ＊lie on one's belly（腹ばいになる）, spare tire（三段腹）, potbelly（太鼓腹〔の人〕）, beer belly [gut]（ビール腹）
脇腹, 横腹	side / flank ＊I have a pain in my right side.（右の脇腹が痛いんです）
へそ	navel [néivl] / bellybutton ＊navel string [cord]（へその緒）, protruding navel（出べそ）
腰（のくびれ）	waist [wéist] ＊胴のくびれた部分。have a slim [narrow] waist（腰が細い）, fit at the waist（〔主語の〕ウエストはちょうどいい）

尻	hips ＊腰の左右に張り出した部分。
臀部, 尻	bottom [bátəm] / buttocks [bátəks] / butt 《米, くだけて》 ＊尻の肉の方全部を指す。tight [loose] buttocks（引き締まった［たるんだ］お尻）
股	crotch [krátʃ]
脚	leg [lég] ＊get [have] (a) cramp in one's leg（脚の筋肉がつる）, Leg cramp!（脚がつってる！）
太腿 (ふともも)	thigh [θái]
ふくらはぎ	calf [kǽf] ＊複数形は calves。
ひざ	knee [níː] / lap [lǽp] ＊knee は「ひざの関節, ひざ小僧」を指し, lap はイスに腰掛けたときの腰からひざまでを指す。on one's hands and knees（四つんばいで）, sit on a person's lap（～の膝の上に座る）
半月板	meniscus [mənískəs] ＊meniscus injury（半月板損傷）
むこうずね	shin [ʃín] ＊kick a person in [on] the shin（～〔人〕のむこうずねを蹴る）
足	foot [fút] ＊くるぶしから下の部分。複数形は feet [fíːt]。
足首	ankle [ǽŋkl] ＊sprain [twist] one's ankle（足首をくじく）
かかと	heel [híːl] ＊sit on one's heels（正座をする）

土ふまず	arch [á:rtʃ] ＊ be flat-footed（扁平足である）
足の裏	sole [sóul]
足の甲	instep [ínstèp]
つま先，足の指	toe [tóu] ＊ toe finger とは言わない。
つま先立ちする ／つま先で歩く	tiptoe [típtòu] ＊ on tiptoe（つま先で）
足の親指	big toe
足の第二指	second toe
足の中指	middle toe
足の第四指	fourth toe
足の小指	little toe
足指の爪	toenail

★皮膚・毛

皮膚，肌，皮	skin ＊ You have clear [nice] skin.（肌がきれいね）, wrinkled skin（しわの多い皮膚）
艶のある肌	glowing skin
サメ肌	scaly [skéili] skin
オイリー肌	oily skin
白い肌	fair skin
鳥肌	gooseflesh／goose pimples／goosebumps ＊ I have gooseflesh on my arms.（腕に鳥肌が立っている）
あか〔垢〕，汚れ	dirt [dá:rt]／grime [gráim] ＊ wash oneself clean／wash off the dirt（あかを落とす）
ふけ（症）	dandruff [dǽndrəf] ＊ have dandruff（ふけが出る）

かさぶた	scab [skǽb] ＊ be scabbed（かさぶたができる）, pick one's scab（かさぶたをはがす）
皮膚呼吸	cutaneous respiration [kjuːtéiniəs rèspəréiʃən]
毛	hair ＊ My hair is thinning.／I'm losing my hair.（髪の毛が薄くなってきた）
うぶ毛	downy [dáuni] hair
毛穴	pore [pó:r]

★筋肉・脂肪・ホルモン

筋肉	muscle [mʌ́sl] ＊ develop [build] one's muscles（筋肉を鍛える [付ける]）, firm muscles（引き締まった筋肉）, flabby muscles（たるんだ筋肉）, knead someone's muscles（筋肉をもむ〔knead の発音は [níːd]〕）
心筋	cardiac muscle [káːrdiæk mʌ́sl]
腹筋	abdominal [æbdáminl] muscles ＊ develop one's abdominal muscles（腹筋を鍛える）, do 100 sit-ups（腹筋運動を100回する）
脂肪	fat [fǽt] ＊ burn fat（脂肪を燃焼させる）, body fat（体脂肪）
ぜい肉，（体の）たるみ，脂肪	flab [flǽb] ＊ fight the flab／burn off flab（ぜい肉を落とす）
皮下脂肪	subcutaneous fat
中性脂肪	neutral fat
ホルモン	hormone [hó:rmoun]

男性ホルモン	male hormone
女性ホルモン	female hormone
脳下垂体ホルモン	pituitary [pitʃúːətèri] gland hormone
甲状腺ホルモン	thyroid [θáiroid] gland hormone
副腎ホルモン	adrenal [ədríːnl] hormone
成長ホルモン	growth hormone
性ホルモン	sex hormone

★骨・関節・靱帯(じんたい)

骨	bone [bóun] ＊ have big [small] bones (骨太 [細] である), dislocate a bone (脱臼する)
骸骨, 骨格；やせこけた人 [動物]	skeleton [skélətn]
骨髄	(bone) marrow [mǽrou]
頭蓋骨	skull [skʌ́l]
背骨 (せぼね)	backbone ／ spine [spáin]
鎖骨 (さこつ)	collarbone
肩甲骨 (けんこうこつ)	shoulder blade
胸骨	breastbone
腰骨	hipbone
肋骨 (ろっこつ)	rib
尾骶骨 (びていこつ)	coccyx [kɑ́ksiks]
骨盤	pelvis [pélvis]
軟骨	cartilage [kɑ́ːrtəliʤ]
関節	joint ＊ the hip joints (股関節 (こかんせつ))
靱帯 (じんたい)	ligament [lígəmənt] ＊ strain [tear] a ligament (靱帯を痛める [切る])

★循環器

循環器	circulatory organ [sə́ːrkjələtɔ̀ːri ɔ́ːrgn]
内臓	internal organs ＊ internal organ fat (内臓脂肪)
心臓	heart [hɑ́ːrt]
血	blood [blʌ́d]
血管	blood vessel [blʌ́d vèsl]
動脈	artery [ɑ́ːrtəri]
静脈	vein [véin]
赤血球	red blood corpuscle [kɔ́ːrpəsl]
白血球	white blood corpuscle
血小板	blood platelet
血清 (けっせい)	serum [síərəm]
血漿 (けっしょう)	plasma [plǽzmə]
脾臓 (ひぞう)	spleen [splíːn]
ヘモグロビン	hemoglobin 〈米〉／ haemoglobin 〈英〉
リンパ腺	lymph(atic) gland ＊ lymph node [límf nòud] (リンパ節)

★呼吸器

呼吸器	respiratory organs
肺	lung [lʌ́ŋ] ＊ lung [vital] capacity (肺活量), air cell (肺胞)
気管	wind pipe ／ trachea [tréikiə]
気管支	bronchial [brɑ́ŋkiəl] tube ／ bronchus [brɑ́ŋkəs]

横隔膜	diaphragm [dáiəfræm]
しゃっくり（する）	hiccup [híkʌp] ／ hiccough
くしゃみ（をする [が出る]）	sneeze [sníːz]

★消化器

消化器官	digestive organs
食道	gullet [gʌ́lət] 《米》, esophagus [isáfəɡəs] 《米》／ oesophagus [isáfəɡəs] 《英》
胃	stomach [stʌ́mək] ＊ have a weak stomach（胃が弱い）, stomachache（胃の痛み，腹痛）, have an upset stomach（胃の調子がおかしい）
胃液	gastric juice
粘液	mucus [mjúːkəs]
胃酸	stomach [gastric] acid [ǽsid]
胃壁	stomach [gastric] wall
十二小腸	duodenum [djùːədíːnəm]
げっぷ（が出る）	belch [béltʃ] ＊ stifle a belch（げっぷをおさえる）, feel a burp coming（げっぷが出そうになる）, burp（授乳後のあん坊に）げっぷをさせる）
肝臓	liver ＊ liver transplant（肝臓移植）
すい臓	pancreas [pǽŋkriəs] ＊ insulin [ínsələn]（インシュリン）
胆嚢（たんのう）	gallbladder [ɡɔ́ːlblædər] ＊ bile [báil] ／ gall（胆汁）

腸	intestines [intéstinz] ／ bowels [báuəlz] ＊ large intestine（大腸）, small intestine（小腸）, ileum（回腸）, colon（結腸）, rectum（直腸）
大腸菌	coli [colon] bacillus [kóulai [kóulən] bəsíləs]
善玉菌	good bacteria
悪玉菌	bad bacteria
虫垂（ちゅうすい）	(vermiform) appendix ＊ appendicitis[əpèndəsáitis]（虫垂炎）
肛門	anus [éinəs] ＊ anal [éinl]（肛門の〔付近の〕）
大便，便	stool(s) [stúːl(z)] ／ feces [fíːsiːz] ＊ empty one's bowels ／ have a bowel movement（大便をする）, have blood in one's stool（〔検便の〕便に血が混じっている）
小便（をする），尿	urine [júərin] ＊ I need to go to the bathroom.（トイレに行きたい）, I have a frequent need to urinate., I need to go to the bathroom frequently.（トイレが近いんです）, hold one's water（小便を我慢する）
おしっこ（をする）	pee ／ wee-wee ＊ pee ／ wee-wee ともに幼児語。have [take] a pee（おしっこをする）, go for a pee（おしっこをしに行く）
おもらしをする	wet one's pants ＊ 婉曲表現で，have a toilet accident（（大便・小便を）もらす）もある。
おならをする	pass gas《米，婉曲》／ break wind《英，婉曲》／ cut the cheese《婉曲》／ fart《直接的な表現なので，使い方に注意》

★泌尿器，生殖器

泌尿器	urinary [júərənèri] organs
腎臓	kidney [kídni]
膀胱	urinary bladder
陰毛，アンダーヘア	pubic hair [pjúːbik hὲər]
性器	sexual [sex] organs／genitals
尿道	urethra [juəríːθrə]
前立腺	prostate (gland)
陰茎	penis [píːnis]
亀頭	glans [glǽnz] penis
睾丸（精巣）	testicle [téstikl]
精巣	testis
陰嚢	scrotum [skróutəm]
精液	sperm [spə́ːrm]／semen [síːmən]
膣	vagina [vədʒáinə]
子宮	uterus [júːtərəs]／womb [wúːm]
卵巣	ovary [óuvəri]
卵子	ovum [óuvəm]／egg ＊ovum の複数形は ova。
月経	period [píəriəd]／menstruation ＊have one's period（生理がある），miss one's period（生理がない）
閉経（期），更年期	menopause [ménəpɔ̀ːz]
胎芽《受精後8週未満》	embryo [émbriòu]
胎児《妊娠3か月以後》	fetus [fíːtəs]

★神経・甲状腺，代謝など

神経	nerve [nə́ːrv] ＊motor nerve（運動神経），optic nerve（視神経）。「彼は運動神経が発達している［鈍い］」は，He has quick [slow] reflexes.。
中枢神経系	central nervous system
自律神経系	autonomous nervous system
交感神経	sympathetic nerve
副交換神経	parasympathetic nerve
甲状腺	thyroid gland [θáirɔid glæ̀nd]
分泌物	secretion [sikríːʃən] ＊the secretion of hormones（ホルモンの分泌）
老廃物	wastes [wéists] ＊eliminate wastes（老廃物を排出する）
新陳代謝	metabolism [mətǽbəlìzm] ＊metabolize（〜を新陳代謝する），speed up one's metabolism（新陳代謝を促す）
汗（をかく）	sweat [swét] ＊break a sweat（汗をかく），armpit sweat（ワキ汗），break out in a cold sweat（冷や汗をかく）
発汗	sweating／perspiration [pəːrspəréiʃən]

★外見・容姿

姿《体の格好》，プロポーション	figure [fígjər | fígə] ＊have a good [poor] figure（スタイルがいい[悪い]）
外見《外見，身なり》	appearance [əpíərəns] ＊Don't judge people by their appearance(s).（人を見かけで判断しないで）
体格，体つき	frame／build／physique [fizí:k] ＊have a good [poor] physique（いい[ひ弱な]体格をしている），She has a slender build.（彼女の体つきはほっそりしている）
がっちりした体	a solidly-built body
（筋骨の）たくましい《体格がいい》	brawny [brɔ́:ni]《形》
筋肉質の	muscular [mʌ́skjələr]
がっちりした，骨太の	sturdily [stə́:rdili] built
足腰が強い	have strong legs
男らしい	manly／masculine [mǽskjələn]
《体格が格好よく》ほっそりした，すらりとした	slender [sléndər]《形》 ＊ほめ言葉。
《体格が》ほっそりしてしなやか	slim [slím]《形》 ＊ほめ言葉。

《体格が》ほっそりして弱々しい	slight [sláit]《形》
《病気・栄養不足などで》やせた，ほっそりした	thin [θín]《形》
《骨と皮ばかりみたいに》がりがりにやせた	skinny [skíni]《形》
太った	fat [fǽt]《形》／stout [stáut]《形》 ＊fat は軽蔑的。他人に対しては NG。stout は fat の婉曲表現。
ぽっちゃりした，まんまるした	chubby [tʃʌ́bi]《形》／plump [plʌ́mp]《形》 ＊軽蔑的な意味はなく，特に赤ちゃんや子ども，女性に対して使える。
太りすぎの	overweight [òuvərwéit]《形》
肥満の	obese [oubí:s | ou-] ＊obesity（肥満），lifestyle diseases（生活習慣病）
太鼓腹の	potbellied ＊potbelly（太鼓腹〔の人〕）
中肉中背の	middle-sized／medium-built
体重	weight [wéit] ＊gain [lose] weight（体重が増える[減る]），I weigh 48 kilograms.（体重は 48 キロです）

体格指数	body mass index [bádi mǽs índeks] ＊略して BMI。
メタボリック・シンドローム	metabolic syndrome [mètəbálik síndroum]
身長	height [háit] ＊measure one's height（身長を計る）. I'm 165 centimeters in height. = I'm 165 centimeters tall.（身長は 165 センチです）
背が高い	tall《形》
背が低い，小柄な	short《形》
姿勢がいい	have a good posture ＊反対は，have a bad [poor] posture。
裸の，《体の一部が》むきだしの	naked [néikid]《形》 ＊be naked from the waist up（上半身裸である）
美しい	beautiful《形》
かわいい	pretty《形》
かわいい，きれい，ハンサム，セクシー	cute《形》
グラマーである	have a nice body ／ have a great figure ／ have a sexy body
ハンサムの，目鼻立ちの美しい	handsome《形》
目鼻立ちの美しい，器量がいい	good-looking《形》
《外見から見て》魅力的な	attractive

《主に女性，顔が》容貌の平凡な	homely《形》／ plain《形》 ＊ugly [ʌ́gli] の婉曲表現。
黒髪	black hair ／ dark hair
白髪	gray hair ／ white hair
茶髪	brown hair
長い髪の	long-haired
短い髪の	short-haired
天然パーマ	naturally curly hair
カーリーヘア	curly hair
スキンヘッド	skinhead
寝癖（がついた髪）	bed hair ／ bedhead
髪のない，髪の薄い，はげた	bald [bɔ́:ld]《形》 ＊直接的な語。thin が婉曲的な言い方。go bald（はげる），lose one's hair（はげる《やわらかい言い方》）
髪のはげた部分	bald spot《米》／ bald patch《英》
《髪の密度が》薄い	thin [θín] ＊He has thin hair.（彼は髪の毛が薄い）
《髪の密度が》濃い，《髪が》ふさふさした	thick [θík]
人相，容貌	looks ＊evil-looking man（人相の悪い男）
顔つき，容貌，目鼻だち	features
顔色，肌の色つや	complexion [kəmplékʃən] ＊He has a healthy [sickly] complexion. ／ He looks healthy [pale].（彼は顔色がいい [わるい]）

色白である	have a fair complexion
色黒である	have a tanned complexion
肌がきれいである	have a good complexion
肌が荒れている	have a rough complexion ＊collagen [kάlədʒən]（コラーゲン）
目つき	look ＊a man with a sharp look（目つきの悪い [鋭い] 男）
えくぼ（ができる）	dimple [dímpl] ＊She has dimples on her cheeks.（彼女はほおにえくぼができる）
鷲鼻	hooked nose ／ aquiline [ǽkwilàin] nose
だんご鼻〔鼻先が丸い〕	button(-shaped) nose ／ bulbous [bΛ́lbəs] nose
しし鼻〔短く低く上を向いている〕	snub [snΛ́b] nose ＊have a snub nose（しし鼻をしている）
にきび，吹き出物	pimple [pímpl] ＊pimpled face（にきびだらけの顔），squeeze one's pimples（にきびをつぶす），have pimples all over one's face（顔中にきびだらけである）
そばかす（ができる）	freckles [fréklz] ＊freckled face（そばかすのある顔）
（顔の）しみ	age spot

《皮膚，衣服などの》しわ；～にしわを寄せる	wrinkles [ríŋklz] ／ line ＊tiny lines around the eyes（目の周りの小じわ）
目の下のたるみ	bags under one's eyes
老化	aging [éidʒiŋ]
ほくろ	mole [móul] ＊have a mole on one's face（顔にほくろがある）
《打撲の後の》あざ（ができる），打撲傷を与える，打ち傷をつける；《人，感情を》傷つける	bruise [brúːz] ＊a bruise on the knee（膝のあざ），heal [treat] a bruise（打ち身を治す [治療する]）
（切り傷やけどなどの）傷跡	scar [skάːr] ＊have a scar on one's arm（腕に傷跡がある）

3. 感情・情緒

★感情・情緒

感情，情緒	emotion [imóuʃən] ＊ betray one's emotions（感情を外に出す），control one's emotions（感情を抑える）	態度	attitude [ǽtitʃùːd] ＊ take [have] an attitude of arrogance（ごう慢な態度をとる）
感情，気持ち	feelings ＊ control one's feelings（気持ちを抑える）	《感情を》害する；《人の》感情を害する，気分をこわす	hurt [hə́ːrt] ＊ I didn't mean to hurt her feelings.（彼女の感情を傷つけるつもりはなかった）
心情，気持ち；考え，意見	sentiment ＊ show [express] a sentiment（気持ちを表す）	《声を出して》笑う	laugh [lǽf] ＊ burst out laughing（爆笑する），have a good laugh（大笑いする），laugh loudly（大声で笑う）
感じ，気持ち，気分	sensation ＊ pleasant sensation（心地よい感じ），strange sensation（奇妙な気分）	《声を立てないで》笑う，微笑する	smile ＊ smile at（〜にほほ笑みかける）／ Everybody, let's have some smiles!（《集合写真を撮るとき》みんな，笑って！）
心の，精神の	mental ＊ mental health（心の健康），mentality（精神力，知性）	《歯を見せ，声を立てずに》にっこり笑う；《軽蔑，悪意などを感じて》にやりと笑う	grin [grín] ＊ with a big grin on one's face（満面の笑みを浮かべながら）
(その時の)気分，機嫌，雰囲気	mood ＊ in a good [bad] mood（上機嫌 [不機嫌] で）		
(一時的な)気分，機嫌；(永続的な)気質，気性	temper ＊ be in a good [bad] temper（機嫌がいい [悪い]）	笑う門には福来たる	Laugh and grow fat.
敏感な，繊細な，気を配る，(〜に)神経質な，(〜を)すぐ気に病む	sensitive ＊ sensitive heart（感じやすい心）	うれしい，幸せな，満足な	happy ＊ be happy about [with]（〜を喜んでいる，満足している）
(事件，影響，刺激などへの)反応，反発	reaction ＊ What was her reaction?（彼女の反応はどうだった？），hide one's reaction（反応 [気持ち] を隠す）	うれしい；(〜を)うれしく思う《at, of, about, for ..., that 節, to do》	glad ＊ I'm very glad to see you.（お目にかかれて本当にうれしいです）

（～に）満足した《with, at, by ..., to do》	satisfied [sǽtisfàid] ＊be satisfied with（～に満足している）	腹を立てた，怒った	angry [ǽŋgri] ＊get angry about [at/over]（～に腹を立てる）
喜び，（～する）楽しみ，快楽	pleasure [pléʒər] ＊take great pleasure in（～に大きな喜びを感じる）	怒った，狂った	mad ＊go mad（頭にくる，激怒する），drive a person mad（～を怒らせる）
大喜びしている	overjoyed ＊be overjoyed at [with]（～に大喜びしている）	腹立たしい，いらいらさせる	offensive [əfénsiv] ＊an offensive remark（人の気にさわる発言［言葉］）
最高の気分で	in seventh heaven ＊I'm in seventh heaven.（最高の気分だ）	怒り狂っている	furious [fjúəriəs] ＊be furious at（～に激怒している）
楽しみ，おもしろみ	fun [fʌ́n] ＊Have fun!（楽しんで！）	大声で叫ぶ，怒鳴る	shout [ʃáut]
悲しい，悲しんでいる；かわいそうな；残念な	sad [sǽd] ＊make a person sad（～を悲しませる），a sad look（悲しそうな表情）	わめく，怒鳴る	yell [jél] ＊Don't yell [shout/roar] at me!（怒鳴らないで！）
悲しむ，悲しくなる	feel sad	怒って怒鳴る，怒鳴る	roar [rɔ́ːr] with anger
《通例，涙を流しながら》泣く，叫び声をあげる，叫ぶ	cry	愛する，恋する，（物事が）大好きである；愛，恋愛，愛情	love ＊love at first sight（ひと目ぼれ），unrequited love（片思い），love triangle（三角関係）
うれし泣きする	cry for [with] joy	失恋する	get a broken heart ／ get one's heart broken ＊lost love（失恋），He has been unlucky in love.（彼は失恋しました）
痛くて泣く	cry with [in] pain		
涙を流す；《悲しみで静かに涙を流して》泣く	weep [wíːp] ＊weep one's eyes out（目を泣きはらす），weep oneself out（心ゆくまで泣く）		
涙を流す	shed tears	好む；好きなこと	like
すすり泣く	sob [sáb] ＊sob quietly（静かにすすり泣く）	いちばん好きな（もの）	favorite [féivərət] ＊an all-time favorite（今までで一番のお気に入り）
泣きじゃくる，泣きながら言う	blubber [blʌ́bər]		

感謝（する）	thank [θǽŋk] ＊Thanks a lot.（どうもありがとう），thank *a person* for（〜に…を感謝する）
感謝して，ありがたく思って	grateful [gréitfl] ＊*be* grateful for（〜をありがたいと思う）
感動［感激］させる；触れる	touch ＊*be* greatly touched by [with]（〜にとても感動する），You really touched my heart.（あなたからたくさんの感動をもらいました）
興奮した，夢中になった	excited ＊get excited at [about]（〜に興奮する）
すばらしい，とてもよい	great ＊That's great!（すごい［よかった／すばらしい］！）
見事な，すばらしい	marvelous [mɑ́ːrvələs] ＊That's really marvelous!（本当にすばらしい！）
とてもすばらしい，すてきな，すごい	fantastic
（〜に）驚いた，びっくりした	surprised ＊*be* surprised at（〜に驚く），I wouldn't be surprised at all.（全然驚かないよ／当り前のことだ）
（〜に）驚いた，びっくりした	amazed ＊*be* amazed at（〜に驚く），I'm amazed!（ビックリ〜！）
みじめな，ひどく不幸な	miserable [mízərəbl] ＊I feel so miserable.（自分が情けない）

かわいそうな，痛ましい，ふびんな	pitiful ＊pitiful sight（痛ましい光景）
哀れみ，同情；残念なこと	pity ＊feel pity for 〜（〜をふびんに思う），That's a pity.（それは残念でしたね）
かわいそうな	poor ＊Poor thing.（かわいそうに）
気の毒な	sorry ＊feel sorry（気の毒だと思う）
孤独の，寂しい，心細い	lonely ＊I feel lonely without you.（あなたがいなくて寂しい）
ホームシックになった，（〜が）恋しい；ホームシック	homesick ＊*be* homesick for Japanese food（日本食が恋しい）
憂うつな，陰うつな	gloomy ＊feel gloomy about the future（将来を考えると憂うつになる）
後悔（する）	regret ＊feel regret about [at/over]（〜を後悔する）
がっかりした	disappointed ＊*be* disappointed at（〜にがっかりする）
絶望（する）	despair ＊out of despair（絶望のあまり），despair of *one's* boss（上司に絶望する）
気落ちした，元気のない，意気消沈した	depressed ＊feel [get] depressed（憂うつな気分になる），feel terribly depressed（ひどくがっかりした気持ちでいる）

（〜に）取り乱している，うろたえている，怒った，動転した	upset [ʌpsét] ＊be upset about（〜のことで動揺している）	（精神的，肉体的に）気持ちよく感じる，気楽［安楽］で（ある），心安まる	comfortable [kʌ́mftəbl]
正気でない，気が狂った；〜に夢中になって	crazy ＊be [go] crazy with worry（心配のあまり頭がおかしくなる），be crazy about（〜に夢中である）	心地よくない，いらいらさせる；心地よく感じない；不愉快な	uncomfortable ＊an uncomfortable silence（気まずい沈黙）
（〜に）ショックを受けて	shocked ＊be shocked at（〜にショックを受ける）	ひどい，嫌な	awful [ɔ́ːfl]
心配（する）	worry [wə́ːri] ＊worry about [over]（〜のことで心配する），be worried about（〜のことで思い悩んでいる，心配している）	混乱させる，困惑させる	confuse [kənfjúːz] ＊be confused about（〜のことで混乱する）
（〜のことで）心配して，案じて	anxious [ǽŋkʃəs] ＊be anxious about（〜のことで心配している）	迷惑，面倒，じゃまする，迷惑［面倒］をかける	bother [bɑ́ðər]
（心配，後悔などのために）取り乱した	distracted [distrǽktid] ＊be[go] distracted（動転している［する］）	つらい，苦しい	hard [hɑ́ːrd] ＊have a hard time（つらい思いをする，苦労する）
（事，人に）いらいらした	irritated ＊be irritated about（〜にいらいらする）	《感情，言葉などが》激しい，乱暴な	violent
いらいらさせる，悩ます	annoy [ənɔ́i] ＊be annoyed about [at/by]（〜にいらだつ），How annoying!（ほんとイライラする！）	恥ずかしさ；残念なこと	shame ＊feel shame at（〜を恥ずかしく思う）
ストレスの多い	stressful ＊stressful work（ストレスの多い仕事）	恥ずかしい思いをさせる，まごつかせる	embarrass [embǽrəs] ＊I was embarrassed to death.（恥ずかしくて死にそうだった）
神経質な，緊張した	nervous ＊be nervous about（〜で神経質になっている）	（〜を）恥じて	ashamed ＊feel ashamed about [at/of]（〜を恥ずかしいと思う）
欲求不満の，苛立っている	frustrated	（〜を）こわがって，恐れて	afraid ＊be afraid of（〜をこわがる）
安らかな	peaceful		

恐怖, 不安；恐れる, 不安がる	fear [fíər] * hopes and fears（期待と不安）
（〜を）こわがる, （〜に）おびえた	scared [skéərd] * I'm scared of riding a roller coaster.（ジェットコースターに乗るのがこわい）
（〜に）おびえた, ぎょっとする；（〜して）どきりとする	frightened [fráitnd]. * be frightened at the noise（物音にドキッとする）
（〜に）ぞっとする；（〜[するの]を）怖く思う	terrified [térəfàid] * be terrified of（〜にゾッとする）, be terrified at the thought of（〜のことを思うとゾッとする）
（一時的に）〜で口がきけない	speechless * be speechless with horror（恐怖のあまり口がきけない）
《興味を失って》〜に飽きる	lose interest in
《興味, 気力を失って》〜に飽きる, 〜に疲れる	get tired of * get tired of the whole business（何もかもいやになる）, get awfully tired of ~ing（〜するのはまったくあきあきする［疲れる］）
《うんざりして》〜に飽き飽きしている, うんざりしている	be fed up with * I'm fed up with this rain.（この雨にはうんざり）
（〜に）うんざりして, 退屈して	bored * I'm bored to death.（死ぬほど退屈だ）
（肉体的, 精神的に）疲れきった, まいっている	weary [wíəri] * My eyes are so weary.（目がとても疲れている）

憎む, （ひどく）嫌う；憎しみ	hate [héit]
憎らしい, （ひどく）嫌な	hateful
憎しみ, 憎悪	hatred [héitrid] * bear a person hatred（人に憎悪の気持ちをもつ）
〜に恨みを抱く	have [hold / bear] a grudge against * work [pay] off a grudge（恨みを晴らす）
嫉妬	jealousy [ʤéləsi] ／ envi [énvi] * feel jealousy（嫉妬する）, invite the jealousy of（〜の嫉妬を招く）, nurse jealousy against（〜に嫉妬を抱く）
《人, 言動などが》ひねくれた；《人, 行動などが》非を認めない, 強情な	perverse [pərvə́:rs] * get perverse（ひねくれる）
《人の地位, 持ち物などが》うらやましい	enviable [énviəbl] * enviable job（うらやましい仕事）
うらやむ	envy ／ be envious of * I envy you.（あなたがうらやましい）
誇りに思う	proud * I'm proud of you.（よくやったね）《ほめ言葉》. be proud of「〜を誇りに思う」「よくやったね, うれしいよ」のニュアンス。

18

4. 思考・判断・感覚

★思考

考える，思う	think ＊think deeply（深く［じっくり］考える），think calmly（冷静に考える）
考える，考慮する	consider [kənsídər] ＊consider a plan（計画をよく練る），consideration（考慮，熟慮）
考える，〜を（…と）みなす	regard [rigáːrd] ＊regard a person as a genius（〜を天才だと思う）
《本当だ，正しいと》思う，信じる	believe
《十分な根拠なしに》思う，推測する	guess [gés]
〜と思う［考える］，〜のような気がする，想像する	imagine [imǽdʒin] ＊根拠なくなんとなく思うときに用いる。I imagine (that) it will rain tomorrow.（明日は雨が降ると思うよ）
〜と思う，（〜と）考える，〜のように思える，〜という気がする	feel ＊感性的な判断を表わし，控えめに考えを述べるときに用いる。I don't feel that it is a very good plan.（それはあまりよい計画とは思えないんだけど）。
（〜であると）思う，当然〜すると思う	expect ＊I expect (that) you can do it.（あなたならできると思う）。好ましいこと，好ましくないこと両方に用いる。
思う，想像する，仮定する	suppose [səpóuz] ＊曖昧な根拠から自分なりに判断して考えを述べるときに用いる。be supposed to be ...（〜だと思われている）。
不思議に思う，〜かと思う；不思議，奇跡	wonder [wʌ́ndər]
〜ではないかと思う，疑いをかける，怪しむ	suspect [səspékt] ＊疑いや好ましくないことがあるのではないかと思うときに用いる。
疑う，〜ではないと思う	doubt [dáut]
思う，意味する，本気で言う［思う］	mean ＊I mean it.（本当にそう思っています），I didn't mean it.（わざとじゃないんです／そういうつもりじゃなかったんです）
意図する，もくろむ，つもりである	intend [inténd] ＊I didn't intend to hurt you.（あなたの気持ちを傷つけるつもりはなかったんです）
（〜についての）考え，見解	thought [θɔ́ːt] ＊express one's thoughts（〜の考えを述べる）
意見，見解，考え	opinion ＊express an opinion（意見を述べる），accept a person's opinion（人の意見を受け入れる）
考え，意見；アイデア	idea [aidíːə] ＊collect one's ideas（考えをまとめる），conceive an idea for（〜の構想が浮かぶ），force one's idea on others（自分の考えを他人に押しつける）

集中する，専念する	concentrate [kánsəntrèit] ＊ have great concentration (とても集中力がある)	経験（する）	experience [ikspíəriəns] ＊ have a pleasant [bitter] experience（楽しい［苦い］経験をする），build up one's experience（経験を積む）
注意（力）	attention ＊ pay attention to（～に注意を払う），attract [catch /get] a person's attention（人の注意を引く）	決心する，決定する，決断する	decide ＊ decide conclusively（最終的に決める），You decide.（あなたが決めて）
確信させる，納得させる	convince [kənvíns] ＊ convince one's boss（上司を納得させる）	（慎重に）決定する，決意する	determine [ditə́ːrmin] ＊ determine a price（価格を決める）
強調する，力説する	emphasize [émfəsàiz] ＊ emphasize the need for（～の必要性を強調する）	あきらめる	give up ＊ Don't give up. You can do it.（あきらめてはだめ。あなたならできるわ）Never give up. Always follow your dreams.（決してあきらめず，常に夢を追い続けて）
知る，知っている	know [nóu]		
わかる，理解する	understand [ʌ̀ndərstǽnd]		
気づく，認識する，悟る	realize [ríːəlàiz, ríə-] ＊ realize one's mistake（間違いに気づく）	示す	indicate [índikèit] ＊ clearly indicate one's intention to do ...（～しようという意思を明確に示す）
わかる，気づく	find ＊ find A (to be) C「A が C であることがわかる」。I found him (to be) a genius.（彼が天才であることに気づいた）	同意する，合意する	agree [əgríː] ＊ agree to the proposal（提案に同意する），agree with reservation（条件付きで同意する）
認める，認識する，～がわかる	recognize [rékəgnàiz] ＊ It is generally recognized that ....（～と一般に認められている）	否定する	deny [dinái]
思い出す，覚えている	remember	主観的な，個人的な	subjective [səbdʒéktiv]
覚える，暗記する，記憶する	memorize ＊ memory（記憶），lose one's memory（記憶〔力〕を失う，記憶喪失になる）	客観的な	objective ＊ with objective eyes（客観的な目で），see things objectively（客観的に物事を見る）
忘れる	forget [fərgét]	論理的な，筋が通った	logical [ládʒikl] ＊ logical thinking（論理的な思考〔力〕），illogical（筋の通らない）
～を度忘れする	forget ... for the moment		

★判断

おもしろい，興味を引く	interesting ＊That sounds interesting.（それはおもしろそうですね）
重要な，重大な，大切な	important
（物・時間・資源などが）貴重な	precious [préʃəs] ＊precious time（貴重な時間）
必要な，必然の	necessary ＊be necessary for [to] good health（健康に欠かせない）
よい，善良な，立派な	good
悪い	bad
完璧な；完璧にする	perfect [pə́ːrfikt]《形》《名》, [pərfékt]《動》
ものすごい，すばらしい	terrific [tərífik]
立派な，みごとな	splendid
信じられない	incredible ＊Incredible!（信じられない！）
注目すべき，注目に値する	remarkable ＊remarkable points（注目すべきポイント）
ふさわしい，適切な	suitable [súːtəbl] ＊be suitable for（〜に適している）
恐ろしい，ひどい	terrible ＊「気分が悪い，つらい」の意味もある。feel terrible（気分が悪い）
ばかげた	ridiculous [ridíkjələs] ＊be totally ridiculous（実にばかげている）

同じ	same ＊Same here.（〔相手と同じように感じているときに〕同感／私も同じだ）
類似の，似た	similar [símələr] ＊be similar to（〜と似ている）
違う，異なる	different [dífərənt]
特有の，独特の	particular [pərtíkjələr] ＊in particular（とりわけ，特に）
奇妙な，特有の	peculiar [pikjúːljər]
妙な，奇妙な，不思議な	strange [stréindʒ]
単純な，簡単な	simple
基本の，基本的な；基本，原理，原則	basic
一般の，一般的な	general [dʒénərl]
普通の，共通の	common [kámən]
普遍的な，全般的な	universal [jùːnəvə́ːrsl]
典型的な	typical [típikl]
複雑な，込み入った	complicated [kámpləkèitəd]
具体的な，現実の	concrete [kɑnkríːt | ɼ–]
抽象的な	abstract [ǽbstrækt]
実際的な，実用的な	practical [prǽktikl]
便利な，手頃な，好都合な	convenient [kənvíːniənt] ＊Call me when it is convenient for you.（都合のよいときに電話をください）

人について知る

21

合理的な，理にかなった，道理をわきまえた	rational [rǽʃənl]
正しい	right ＊You're quite right.（まったくきみの言うとおりだよ）
間違った，悪い	wrong
公正な，公平な	fair [féər] ＊unfair（不公平な，偏った）
（意見などが）もっともな，十分根拠のある	just ＊形容詞。just opinion（もっともな意見）
本当の，真実の	true
間違った，虚偽の，偽りの	false [fɔ́:ls]
正確な	accurate ／ exact ＊accurate figures（正確な数字），exact time（正確な時間）
大体の，大まかな	rough [rʌ́f] ＊at a rough guess（大ざっぱに見て）
主な，主要な	chief ＊the chief reason（主な理由）
ささいな，取るに足らない	trivial [tríviəl] ＊trivial problems（取るに足りない問題），quarrel about a trivial matter（ささいなことで口げんかする）

★感覚

感覚，分別；感づく，（感覚器官，機械などが）感知する	sense ＊have a sense of humor（ユーモアの感覚［センス］がある），common sense（常識，良識）

触る，触れる；接触，手触り	touch
固い	hard
柔らかい	soft
（表面が）ざらざらした，粗い	rough ＊rough skin（荒れた肌）
なめらかな	smooth [smú:ð] ＊表面がでこぼこしていないニュアンス。smooth skin（なめらかな肌）
鋭い，鋭利な	sharp
熱い，暑い，からい	hot [hát] ＊(hot) spicy food（香辛料の利いた辛い食べ物）
（液体が）ぬるい	lukewarm [lú:kwɔ́:rm] ＊態度などについて「生ぬるい，気乗りしない，熱のない，煮え切らない」のニュアンスもある。
暖かい，温かい	warm [wɔ́:rm]
冷たい，寒い；寒さ，風邪	cold ＊不快なほど温度が低くて寒いのニュアンス。
ひんやりする，寒気がする，肌寒い	chilly 《形》 ＊天気，場所，身体が不快なほど「寒い」のニュアンス。
（凍えるほど）寒い	freezing 《形》 ＊I'm freezing.（凍えそう）
涼しい；冷やす，冷える	cool
においがする，かぐ；におい	smell
《特に不快な》におい	odor [óudər]
いやなにおいがする，悪臭を放つ；悪臭	stink

5. 性格・人柄

★性格・人柄・特徴

性格，人柄	character [kǽrəktər] ＊good [bad] character（いい [悪い] 性格）
性質，気質	nature ＊suit one's nature（性に合う），by nature（生まれつき，生来）
印象；感銘，感動	impression [impréʃən] ＊the first impression（第一印象），impress（印象を与える），create a good [bad] impression（好 [悪] 印象を与える）
欠点，短所；責任，罪；誤り，過失	fault [fɔ́ːlt] ＊correct a fault（欠点 [過ち] を改める），Everybody has faults.（だれにも欠点はあるよ），find fault with（～のあら探しをする）
明るい，陽気な，快活な	sunny／cheerful ＊sunny [cheerful] personality（明るい性格）
暗い	gloomy
話好きの，おしゃべり	talkative ＊I'm a talkative person by nature.（私って生まれつきおしゃべりなの）
うるさい	loud [láud] ＊loud personality（騒々しい性格）
おとなしい，もの静かな，控えめな	quiet
社交的な	sociable ＊She is sociable.（彼女は社交的だ）
社交的な，外向的な，（対人関係で）積極的な	outgoing
率直な，ストレートな，包み隠さない	frank
率直な，正直な，ストレートな	straight
開けっぴろげな，心の広い	expansive [ikspǽnsiv]
おおらかな，あくせくしない，おっとりした	easygoing
内向的な（人）	introvert [ìntrəvə́ːrt] ＊extrovert（外向的な〔人〕），introverted personality（内向的な性格）
恥ずかしがりの，内気な	shy [ʃái]
楽観的な	optimistic [ɑ̀ptimístik]
悲観的な	pessimistic [pèsəmístik]
《性格が》やさしい，寛大な	gentle ＊gentle personality（穏和な性格）
やさしい，思いやりがある	sweet ＊That's really sweet of you to say so.（そう言ってくれるなんて〔あなたって〕やさしいのね）／That's very sweet of you.（ご親切にどうも）相手に何か親切にされたときに返す言葉。

23

親切な，やさしい	kind	尊敬すべき，立派な，名誉ある	honorable [ánərəbl]
親切な，すてきな	nice	人気のある	popular
親しみやすい，気さくな	friendly ＊「彼は気取らない性格だ」なら，He never puts on airs.。	有名な	famous
		気前のよい，寛大な	generous
思いやりのある	thoughtful ＊thoughtless は（思いやりがない）	けちな	stingy [stíndʒi]
		お人好しな	good-natured
《人，心，態度などが》穏やかな，落ち着いた，しとやかな	calm [kάːm]	意地悪な	mean ／ ill-natured ／ nasty [nǽsti]
		短気な	impatient [impéiʃənt] ／ short-tempered
《人体の動きなどが》優雅な，しとやかな	graceful	勝ち気な	strong-minded ／ strong-willed
		我慢強い	patient
上品な	elegant ＊have elegant manners （立ち居振る舞いに品がある）	好奇心の強い	curious [kjúəriəs]
		自立心の強い，自立した	independent
下品な	vulgar [vʌ́lgər]	のんきな，成り行き任せの	happy-go-lucky
積極的な，前向きな	positive [pάzətiv] ／ active	几帳面な，とても注意深い	meticulous ／ methodical ＊a methodical person （几帳面な人）
消極的な	negative ／ passive		
勤勉な，仕事熱心な	hardworking ／ diligent	純粋な	pure ＊be pure in heart （心が純真である）
まじめな	earnest		
頭がよい	smart	誠実な，正直な	honest [άnəst] ／ sincere [sinsíər]
きまじめな	serious [síəriəs] ＊He is very serious. （彼はとてもまじめだ）		
		頼りになる	reliable
怠惰な，無精な	lazy [léizi] ＊get lazy （怠け癖がつく）	頼りにならない	unreliable
		柔軟な	flexible ＊a flexible person （柔軟性のある人）
ユーモアのある	humorous [hjúːmərəs]		
おかしい	funny		

優柔不断な	wishy-washy [wíʃiwàʃi] / indecisive [ìndisáisiv] * wishy-washy [indecisive] personality（優柔不断な性格）
奇妙な，風変わりな	odd / strange
《非難して》自慢げな，自尊心のある，高慢な	proud * proud には「誇りに思う，誇るべき，うれしい，喜ばしい」の意味合いもある。be proud of（～を誇りに思う）。
高圧的な，高飛車な	high-handed / coercive [kouə́ːrsiv] * take a high-handed [coercive] attitude（高飛車な態度を取る）
横柄な	arrogant [ǽrəgənt]
強引な	forceful / pushy [púʃi] * forceful は，ほめて「（強力で）説得力のある」の意味もある。pushy は「《非難して》でしゃばりの，あつかましい，強引な，ごり押しの」のニュアンス。
うぬぼれの強い，思いあがった，自信過剰な	conceited [kənsíːtid] / vain [véin]
頑固な	stubborn [stʌ́bərn]
生意気な	saucy [sɔ́ːsi] ◀ get saucy with（・に生意気な態度を取る）。saucy は米口語で「（どぎつくなく）セクシーな，（衣服などが）しゃれた」の意味もある。
憎たらしい	hateful
謙虚な，低姿勢な	modest [mádəst] / humble

温厚な，寛容な	clement * 「（気候の）温暖な」の意もある。
乱暴な	violent
心が広い	tolerant
大胆な，厚かましい	bold / impudent [ímpjudənt]
小心な，臆病な	timid [tímid]
勇敢な	brave [bréiv] / courageous [kəréidʒəs] * be courageous to（～する勇気がある），an act of courage（勇気ある行為）
しつこい，くどい	persistent
なれなれしい，よく知っている，ありふれた	familiar * get too familiar（なれなれしくする，〔人間関係で〕深みにはまる）
ずるい	cunning [kʌ́niŋ] / sly [slái]
わがままな，自己中心的な	selfish / egoistic
自己中心的な	self-centered
ばかな，ばかげた	foolish
愚かな，ばかな	silly
独特の	unique * have a unique personality（独特の個性がある）
普通の，ありきたりの	ordinary * an ordinary person（普通〔ありきたり〕の人）
男らしい	manly 〈形〉
女らしい	womanly 〈形〉

★ 一日の行動

目覚める	wake up
起きる	get up
メガネをかける [はずす]	put on [take off] one's glasses
明かりをつける [消す]	turn on [off] the light
窓を開ける [閉める]	open [close] the window
トイレに行く	go to the bathroom
シャワーを浴びる	take a shower
歯を磨く	brush one's teeth
口をすすぐ	rinse one's mouth
ひげをそる	shave [ʃéiv]
顔を洗う	wash [rinse] one's face
化粧をする	put on makeup
髪をブラッシングする	brush one's hair
髪に櫛を入れる	comb one's hair
服を着る [脱ぐ]	put on [take off] one's clothes
服を着替える	change one's clothes

お湯を沸かす	boil some water
料理を作る，（火を使って）料理をする	cook
食事を用意する	prepare meals

テーブルに皿を並べる	arrange the dishes on the table
朝食を食べる	eat breakfast
昼食を食べる	eat lunch
夕食を食べる	eat dinner
（食後の）食器を下げる	put away the dishes / clear the table
（食後の）食器を洗う	do [wash] the dishes
コーヒーを飲む	drink [have] (a cup of) coffee

風呂に入る	take a bath
体をタオルで拭く	dry oneself with a towel
新聞を読む	read a newspaper
テレビを見る	watch television [TV]
テレビをつける [消す]	turn on [off] the television
ボリュームを上げる [下げる]	turn up [turn down] the volume
（6時に）目覚ましをセットする	set one's alarm (for 6:00)
寝る	go to bed
睡眠	sleep

★家族・親族

家族	family		義理の母親，しゅうとめ	mother-in-law
世帯，家族	household		独身の母親	single mother
家族写真	family picture		継母	stepmother
家系図	family tree		子供たち	children [tʃíldrən]
親戚	relative 〈名〉		息子	son [sʌ́n]
近縁の親戚	close relative		娘の夫，婿	son-in-law
遠戚の親戚	distant relative		継子《男》	stepson
親類縁者	relatives in blood and law		娘	daughter [dɔ́ːtər]
血縁，親族，親類	kin		息子の妻，嫁	daughter-in-law
親戚関係	kinship		継子《女》	stepdaughter
先祖	ancestor [ǽnsestər]		兄／弟	brother
子孫	descendant [diséndənt]		兄	elder brother
			弟	younger brother
			義理の兄／弟	brother-in-law
夫婦	couple／husband and wife		異母兄弟／異父兄弟	half brother
夫	husband		継父［継母］の息子	step brother
妻	wife		姉／妹	sister
配偶者	spouse [spáus]		姉	elder sister
			妹	younger sister
親	parent [péərənt]		義理の姉／妹	sister-in-law
保護者（未成年者などの）	guardian		異母姉妹／異父姉妹	half sister
父親	father [fáːðər]		継父［継母］の娘	step sister
義理の父親，しゅうと	father-in-law		祖父／祖母	grandparent
独身の父親	single father		曽祖父母，曽祖父と曽祖母	great-grandparents
継父	stepfather		祖父	grandfather
母親	mother [mʌ́ðər]			

曽祖父	great-grandfather
祖母	grandmother
曽祖母	great-grandmother
孫	grandchildren
ひ孫	great grandchild
孫息子	grandson
ひ孫（息子）	great-grandson
孫娘	granddaughter
ひ孫（娘）	great-granddaughter
叔父	uncle [ʌ́ŋkl]
叔母	aunt [ǽnt | áːnt]
いとこ	cousin [kʌ́zn]
はとこ	second cousin
甥	nephew [néfjuː]
姪	niece [níːs]

★その他の身近な人

隣人，近所の人	neighbor [néibər]
友だち	friend
知り合い／知人	acquaintance [əkwéintəns]
幼なじみ	childhood friend
他人	other people ／ stranger ＊自分以外のすべての人を指す場合。
ライバル	rival

★人の一生

生涯，一生	lifetime
生きる	live
人生，生活	life

生まれる	*be* born
誕生日	birthday ＊ celebrate *a person's* birthday（〜の誕生日を祝う）
洗礼（式）	baptism
洗礼を施す，命名する	christen [krísn]
年齢；歳をとる	age
子供	child
幼年時代	childhood
幼稚園から第12学年（高校3年）まで(の)	K-12 [kéiθruːtwélv]
学校に通い始める	start school
卒業する	graduate ＊ graduation（卒業）
若者	youth ＊ in *one's* youth（若い頃に）
思春期	adolescence ／ puberty
大人，成人	adult [ədʌ́lt | ǽdʌlt]
育つ	grow
成長	growth
育てる	raise ／ bring up ＊ bring up *one's* children strictly（子供を厳しく育てる）
若い	young
年とった，年老いた	old ＊ elderly（お年寄りの；《the ~》高齢者，お年寄り）
運転を学ぶ	learn to drive
入隊する	join the army
仕事を得る	get a job

市民権を得る	become a citizen		独身の	single ＊stay single（独身でいる）
アパートを賃借する	rent an apartment		旅行をする	travel
大学に通う	go to college		家を買う	buy a house
恋をする	fall in love		引退	retirement
キスをする	kiss ／ give someone a kiss		（60歳で）定年退職する	retire (at the age of 60)
キスマーク	hickey《米》／ love bite《英》／ lipstick mark《口紅の》		余生を楽しむ[過ごす]	enjoy [spend] the rest of one's life
結婚する	get married ＊get married to a person（～と結婚する）		死ぬ	die
			《婉曲的に》亡くなる	pass away
事実婚	common-law marriage		葬儀	funeral (service) ＊attend a funeral（葬儀に参列する）
花嫁，新婦	bride [bráid]	
花婿，新郎	(bride)groom	

★パーティーなど

別れる，別居する	separate ＊be separated from one's wife（妻と別居している）		主催者／ホスト	host
			客	guest
～とセックスする	have sex with ... ／ make love to ...		招待	invitation
妊娠する	get [become] pregnant [prégnənt] ＊be three months pregnant（妊娠3か月である）		パーティーを開く	throw (hold) a party
			誕生会	birthday party
			晩餐会	dinner party
妊娠している	be expecting a baby ＊I'm expecting a baby.（赤ちゃんが生まれるの）		変装パーティー	costume party
			ビックリ・パーティー	surprise party
赤ちゃんができる，赤ん坊を生む	have a baby ＊have a baby boy [girl]（男の子［女の子］を産む）		新築（移転）祝いのパーティー	housewarming party
			記念日	anniversary ／ red-letter day ＊red-letter day：カレンダーに赤文字で示すことから。
離婚（する）	divorce [divɔ́:rs] ＊get a divorce from one's wife（妻と離婚する）	

結婚式	wedding (ceremony) ＊hold [have] a wedding （結婚式を挙げる）
園遊会	garden party
宴会	banquet
昼食会パーティー	luncheon party
合コン	matchmaking party
花見パーティー	cherry-blossom viewing party
カクテルパーティー	cocktail party
歓迎会	welcome party
送別会	farewell party
男だけのパーティー／結婚直前に男性だけで開くパーティー	stag party

女性だけのパーティー／結婚直前に女性だけで開くパーティー	hen party
世間話	small talk
スピーチをする	make a speech
紹介する	introduce
自己紹介	self-introduction
挨拶する	greet
握手する	shake hands

マンハッタンをパトロールする騎馬警官
時には写真撮影にも応じてくれる

★いろいろな格言・名言

格言	proverb ／ adage [ǽdidʒ] ／ aphorism [ǽfərìzm]
名言	(wise) saying ／ maxim ／ wise saw
一日１個のリンゴで医者いらず	An apple a day keeps the doctor away.
光る物必ずしも金ならず	All that glitters is not gold.
離れていることが情をいっそう深める	Absence makes the heart grow fonder.
困ったときに助けてくれる友こそ真の友	A friend in need is a friend indeed.
言葉よりも行動は雄弁である	Actions speak louder than words.
手中（しゅうちゅう）の一羽は，藪の中の二羽に値する	A bird in the hand is worth two in the bush.
遅くともやらないよりはいい	Better late than never.
転ばぬ先の杖	Better safe than sorry. ／ Look before you leap.
悪事千里を走る	Bad news travels fast.
英雄として死ぬより，臆病者として生きながらえた方がよい	Better a live coward than a dead hero.

美しさは，見る人次第	Beauty is in the eye of the beholder.
血は水よりも濃し	Blood is thicker than water.
類は友を呼ぶ	Birds of a feather flock together.
好奇心もほどほどに	Curiosity killed the cat.
取らぬ狸の皮算用はしないように	Don't count chickens before they're hatched.
外見で物事を判断するなかれ	Don't judge a book by its cover.
中途で計画や決断したことを変更するべからず	Don't change horses in midstream.
本末転倒	Don't put the cart before the horse.
手に負えないほどの責任を引き受けるな	Don't bite off more than you can chew.
得やすいものは失いやすい	Easy come, easy go.
タンゴは一人じゃ踊れない	It takes two to tango.
長いものには巻かれろ	If you can't beat them, join them.
覆水盆に戻らず	It's no use crying over the spilt milk.
恋は盲目	Love is blind.
お金は簡単に手に入るものではない	Money does not grow on trees.

1

人はパンのみにて生くるにあらず	Man does not live by bread alone.
真実ほど厳しいものはない	Nothing hurts like the truth.
苦労なくして得るものなし	No pain, no gain.
必要は発明の母なり	Necessity is the mother of invention.
習うより慣れろ	Practice makes perfect.
鉄は熱いうちに打て	Strike while the iron is hot.
魂は望んでいても肉体は弱し	The spirit is willing, but the flesh is weak.
老いた者ほど愚考は目立つ	There's no fool like an old fool.
我が家に勝るところはない	There's no place like home.
船頭多くして船山に登る	Too many cooks spoil the broth.
知恵を出すなら一人より二人	Two heads are better than one.
よその芝生のほうが青く見える	The grass is always greener on the other side of the fence.
郷にいれば郷に従え	When in Rome, do as the Romans do.
老犬に新しい芸当を教えることはできない	You can't teach an old dog new tricks.

もし世界が一つの舞台であるならば，すべての人々は演者である（by シェークスピア）	All the world's a stage, and all the men and women are merely players.
命ある限り希望がある	While there's life, there's hope.
セオリーどおりに行かないのが人生	Life is so unlike theory.
芸術が人生を模倣するよりも，人生はより芸術を模倣する（by オスカー・ワイルド）	Life imitates art far more than art imitates life.
他の事を考えている最中に，起きるのが人生（by ジョン・レノン）	Life is what happens to you while you're busy making other plans.
答えは愛…質問はなんだっけ？（by ジョン・レノン）	Love is the answer ... What was the question?
見た目と実際は異なる	Nothing is as good or bad as it appears.
人生で素晴らしいものは，ほとんど全て，短い言葉（一音節）である：平和，愛，喜び，信頼，家，希望	Most of the great things in life are one-syllable things; peace, love, joy, trust, home, hope.

人生において欠かせないのはタイミング	The essential ingredient of life is timing. ＊ingredient は「(成功の) 要因, 要素」。

★迷信

迷信	superstition [súːpərstíʃən]
神のご加護を (くしゃみをした相手に, くしゃみをしたはずみで魂が抜けないよう願っていう)	(God) bless you.
幸運を祈っていてください	Keep your fingers crossed.
かゆい鼻 (鼻がかゆくなるのは喧嘩をする予兆)	an itchy nose ＊itchy の発音は [ítʃi]。
ライスシャワー (新郎新婦が子宝に恵まれるように)	throwing rice ／ rice shower
何か古いもの, 何か新しいもの, 何か借りたもの, そして何か青いもの (結婚式で花嫁が身につけるとよいとされている 4 つのもの)	Something old, something new, something borrowed, something blue.

ネコは 9 つの命を持つ (古代エジプトでは, ネコは神に似た存在だった)	Cats have nine lives.
7 年目の浮気 (人の肉体と精神は 7 年毎に変わるということから)	the seven-year itch
13 人がテーブルにつく (13 人目の客になるのは縁起が悪い)	thirteen at a table
黒猫 (黒猫が目の前を横切ると縁起が悪い)	a black cat
鏡を割ること (自分の姿を映す鏡を割ると 7 年の間不運に恵まれる)	breaking a mirror
起きるときベッドの左側から出た (ベッドを出るときに, 悪い方の側, 左側から降りると機嫌が悪くなる)	getting up on the wrong side of the bed
四つ葉のクローバー (四つ葉のクローバーを見つけると幸運に恵まれる)	four-leaf(ed) clover

木を叩くこと（木を三回叩いて木の精霊に運に恵まれるよう祈る）	knocking on wood	歯の妖精（子供の歯が抜けるとその歯を枕の下に入れて寝ると，歯の妖精が夜中にやってきてお金を置いていく）	tooth fairy
ビギナーズ・ラック（素人のまぐれ当たり）	beginner's luck		
13日の金曜日（縁起の悪い金曜日と縁起の悪い数字13の組合せ）	Friday the 13th	星に願いをかける（流れ星や一番星にお願い事をすると叶う）	wish on a star

2.

食べる・飲む

1. 飲食のキーワード & フレーズ

★基本単語&表現

食習慣	eating habits [íːtiŋ hǽbits] ＊ develop healthy eating habits（健康的な食習慣を身につける）
食べ物，食料品	food [fúːd] ＊ food additives to avoid（避けるべき食品添加物）
食事	meal [míːl] ＊ have [take] a meal（食事する）
（品質，成分，健康への影響などから見た）食事，食生活；《食事の質・量》ダイエット，食事制限	diet [dáiət] ＊ be [go] on a diet（ダイエットしている［し始める]）
朝食	breakfast [brékfəst] ＊ have a late breakfast（遅い朝食を取る），skip breakfast（朝食を抜く）
（喫茶店などの）モーニングサービス	breakfast special
ブランチ	brunch [brʌ́ntʃ] ＊ have brunch（ブランチを取る）
昼食	lunch ＊ have [eat] lunch（昼食を取る）
お茶の時間	coffee break 《米》 / tea break 《英》 ＊ take a coffee [tea] break（一休みしてコーヒー［紅茶］を飲む）
ティータイム，（午後の）お茶の時間	teatime 《主に英》
（軽い）夕食	supper [sʌ́pər]
夕食	dinner [dínər] ＊ have dinner（夕食［ディナー］を取る）。
軽食，間食，スナック	snack [snǽk] ＊ have a snack（軽く食事をする，腹ごしらえをする，おやつにする）
間食	in-between snacks
間食をする	eat between meals ／ nosh [nɑ́ʃ]《米》
外食する	eat out ＊ eat out once a week（週1回外食する）
夜食	midnight snack
暴飲暴食をする	eat and drink too much ／ overeat and overdrink
食べる	eat
飲む	drink
食べる，飲む	have ＊ Would you like to have another cup of coffee?（コーヒーをもう一杯いかがですか）
かむ	chew [tʃúː]
かじる，かむ	bite [báit] ＊ bite into an apple（リンゴを丸かじりする）／ bite ~ off with one's teeth（歯で~をかみちぎる）
少しずつかじる，（酒を）ちびちび飲む	nibble [níbl] ＊ nibble on a piece of celery（セロリを〔少しずつ〕かじる）

なめる	lick [lík] ＊lick the candy（キャンディをなめる）
飲み込む	swallow [swálou] ＊swallow food（食べ物を〔かまずに〕飲みこむ）, swallow one's saliva（つばを飲み込む）
ごくごく〔ぐいぐい〕飲む	gulp [gʌlp] ＊gulp water（水をがぶ飲みする）, drink ~ in a gulp（～を一気飲みする）
むしゃむしゃ〔もぐもぐ〕食べる	munch [mʌntʃ] ＊munch on chips（ポテトチップスをパリパリ食べる）
（人が）がつがつ食べる，（動物が）むさぼり食う	devour [diváuər] ＊devour a book で「本をむさぼり読む」。
がつがつ食べる	wolf down
お腹がすいています。	I'm hungry.
お腹ペコペコ。	I'm starving. ／ I'm very hungry.
お腹いっぱいです。	I'm full [stuffed] . ＊Are you getting full?（お腹一杯になってきた？）
のどが渇いた。	I'm thirsty.
のどの渇き，酒を飲みたい気持ち	thirst [θə́ːrst] ＊I have a thirst for beer.（ビールが飲みたい）
食べられる（状態の）《食べ物の状態から》	eatable ＊「《通例，複数形で》食料品」の意味もある。
食べられる《食べ物の性質から》	edible [édəbl] ＊「食用の」「食用に適する」。edible frog（食用蛙）

飲める	drinkable ＊「飲用に適する」。drinkable water（飲用水）
食費	food expenses
パーティー	party ＊throw [give / have / hold] a party for（～のためにパーティーを催す）
（水以外の）飲み物	beverage [bévəridʒ] ＊coffee，milk，tea，beer など。「アルコール飲料」は drinks が一般的。
食欲	appetite [ǽpiàit] ＊have a good [poor] appetite（食欲がある〔ない〕）
彼は食べ物の好き嫌いが激しい。	He has strong likes and dislikes in food.
グルメ	gourmet [guərméi]
グルメ，料理するのが好きな人	foodie [fúːdi]
ごちそうを食べる，満喫する，もてなす；祝宴	feast [fíːst]
食いしん坊	big eater
少食である	do not eat much ／ eat lightly
菜食主義者	vegetarian [vèdʒətéəriən]
（酒好き，酒飲みの意味で）辛党	drinker ＊菓子などの甘いものよりも，お酒のほうを好む人のこと。
私は甘党です。	I have a sweet tooth.

2 食べる・飲む

食事の支度をする	prepare a meal
テーブルクロスをかける	spread [spréd] the tablecloth
配膳する，食卓の用意をする	set the table
（ナイフ，フォーク，スプーンなどの）食卓用金物類	silverware 《米》／ cutlery [kʌ́tləri] 《英》
テーブルナプキン	table napkin
食事だよ！／ご飯だよ！	Time to eat! ／ Chow [tʃáu] time! ＊chow（食事，食べ物），Dinner is ready.（夕飯できたよ）
夕食［昼食／朝食］だよ！	It's dinner [lunch ／ breakfast] time!
食事の席に着く	sit down at the table
（食事を形容して）豪華な，豪勢な	sumptuous [sʌ́mptʃuəs] ／ lavish [lǽviʃ]
（食事を形容して）質素な，粗末な	humble [hʌ́mbl]
（食前の）お祈り	grace [gréis]
（食前の）お祈りをする	say grace
社員食堂，学食	cafeteria [kæ̀fətíəriə] ＊canteen《英》
弁当	packed [box] lunch
おかず	(side) dish
お袋の味	the taste of Mom's cooking

〜を試食［試飲］する	sample ／ try

★味・食感

味見する；味	taste [téist]
おいしい	good ／ delicious [dilíʃəs]
まずい	bad
味がしない	tasteless
風味に富んだ	flavory [fléivəri]
風味がある，おいしい	tasty [téisti]
風味がない，味が薄い	bland
酸っぱい	sour [sáuər]
スパイスがきいている	spicy [spáisi]
辛い	hot [hát	hɔ́t]
塩辛い	salty [sɔ́:lti]
甘い	sweet
まろやかな	mild
苦い	bitter ＊bitter tea（渋いお茶）のように，「渋み」を表す場合にも使われる。
油っこい	oily ＊サラダ油などの「油分」が多いとき。 greasy [grí:si, grí:zi] ＊「脂肪分」が多いとき。
水分が多い，汁の多い	juicy
クリーム状の	creamy
水っぽい	watery

チーズ入りの，チーズ風味の	cheesy [tʃíːzi]
固い	hard
やわらかい	soft [sɔ́(ː)ft]
（肉などが）固い	tough [tʌ́f]
（肉などが）やわらかい	tender
（茶，スープなど味が）濃い	strong
（飲み物が）薄い，味がない	weak
（飲食物，味などが）軽い	mild
（液体が）濃い，どろどろした	thick [θík] ＊thick soup（濃いスープ）
（液体が）薄い	thin [θín] ＊thin soup（薄いスープ）
パサパサした	dry [drái]
パリパリした，カリカリした	crispy [kríspi]
かみごたえのある，（うどんなどが）腰のある	chewy [tʃúːi]
ねばねばしている	sticky [stíki] ＊sticky day（蒸し暑い日），sticky problem（やっかいな問題）も覚えておこう。

★食品

ダイエット補助食品	dietary aid
食品成分	dietary constituent
加工食品	processed food
レトルト食品	retort-packed food ／ food in a sealed pouch
インスタント食品	instant food ／ convenience food
冷凍食品	frozen food
冷凍インスタント食品（テレビディナー）	TV dinner ＊加熱すればすぐ食べられる調理済みの冷凍食品のこと。
健康食品	health food(s)
自然食品	natural food(s)
真空パックの食品	vacuum-packed foods
賞味期限５月24日《表示》	Best-by May 24 ／ Best-before May 24
消費期限６月10日《表示》	Use by June 10 ／ Expiration date June 10

★主な栄養素など

栄養	nutrition [njuːtríʃən] ＊get enough nutrition（十分な栄養を取る）
栄養士	dietitian [dàiətíʃən]
栄養失調	malnutrition
栄養強化	nutritional enhancement
栄養バランス	nutritional balance
栄養不良の	undernourished

2 食べる・飲む

栄養分が多い	nutritious
栄養分が少ない	innutritious
二大栄養素	the three major nutrients
炭水化物	carbohydrate [kàːrbouháidreit]
食物繊維	dietary fiber [dáiəteri fáibər]
たんぱく質	protein [próutiːn]
脂肪（分）	fat ＊be high [low] in fat（脂肪分が多い [少ない]）
コラーゲン	collagen [kálədʒən]
脂質	lipid [lípid]
コレステロール	cholesterol [kəléstəròul]
カロリー	calorie [kǽləri] ＊keep a daily calorie count（一日のカロリー摂取量を守る）
ビタミン	vitamin [váitəmin, vítə-] ＊lack of vitamin C（ビタミンCの不足）
ミネラル	mineral [mínərl] ＊mineral-rich water（ミネラル豊富な水）
カルシウム	calcium [kǽlsiəm] ＊consume adequate amounts of calcium（適度の量のカルシウムを摂る）
鉄分	iron [áiərn]
ナトリウム	sodium [sóudiəm]
カリウム	potassium [pətǽsiəm]
マグネシウム	magnesium
ヨード	iodine [áiədàin]

リン	phosphorus [fásfərəs]
亜鉛	zinc [zíŋk]
クロム	chrome [króum]
ブドウ糖	glucose [glúːkous]
果糖	fructose [frʌ́ktous]
乳糖	lactose [lǽktous]
オリゴ糖	oligosaccharide [òuligousǽkəraid]
アミノ酸	amino acid [əmíːnou ǽsid]
クエン酸	citric acid [sítrik ǽsid]
タウリン	taurine [tɔ́ːriːn, -rən]
酸化防止剤	antioxidant [æntiáksidnt]
葉酸（ようさん）	folic acid [fóulik ǽsid] ＊ビタミンMと呼ばれるビタミンB群の一つ。ほうれん草（spinach [spínitʃ]）、ブロッコリー（broccoli [brákəli]）などの葉物野菜、レバーなどに含まれる。

2. 食材 & 食料品

★肉類・牛肉

牛肉	beef
牛ひき肉	ground beef ＊「ひき肉」は ground meat, hamburger meat《米》／ minced meat《英》。
ロースト用肉	roast [róust]
ステーキ用肉	steak [stéik]
シチュー用肉	stewing [stjúːɪŋ] meat
肩肉	chuck [tʃʌ́k]
あばら肉	rib
腰肉, サーロイン	sirloin
トップサーロイン	top sirloin
腰肉の前方部	short loin
もも肉	round
しり肉	rump
ヒレ肉	tenderloin
すね肉	tip
わき腹肉	flank
バラ肉	short plate
胸肉	brisket [brískit]
すね肉《前脚》	fore shank
すね肉《後ろ脚》	hind shank
牛のしっぽ	oxtail
舌, タン	tongue [tʌ́ŋ]
腎臓《主に子牛》	kidney
レバー	liver
ハラミ	outside skirt
胃	tripe [tráip]

★牛肉・切り身

モック・テンダー・ロースト	mock tender roast
骨なし肩ロースト	boneless chuck roast
骨なしトップ・ブレード・ステーキ	boneless top blade steak
骨なし肩肉ポット・ロースト	boneless chuck pot roast
骨なし肩ステーキ	boneless shoulder steak
骨なしアーム・ポット・ロースト	boneless arm pot roast
7ボーン・ポット・ロースト	7-bone pot roast
田舎風リブ	country-style ribs
ショートリブ	short ribs
リブロース	rib roast
リブアイ・ロースト	rib eye roast
リブアイ・ステーキ	rib eye steak
背側リブ	back ribs
上級切り身	grade "A" cut meat
ヒレ肉ロースト	tenderloin roast
上部腰肉ステーキ	top loin steak
ティーボーン・ステーキ	T-bone steak

2

食べる・飲む

ヒレ肉ステーキ	tenderloin steak
上部サーロイン・ステーキ	top sirloin steak
下部サーロイン・ステーキ	bottom sirloin steak
サーロイン・ステーキ	sirloin steak
上部サーロイン・ロースト	top sirloin roast
3チップステーキ	tri-tip steak
3チップロースト	tri-tip roast
チップ・ステーキ	tip steak
もも肉チップ・ロースト	round tip roast
もも肉ステーキ	round steak
アイ・ラウンド（もも肉）・ステーキ	eye round steak
上部もも肉ステーキ	top round steak
下部もも肉ステーキ	bottom round steak
上部もも肉ロースト	top round roast
下部もも肉ロースト	bottom round roast
アイ・ラウンド（もも肉）・ロースト	eye round roast
骨なし臀部ロースト	boneless rump roast

すね肉クロスカット	shank crosscut
わき腹肉ステーキ	flank steak

★肉類・豚肉

豚肉	pork
肩ロース	Boston butt [bʌ́t] ／ shoulder
腰肉，ロース	loin [lɔ́in]
もも肉	leg
わき腹肉	side
ヒレ肉	tenderloin
三枚肉	belly [béli]
豚足	pork feet
子豚の背あばら肉	baby back ribs

★豚肉・切り身

肩甲骨部ステーキ	blade steak
肩甲骨部ロースト	blade roast
骨なし肩甲骨部ロースト	boneless blade roast
燻製肩肉	smoked picnic
燻製足肉	smoked hock
燻製骨なし肩肉	smoked boneless shoulder
スペアリブ	spareribs
ベーコン	bacon
ハム	ham
ソーセージ	sausage [sɔ́(ː)sidʒ]

ハム・センター・スライス	ham center slice
燻製骨なしハム	boneless smoked ham
骨なし上部腰肉ロースト	boneless top loin roast
センター・リブロースト	center rib roast
あばら肉王冠型ロースト	rib crown roast
上部腰肉チョップ	top loin chop
蝶型チョップ	butterfly chop
腰肉チョップ	loin chop
あばら肉チョップ	rib chop
骨なしサーロイン・チョップ	boneless sirloin chop
サーロイン・チョップ	sirloin chop
カナディアン・スタイル・ベーコン	Canadian-style bacon
燻製腰肉チョップ	smoked loin chop

★肉類・羊肉

肩	shoulder
あばら骨	rib
腰	loin
脚	leg
前脚肉と胸肉	foreshank & brisket

★羊肉・切り身

アームチョップ	arm chop
骨なし肩ロースト	boneless shoulder roast
肩甲骨部チョップ	blade chop
あばら肉チョップ	rib chop
リブロース	rib roast
フレンチ・スタイル・リブロース	French-style rib roast
腰肉チョップ	loin chop
腰肉ロースト	loin roast
前脚のすね肉	foreshank
内腿肉のロースト	top round roast
脚全体	whole leg
すね肉半分	shank half of leg
腰肉半分	sirloin half of leg
後ろ脚のすね肉	hind shanks
羊の脚肉全体	whole leg of lamb
脚肉センタースライス	leg center slice

★肉類・鳥肉

鳥肉	poultry [póultri]
鶏肉	chicken
七面鳥の肉	turkey
鴨肉	duck
去勢した雄鶏	capon [kéipɑn]
ロースター	roaster

2 食べる・飲む

ロック種とコーニッシュ種を混ぜた雌鳥	Rock Cornish hen
シチュー用鶏肉	stewing chicken

★鳥肉・切り身

骨なし胸肉	boneless breast
胸肉	breast
鶏肉レバー	chicken liver
足（関節から下の足肉）	drumstick
砂肝	gizzard [gízərd]
脚	leg
もも	thigh [θái]
ささみ	tender
丸ごと一羽の鶏肉	whole chicken
手羽先	wing
手羽元	drumette

★魚貝類

背びれ	fin
えら	gill
尾びれ	tail
魚	fish
貝	shellfish
海草	sea weeds
昆布	kelp ／ tangle
シーフード	seafood
小エビ	shrimp
甘エビ	sweet shrimp
シャコ	mantis shrimp
車エビ	prawn [prɔ́:n]

ロブスター，伊勢エビ	lobster [lábstər]
ザリガニ	crawfish [krɔ́:fiʃ]
カキ	oyster [ɔ́istər]
ハマグリ	clam [klǽm]
アサリ	short-necked clam
ミル貝	geoduck clam
シジミ	corbicula
赤貝	red clam
ムール貝	mussel [mʌ́sl]
ホタテ貝	scallop [skǽləp, skáləp]
とり貝	cockle [kákl]
ホッキ貝	surf clam
青柳（あおやぎ）	the meat of surf clams
サザエ	top shell
アワビ	abalone [æ̀bəlóuni]
メカジキ	swordfish
サンマ	saury [sɔ́:ri]
カレイ	right-eye flounder [fláundər] ／ flatfish
ヒラメ	left-eyed flounder ／ flatfish
舌平目	sole [sóul]
タラ	cod [kád]
ハドック（タラの一種）	haddock [hǽdək]
イワシ	sardine [sɑːrdíːn]
アンチョビ，カタクチイワシ	anchovy [ǽntʃəvi, ǽntʃouvi]
サバ	mackerel [mǽkərl]

アジ	horse mackerel / jack mackerel
サワラ	Spanish mackerel / spotted mackerel
コハダ	gizzard shad
タイ	porgy [pɔ́ːrgi]
ティラピア	tilapia [təléipiə, -láː-, -lǽp-] ＊日本ではイズミダイ, チカダイと呼ばれている。
バス《スズキの類》	bass [bǽs]
キンメダイ	red snapper
マス	trout [tráut]
ニジマス	rainbow trout
マグロ	tuna ＊「大とろ」は most fatty tuna, 「中とろ」は medium fatty tuna。「赤身」は red tuna。canned tuna (ツナ缶, シーチキン)
ハマチ, イナダ	(young) yellowtail
ブリ	yellowtail
カンパチ	great amberjack
カツオ	skipjack (tuna) / bonito
トビウオ	flying fish
ニシン	herring [hériŋ]
カズノコ	herring roe [róu]
カサゴ	scorpion fish
サメ	shark
サメのヒレ	shark fin
チョウザメ	sturgeon [stə́ːrdʒən]
キャビア	caviar [kǽviɑ̀ːr]
サケ	salmon [sǽmən]

イクラ	salmon roe
ボラ	mullet [mʌ́lət]
からすみ	botargo [bətɑ́ːrgou] / dried mullet roe
ウニ	sea urchin [ə́ːrtʃən]
タコ	octopus [áktəpəs]
イカ	squid [skwíd]
ホタルイカ	firefly squid
クラゲ	jellyfish
ナマコ	sea cucumber
ウナギ	eel [íːl]
アナゴ	conger eel / sea eel
ドジョウ	loach [lóutʃ]
アンコウ	monkfish / angler
ナマズ	catfish [kǽtfìʃ]
フグ	swellfish / globefish
カニ	crab [krǽb]
ズワイガニ	snow crab
タラバガニ	king crab

2 食べる・飲む

★果物

リンゴ	apple [ǽpl] ＊ peel an apple (リンゴの皮をむく)
アンズ	apricot [ǽprikɑ̀t]
アボカド	avocado [æ̀vəkɑ́ːdou]
バナナ	banana [bənǽnə]
ベリー	berries
チェリー, サクランボ	cherry
柑橘類	citrus [sítrəs]
オレンジ	orange [ɔ́(ː)rindʒ]

タンジェリン	tangerine orange [tǽndʒərí:n ɔ́(:)rindʒ]
温州(うんしゅう)みかん	mandarin orange
ネーブル	navel orange [néivl ɔ̀(:)rindʒ]
グレープフルーツ	grapefruit [gréipfrù:t]
レモン	lemon
ゆず	citron
クランベリー	cranberry [krǽnbèri]
ラズベリー	raspberry [rǽzbèri] *スペル注意。p は発音しない。
ブルーベリー	blueberry
ブラックベリー	blackberry
イチゴ	strawberry [strɔ́:bèri]
ブドウ	grapes
キウイ	kiwi fruit [kí:wi: frù:t]
マンゴー	mango [mǽŋgou]
イチジク	fig
グァバ	guava [gwá:və]
メロン	melon
スイカ	watermelon
ネクタリン	nectarine [nèktərí:n]
桃	peach
パパイア	papaya [pəpáiə]
パッションフルーツ	passion fruit
洋梨	pear [péər]
パイナップル	pineapple
プラム	plum [plʌ́m]

ビワ	loquat [lóukwɑt]
ダイオウ(大黄)	rhubarb [rú:bɑːrb]
プルーン	prune
柿(の木)	persimmon [pərsímən]
梅	Japanese apricot / ume
ココナッツ	coconut [kóukənʌ̀t]
ザクロ	pomegranate [páməgrænət]

★野菜&豆類

アーティチョーク(朝鮮アザミ)	artichoke [á:rtitʃòuk]
(サラダ用の)キバナスズシロ	arugula [ərúgələ]
もやし	bean sprouts
アルファルファもやし	alfalfa sprouts [ælfǽlfə spràuts]
アスパラガス	asparagus [əspǽrəgəs]
ビート、赤カブ	beet
ブロッコリー	broccoli [brákəli]
カリフラワー	cauliflower [kɔ́(:)liflàuər]
タケノコ	bamboo shoot / bamboo sprout
メンマ	braised bamboo shoots
チンゲン菜	bok-choy [bák-tʃói]
キャベツ	cabbage [kǽbidʒ]
紫キャベツ	red cabbage
芽キャベツ	Brussels sprouts

白菜	Chinese cabbage / nappa cabbage / celery cabbage		キノコ, マッシュルーム	mushroom
コラードの若葉	collard greens		えのき茸	enoki mushroom / velvet shank
エンダイブ	endive / escarole ＊店によっては chicory (チコリー) と呼ばれる。		エリンギ	eryngii mushroom
			なめこ	nameko mushrooms
ケール, 緑葉キャベツ	kale [kéil] / kail [kéil]		ワラビ	bracken [brǽkn]
			オクラ	okra [óukrə] / gumbo [gΛmbou]
レタス	lettuce [létəs]		たまねぎ	onion [Λnjən]
サラダ菜	leaf lettuce		ネギ	green onion / leek / scallion
水菜	potherb mustard / mizuna		エシャロット	(e)shallot
ほうれん草	spinach [spínitʃ] ＊boiled spinach (ホウレンソウのおひたし)		ニラ	(Chinese) chive [tʃáiv] / garlic chive
			唐辛子	red pepper / chili pepper
小松菜	Japanese mustard spinach		しし唐	sweet green pepper
春菊	garland chrysanthemum [krəsǽnθəməm]		ピーマン	green pepper / bell pepper
青じそ, 大葉	green perilla [pərílə]		赤ピーマン	red bell pepper
			大根	Japanese radish / daikon radish
クレソン	watercress		カイワレ大根	radish sprouts
ニンジン	carrot		パースニップ (根部野菜)	parsnip ＊ニンジンに似た根菜。
セロリ	celery [séləri]			
三つ葉	honewort		カブハボタン, ルタバガ (根が黄色のカブの一種)	rutabaga [rùːtəbéigə]
キュウリ	cucumber [kjúːkΛmbər]			
冬瓜 (トウガン)	wax gourd [góːrd]		カブ, カブラ	turnip [tóːrnəp]
ニガウリ, ゴーヤー	bitter gourd / bitter melon		ジャガイモ	potato [pətéitou]
ヘチマ	loofa(h) [lúːfə]		サツマイモ	sweet potato
ナス	eggplant 《米》 / aubergine 《英》		里芋	taro [táːrou]

2 食べる・飲む

ヤムイモ, 山芋	yam [jǽm]
ユリ根	lily root
トマト	tomato [təméitou, -mɑ́:tou]
缶入りホールトマト	canned whole tomatoes
プチトマト	cherry tomato
カボチャ	pumpkin [pʌ́mpkin]
冬カボチャ（ニホンカボチャ, セイヨウカボチャなどのウリの類）	winter squash
夏カボチャ（ヘチマカボチャ, ズッキーニなどのウリの類）	summer squash
ズッキーニ	zucchini [zu(:)kí:ni] 〈米〉／ courgette [kuərʒét, kɔ:-] 〈英〉
しょうが	ginger
みょうが	Japanese ginger
ニンニク	garlic
ごぼう	burdock [bə́:rdɑ̀k] root
れんこん	lotus root
クワイ	arrowhead bulb [bʌ́lb]
豆	bean
大豆	soybean
小豆	red bean
ライマメ	lima bean [láimə bì:n]
ソラマメ	broad bean
いんげん豆	kidney bean

さやいんげん	string bean
エンドウ（豆）	pea [pí:]
枝豆	green soybean
絹さや	snow pea
グリーンピース	green peas

★穀物類

米	rice
短い粒米	short-grain rice
中型の粒米	medium-grain rice
長粒米	long-grain rice
玄米	brown rice
粟（あわ）	foxtail millet
小麦粉	flour [fláuər]
中力粉	all-purpose flour
グルテン麦粉／強力粉	bread flour
ケーキ用小麦粉／薄力粉	cake flour
オートミール用小麦粉	oat bran flour [óut brǽn flàuər]
全粒小麦粉	whole wheat flour [hóul hwí:t flàuər]
片栗粉	potato starch
小麦	wheat [hwí:t]
大麦	barley [bɑ́:rli]
ライ麦	rye [rái]
トウモロコシ	corn 〈米〉／ maize [méiz] 〈英〉
そば粉, そば（の実）	buckwheat [bʌ́khwì:t]

3. 料理

★調理する

料理する	cook [kúk]
料理法, 調理法, レシピ	recipe [résəpi]
料理	cuisine [kwizíːn]
あり合わせの料理	potluck [pàtlʌ́k]
ざっと洗う	rinse [ríns]
水気を切る	drain [dréin] ＊drain with paper towels（ペーパータオルで水気を切る）
魚のうろこをこそぎ落す	scrape [skréip] the scales off a fish
（魚や肉を骨のない）切り身にする,（魚を）三枚におろす	fillet [fílit],《米》[filéi]
（魚や鶏の）はらわたを取る	gut [gʌ́t]
骨を抜く[取り除く]	bone [bóun] ＊bone a fish ／ take the bones out of a fish（魚の骨を取る）
皮をむく	peel ＊peel a carrot（ニンジンの皮をむく）
（ナイフなどで果物などの）皮をむく	pare [péər]
豆のさやをむく, 殻をむく	shuck [ʃʌ́k] ／ shell [ʃél]
（おろし金で）おろす, すりつぶす	grate [gréit]

切る	cut
～を半分に切る	cut ~ in half ＊cut into thirds [quarters]（3分の1 [4分の1] に切る）
大きく切り分ける	carve [káːrv]
一口大に切る	cut into bite-size chunks
縦 [斜め] に切る	cut lengthwise [crosswise]
くし形に切る	cut into wedges
薄切りにする	slice
角切りにする, さいの目に切る	dice [dáis]
細切れにする	mince [míns]
千切りする	shred [ʃréd] ＊shred cabbage（キャベツの千切り）
乱切りにする	chop [tʃáp]
みじん切りにする	chop ~ into fine pieces ／ chop finely
搾る	squeeze [skwíːz] ＊squeeze a lemon（レモンを搾る）
（ドレッシングなどと）あえる, 軽く混ぜ合わせる	toss ＊toss the pasta in the sauce（パスタにソースをからめる）
すりつぶす	mash
ピューレにする	puree [pjuréi]
泡立てる（卵・クリームなどかき回して）	whip [hwíp] ／ whisk [hwísk]

2

食べる・飲む

（卵などを）強くかき混ぜる，（クリームなど を）泡立てる	beat ＊beat butter until smooth and fluffy（バターをなめらかでフワフワになるまで混ぜる）
練る，こねる	knead [níːd]
クリーム状にする	cream
混ぜ合わせる	mix
よく混ぜ合わせる	blend
（コーヒーなどを）かき混ぜる	stir [stə́ːr] ＊stir sugar into one's coffee（コーヒーに砂糖を入れてかき混ぜる）
マリネにする	marinate [mǽrənèit]
振りかける	sift [síft] ＊sift flour [fláuər]（小麦粉を振りかける）
浸す	soak [sóuk] ＊soak potatoes in water（じゃがいもを水に浸す）
（液体などに）ちょっとつける，さっと浸す	dip ＊dip in sauce（タレにつける）
裏ごしする	strain [stréin] ＊strain boiled potatoes（ジャガイモを裏ごしする）
衣をつける	dip into batter
挽（ひ）く	grind [gráind]
解凍する	defrost [difrɔ́(ː)st]
（料理する前に魚・肉などを）下ごしらえする	dress ／ prepare ＊dress meat（肉の下ごしらえをする）
（サラダなどに）ドレッシングをかける	dress ＊dress a salad ／ put dressing on a salad（サラダにドレッシングをかける）
～を電子レンジでチンする	microwave ／ nuke [njúːk] ~ in a microwave
～を…分間電子レンジで温める	nuke ~ for ... minutes
予熱する	preheat ＊heat a frying pan（フライパンを温める），reheat（温め直す）
火にかける，熱する，温める	heat
強火にする	turn up the heat
弱火にする	turn down the heat
火を止める	turn off the heat
注ぐ，（液体を）つぐ	pour [pɔ́ːr] ＊pour A B ／ pour B for A（A〔人〕にB〔飲み物〕をつぐ）
（オーブンなどで肉などを）焼く，あぶる，（豆などを）炒る	roast [róust]
（焼き網，グリルを使って直火で）焼く	broil [brɔ́il] ／ grill [gríl]
（オーブンでパンやケーキを）焼く	bake [béik]
（パン，チーズなどを）こんがり焼く	toast [tóust]
～を炭火焼にする	char-grill
真っ黒に焦げる	be burned black
生焼けである	be undercooked
焼きすぎである，煮すぎである	be overcooked
（フライパンで）炒める，ソテーにする	sauté [soutéi] ／ pan-fry

強火で素早く炒める [炒めた料理]	stir-fry		凍らせる	freeze
（油で）揚げる，炒める，焼く	fry		冷やす，冷蔵する	chill
（たっぷりの油で）揚げる	deep-fry		冷蔵庫で一晩寝かせる	let stand overnight in fridge
ゆでる	boil ＊boil until tender（しんなりするまでゆでる）		（調味料で）味付けする	season
短時間ゆでる	poach [póuʧ]		塩・コショウする	season with salt and pepper
煮こぼれる	boil over [bɔ̀il óuvər]		加える，足す	add ＊add black pepper to the soup（スープにブラックペッパーを足す）
湯がく，湯通しする	blanch [blænʧ]			
湯通しする，半ゆでにする	parboil [páːrbɔ̀il]		（塩，胡椒などを）ふる	sprinkle ＊sprinkle salt on a steak（ステーキに塩をふる），put pepper on（～にコショウをふりかける）
煮込む，とろ火でぐつぐつ煮る	simmer [símər] ＊simmer over low heat for 10 minutes（弱火で10分間煮込む）			
とろ火で長時間煮込む	stew [stjúː]		たれ（をつける）	baste [béist]
蒸す	steam ＊steam potatoes（ジャガイモをふかす）		～にマヨネーズをつける	put mayonnaise on ...
			～に…を付け合わせる	garnish ~ with ...
（肉・野菜を油でいためてからとろ火で）蒸し煮にする	braise [bréiz]		～を皿に盛りつける	arrange [serve] ... on a plate

★調味料・だし

（豆などを）炒る	parch [páːrʧ]

調味料，味付け	seasoning ＊adjust the seasoning（味を調える）
燻製にする	smoke
ひっくり返す	turn (over)
調味料，香辛料	spice
アクをとる	remove the scum [skʌm]
薬味，調味料，付け合わせ	relish [réliʃ]
焦げ目を付ける	sear [síər]
砂糖	sugar [ʃúgər]
粉砂糖	powdered sugar 〈米〉／icing sugar 〈英〉
冷ます	cool
塩	salt [sɔ́ːlt]

コショウ	pepper	ディジョンマスタード	Dijon mustard
黒こしょう	black pepper	セイヨウワサビ	horseradish
粉末唐辛子	cayenne pepper [kaién pépər]	ワサビ	wasabi ／ green horseradish paste ／ Japanese horseradish
ソース	sauce [sɔ́ːs]		
醤油	soy sauce		
酢	vinegar [vínigər]	トウガラシ製の辛いソース（タバスコ）	Tabasco sauce [təbǽskou sɔ̀ːs]
みりん	sweet cooking sake ／ mirin		
ワインビネガー	wine vinegar	ケチャップ	ketchup 《米》／ tomato sauce 《英》
オリーブ油	olive oil		
サラダ油	salad oil	マヨネーズ	mayonnaise [méiənèiz]
胡麻油	sesame oil		
食品添加物	additive	タルタルソース	tartar sauce [táːrtər sɔ̀ːs]
防腐剤	preservative [prizéːrvətiv]		
		はちみつ	honey [hʌ́ni]
オールスパイス	allspice [ɔ́ːlspàis]	ジャム	jam
マーガリン	margarine [máːrdʒərən]	マーマレード	marmalade [máːrməlèid]
バター	butter [bʌ́tər]	ピーナッツバター	peanut butter
ラード	lard [láːrd]		
ブイヨン	bouillon [búljan]		
固形スープの素	bouillon cube	**★ドレッシング**	
だしの素	instant bouillon	サラダドレッシング	salad dressing [sǽləd drèsiŋ]
ブロス，だし汁	broth [brɔ́(ː)θ] ＊肉・魚・野菜などを煮出したスープ。		
		シーザー・ドレッシング	Caesar dressing [síːzər drèsiŋ]
昆布だし	kelp stock		
カツオだし	bonito stock	フレンチ・ドレッシング	French dressing
だしを取る	make soup stock		
隠し味	secret ingredients	イタリアン・ドレッシング	Italian dressing
カラシ，マスタード	mustard [mʌ́stərd]	オイル・ビネガー・ドレッシング	oil and vinegar dressing

ガーリック・ペパー・ドレッシング	garlic pepper dressing
当店製ドレッシング	house dressing
サウザンアイランド・ドレッシング	Thousand Island dressing
ブルーチーズ・ドレッシング	blue cheese dressing
ノンオイル・ハーブ・ドレッシング	oil-free herb dressing

★ハーブ類

ハーブ，香味（植物）	herb [ə́:rb, hə́:rb]
バジル	basil [bǽzl, béizl]
チャービル	chervil [tʃə́:rvl]
エゾネギ	chives [tʃáivz]
コリアンダー	cilantro [səlá:ntrou] ／ coriander
ディル	dill
ミント	mint
オレガノ	oregano [ərégənòu]
パセリ	parsley [pá:rsli]
ローズマリー	rosemary [róuzmèri]
セージ	sage [séidʒ]
タラゴン	tarragon [tǽrəgàn]
タイム	thyme [táim]
シナモン	cinnamon [sínəmən]
ナツメグ	nutmeg [nʌ́tmèg]

レモングラス	lemongrass
アニス	anise [ǽnis]
ターメリック，うこん	turmeric [tə́:rmərik]
サフラン	saffron [sǽfrən]
ベイリーフ，月桂樹の葉	bay leaf
セロリシード	celery seed
クミン	cumin [kʌ́min]
アニスヒソップ	anise hyssop [hísəp]
アルカンナ	alkanet
アロエ	aloe [ǽlou]
アンジェリカ	angelica [ændʒélikə]
イタリアンパセリ	Italian parsley
エキナシア	echinacea [èkinéiʃə]
オオグルマ	elecampane [èlikæmpéin]
ニワトコ	elder
オリーブ	olive [áliv]
カモミール	chamomile [kǽməmàil]
カレープラント	curry plant
キャットニップ	catnip
ヒメウイキョウ	caraway [kǽrəwèi]
ムラサキツメクサ	red clover [réd klóuvər]
ヒレハリソウ	comfrey [kʌ́mfri]
オランダワレモコウ	salad burnet
サフラワー	safflower [sǽflàuər]
山椒	Japanese pepper
サントリーナ	santolina

ヒマワリ	sunflower
シソ	shiso / Japanese basil
ジャスミン	jasmine [ʤǽzmin, ʤǽs-]
ステビア	stevia
ゼラニウム	geranium [ʤəréiniəm]
シャボンソウ	soapwort
カタバミ	sorrel
ヨモギギク	tansy [tǽnzi]
タンポポ	dandelion
チコリ	chicory [tʃíkəri]
キンレンカ	nasturtium [nəstə́ːrʃəm]
クロタネソウ	nigella [naiʤélə]
スミレ	heartsease / violet
ハイビスカス	hibiscus
ヤナギハッカ	hyssop [hísəp]
ウイキョウ	fennel [fénl]
アマ（亜麻）	flax
ベルガモット	bergamot [bə́ːrgəmɑ̀t]
ホップ	hop [hɑ́p]
ルリヂサ	borage [bɔ́(ː)riʤ]
ビロードアオイ	marsh mallow
マージョラム，マヨラナ	marjoram [mɑ́ːrdʒərəm]
マリーゴールド	marigold
セイヨウノコギリ草	yarrow [jǽrou]
ゴムの木	gum tree [gʌ́m trìː]
ラベンダー	lavender [lǽvəndər]
ラムズイヤー	lamb's ears
シナノキ	linden [líndən]

ヘンルーダ	rue [rúː]
ハゴロモ草	lady's mantle
香水木	lemon verbena [lémən və(ː)rbíːnə]
レモンバーム	lemon balm [bɑ́ːm]
バラ	rose
月桂樹	laurel [lɔ́(ː)rl]

★前菜系

前菜	appetizer [ǽpitàizər] 《米》／ starter 《英》
（フランス料理の）前菜	hors d'oeuvre [ɔ́ːrdə́ːrv]
（イタリア料理の）前菜	antipasto [æ̀ntipɑ́ːstou]
（スペイン料理の）前菜	tapas
フルーツカクテル，フルーツポンチ	fruit cup ／ fruit cocktail [flúːt kɑ̀kteil]
小エビのカクテル	shrimp cocktail
ナッチョス	nachos [nɑ́ːtʃouz]
コーンチップス	corn chips
クニッシュ	knish [kəníʃ] ＊ユダヤ料理。ジャガイモや肉を薄く練った小麦粉の皮で包んで揚げたり焼いたもの。
鳥の手羽焼	grilled chicken wings
肉の腸詰め	stuffed derma [stʌ́ft də́ːrmə]
カナッペ	canapé [kǽnəpi]

生野菜の前菜（フランス料理）	crudités [krùːditéi]
ビネグレットソース	vinaigrette sauce [vinəgrét sɔ́ːs]
セロリスティック	celery sticks
ニンジンスティック	carrot sticks
ピーマンの薄切り	bell pepper strips
ブルーミングオニオン	blooming onion ＊花のように盛りつけた玉葱の前菜。
ブルスケッタ（イタリア料理）	bruschetta ＊オリーブ油に浸しガーリックやトマトを添えたパン。
デビルズオンホースバック	devils on horseback ＊漬けたマンゴーとかをプルーンに詰めベーコンで包み調理した料理。
エンジェルオンホースバック	angels on horseback ＊オイスターをベーコンで包み焼いたもの。
ドランクンチキン	drunken chicken ＊アルコールを使って調理する鳥料理。
卵とじスープ	egg-drop soup
春巻き	egg roll 《米》／spring roll 《英》
ナスのサラダ	eggplant salad
フルーツサラダ	fruit salad
パコラ	pakora [pəkɔ́ːrə] ＊インドやパキスタンなど南アジアなどが発祥の揚げ物料理。
酢漬けキュウリ	pickled cucumber
ロッキーマウンテンオイスター	Rocky Mountain oysters ＊北米のバッファローや牛の睾丸を調理した前菜。

シュリンプトースト（広東料理）	shrimp toast ＊細かく刻んだエビを揚げた料理。
トルティーヤ（メキシコ料理）	tortilla [tɔːtíːə] ＊小麦粉やコーンの生地を薄く焼いたもの。
揚げラビオリ	toasted ravioli [rævióuli]

★朝食系

グラノーラ	granola [grənóulə] ＊麦の一種に干しぶどうや赤砂糖を混ぜた健康食品。
パンケーキ，ホットケーキ	pancake
そば粉のパンケーキ	buckwheat pancake
ワッフル	waffles [wáflz]
マフィン	muffin [mʌ́fin]
コーンブレッド	corn bread
クレープ	crepe [kréip]
ブリトー	burrito [bəríːtou]
キッシュ	quiche [kíːʃ] ＊チーズ，ベーコンなどで味つけしたパイの一種。
ベーコン	bacon [béikn]
ソーセージ	sausage [sɔ́(ː)siʤ]
ハッシュブラウン	hash browns ＊ジャガイモをすりつぶして油で揚げたもの。
テイタータッツ	tater tots [téitər táts] ＊tater ジャガイモ，tot は一口のこと。つぶしたポテトを一口サイズにして揚げたもの。
シリアル（穀物を加工した朝食）	cereal [síəriəl]

オートミール	oatmeal [óutmìːl] 《米》／ porridge [pɔ́(ː)ridʒ] 《英》 ＊麦をお粥のように煮て調理したもの。
ミルク	milk
コーヒー	coffee [kɔ́ːfi, káfi] ＊iced coffee（アイスコーヒー），make [fix] coffee（コーヒーを入れる）
紅茶	tea
レモンティー	tea with lemon
ミルクティー	tea with milk
ヨーグルト	yogurt [jóugərt]
コンチネンタル・ブレックファースト（コーヒーとパンだけの軽い朝食）	continental breakfast
イングリッシュ・ブレックファースト（卵やベーコン，ハムがつくたっぷりした朝食）	English breakfast
朝食用加工品	breakfast food
朝食時のテレビ番組	breakfast television
朝食会	breakfast meeting
朝食用コーナー	breakfast nook
トーストとコーヒーの朝食	breakfast of toast and coffee
オートミールの朝食	breakfast of oatmeal
朝食用プチパンの盛り合わせ	breakfast pastry platter
朝食を食べない人	breakfast skipper

朝食用トレー	breakfast tray
大急ぎで食べられる朝食	breakfast on-the-run
チョコレートミルク	chocolate [tʃɔ́(ː)kələt] milk
カテージチーズ	cottage cheese
モッツァレラチーズスティック	mozzarella cheese stick
ストリングチーズ	string cheese
赤身のハム	lean ham
七面鳥の赤身	lean turkey
新鮮なフルーツ	fresh fruit
ドライフルーツ	dried fruits
ドライレーズン	dried raisins
ドライクランベリー	dried cranberries
ドライアプリコット	dried apricots
生のベイビーキャロット	raw baby carrots
生のセロリ	raw celery
クラッカー	crackers
クッキー	cookie 《米》／ biscuit 《英》
くし切りのオレンジ	orange wedges
スープ	soup [súːp]

★パン類

ホットドッグ	hot dog
ドーナツ	doughnut / donut
ハンバーガー	hamburger

チーズバーガー	cheeseburger
ベーグル	bagel [béigl]
デーニッシュ ペストリー	Danish pastry [déiniʃ péistri] ＊フルーツやナッツなど を加えたパイ状の菓子パン。
小さくて丸いパン，香料や干し ぶどうが入った 菓子パン	bun [bán]
砂糖衣が十字 状にのった菓 子パン	hot cross bun
サンドイッチ	sandwich [sǽndwitʃ]
ピザ	pizza [pí:tsə]
（小型の）さ っくりしたパ ン	biscuit [bískit] 《米》／ scone [skóun, skán]《英》 ＊イギリスで biscuit は 「ビスケット」。米語で 「（塩味の）ビスケット」 は cracker，「（甘い味の） ビスケット」は cookie。
スコーン	scone [skóun, skán] ＊小麦粉，バター，牛乳を 混ぜて焼いた小さなパン。
クロワッサン	croissant [kwɑːsáːnt, krə-	kwǽsɑːŋ]
タコス	taco [táːkou]
シュークリーム	cream puff
BLT（ベーコン，レタス，トマトを挟んだサンドイッチ）	BLT ＊ Bacon, Lettuce, Tomato の頭文字から。
精白パン	white bread
ライ麦パン	rye bread
全粒粉パン	whole wheat bread

ピタパン	pita bread
ロールパン	roll [róul]
サワードウで 作ったパン	sourdough bread
（潜水艦の形 に似た）長細 いロールパン	submarine roll
トースト	toast [tóust]
食パン	bread ＊a loaf [roll ／ slice ／ piece] of bread（パン 1本 [1個／1枚／1切れ]）。
フランスパン	baguette [bægét]
ハム＆チーズ サンド	ham and cheese sandwich

★パスタ類

麺	noodle
パスタ	pasta [páːstə]
マカロニ	macaroni [mækəróuni]
フジッリ	fusilli [fjuːsíli] ＊らせん型にねじれたパスタ。
フェットゥチ ーネ	fettuccine [fètətʃíːni] ＊ひもかわ状のパスタ。
ボウタイズ	bow ties ＊蝶ネクタイのような形 をしたパスタ。
リングィーニ	linguine [liŋgwíːni] ＊平打ちパスタ。
ラザニア	lasagna [ləzáːnjə]
スパゲティ	spaghetti [spəgéti]
ミートソース	spaghetti bolognese ／ spaghetti with meat sauce
ラビオリ	ravioli [rævióuli]

★ジャガイモ料理

ポテトスキン	potato skins
ベイクドポテト, 皮付きポテト	baked potato 《米》／ jacket potato 《英》
ハッシュドポテト	hashed potatoes [hǽʃt pətéitouz] ＊ゆでたジャガイモを細切りにし小麦粉をまぶしてフライパンで焼いたもの。
ハッシュドブラウン	hash(ed) browns ＊＝ハッシュポテト。
マッシュポテト	mashed potatoes ＊ゆでたジャガイモをつぶしたもの。
フライドポテト	French fries／fries／fried potatoes ＊英では chips。「ポテトチップス」は chips 《米》, crisps 《英》。

★卵料理

卵	egg
生卵	raw egg [rɔ́ː ég]
卵の殻	eggshell
卵の黄身	yolk [jóuk], vitellus [vətéləs]
卵の白身	egg white, albumen [ælbjúːmən]
卵を割る	crack [break] an egg
卵をかき混ぜる	beat an egg
ゆで卵	boiled egg
かたゆで卵	hard-boiled egg
半熟卵	soft-boiled egg
オムレツ	omelet(te) [ámələt]
卵焼き	Japanese rolled omelet(te)

プレーン・オムレツ	plain omelet(te) [pléin áməlet]
チーズオムレツ	cheese omelet(te)
（半熟片面焼きの）目玉焼き	eggs sunny-side up ＊ I'd like my eggs sunny-side up.《注文》半熟目玉焼きでお願いします), eggs sunny-side down（黄身の側を下にした目玉焼き）, eggs over-easy（両面焼いた目玉焼き）, eggs over-medium（両面中焼きの目玉焼き）, eggs over-hard（両面堅焼きの目玉焼き）
いり卵, スクランブルエッグ	scrambled egg
ポーチドエッグ	poached egg
ウズラの卵	quail's egg [kwéilz ég]

★料理全般

食前酒	aperitif [əpèritíːf]
メインディッシュ	main dish
メインコース, 主菜	main course
アントレ, 主菜	entrée [áːntrei]
サイドディッシュ, 副菜	side dish
アラカルト	à la carte [àː lɑː káːrt]
お薦め料理	specialty [spéʃlti]
軽めの［分量が多い］料理	light [heavy] dish
注文（する）	order
オニオンリング	onion rings
アメリカンドッグ	corn dog
ポップコーン	popcorn [pápkɔ̀ːrn]
キュウリの酢漬け	pickles [píklz]
チリスープ；チリトウガラシ	chili

カリフォルニア・ロール	California roll ＊カリフォルニア生まれの巻きずし。
カツレツ	cutlet [kʌ́tlət]
フィッシュ・アンド・チップス	fish and chips
フリッター	fritter [frítər]
フォンデュ	fondue [fɑndʲúː]
ピラフ	pilaf [pilάːf]
チャーハン	fried rice
グラタン	gratin [grǽtn]
ドリア	rice gratin
コロッケ	croquette [kroukét]
ジャンバラヤ《米国南部の料理》	jambalaya [ʤʌ̀mbəláiə]
ミートパイ	meat pie
ポットロースト（なべ焼き牛肉）	pot roast
菜食主義者用の料理	vegetarian dish

★サラダ系

サラダ	salad [sǽləd]
コールスロー	coleslaw [kóulslɔ̀ː]
チキンサラダ	chicken salad
シーザーサラダ	Caesar salad
ガーデンサラダ	garden salad
ギリシャ風サラダ	Greek salad
マカロニサラダ	macaroni salad
ポテトサラダ	potato salad
シーフードサラダ	seafood salad
シェフサラダ	chef's salad
（ドレッシングであえた）グリーンサラダ	tossed salad [tɔ́(ː)st sǽləd]

★スープ系

豆スープ	bean soup
ポタージュ	potage [pɔ(ː)tάːʒ]
コンソメ	consommé [kὰnsəméi]
ビーフ・ストロガノフ	beef stroganoff [bíːf strɔ́(ː)gənɔ̀(ː)f]
チキンスープ	chicken soup
クラムチャウダー	clam chowder [klǽm ʧáudər]
オニオンスープ	onion soup
ガスパッチョ	gazpacho [gəspάːʧou]
オクラスープ	gumbo [gʌ́mbou]
ミネストローネ	minestrone [mìnəstróuni]
コーンスープ	corn soup
エンドウ豆のスープ	pea soup
シチュー	stew [stʲúː]

★デザート系

デザート	dessert [dizə́ːrt] 《米》／ pudding [púdiŋ]《英》
パイ	pie
アップルパイ	apple pie
パンプキンパイ	pumpkin pie
ケーキ	cake [kéik] ＊ birthday cake (バースデーケーキ), Christmas cake (クリスマスケーキ)。
ショートケーキ	strawberry sponge cake
デコレーションケーキ	fancy cake ／ decorated cake
ゼリー	jello 《米》／ jelly 《英》

2

食べる・飲む

プディング, プリン	pudding [púdiŋ] / custard pudding
アイスクリーム	ice cream [áis krìːm]
アイスクリームサンデー	ice cream sundae [sʌ́ndei]

★日本食・B級グルメなど

寿司	sushi ＊ = a hand-shaped vinegared rice topped with raw fish
刺身	sashimi ＊ = a Japanese dish of bite-sized pieces of raw fish eaten with soy sauce and wasabi paste
天ぷら	tempura / Japanese deep-fried food ＊ = a Japanese dish of fish, shellfish, or vegetables, fried in batter
カレーライス	curry [kə́ːri] and rice
ハヤシライス	hashed meat [beef] and rice
すき焼き	sukiyaki ＊ = a Japanese dish of thin slices of beef cooked in a pan with vegetables and tofu
しゃぶしゃぶ	thinly-sliced beef fondue
とんかつ	deep-fried pork cutlets
丼物	a bowl of rice with food on top
牛丼	a bowl of rice topped with boiled beef and onion(s)
カツ丼	a bowl of rice topped with pork cutlet
天丼	a bowl of rice topped with deep-fried prawns

鉄火丼	a bowl of rice topped with slices of raw tuna
中華丼	a bowl of rice topped with stir-fried vegetables and seafood
うなぎの蒲焼	charcoal-broiled eel
ハンバーグステーキ	Salisbury steak / hamburger steak [patty]
おにぎり	rice ball
焼きそば	pan-fried noodles
そば	buckwheat noodle
うどん	Japanese wheat noodle
ラーメン	ramen / Chinese noodle ＊ ramen with soy sauce based soup（醤油ラーメン）
焼き鳥	skewered grilled chicken
お好み焼き	meat [seafood] and vegetable pancake
たこ焼き	spherical fried dumplings of batter with bits of octopus inside
おでん	a stew made with fish cakes, vegetables, and boiled eggs
団子	rice dumpling [dʌ́mpliŋ]
味噌汁	miso soup ＊ fermented soybean paste（味噌）
豆腐	bean curd [kə́ːrd]
納豆	fermented [fərméntid] soybeans

4. 外食

★レストランの予約

手頃な値段のレストラン	restaurant with reasonable prices	シーフード・レストラン	seafood restaurant
ファミレス	casual dining restaurant	ダイナー，小レストラン	diner [dáinər]
高価なレストラン	expensive restaurant [ikspénsiv[eks-] réstərənt]	ビュッフェ，セルフサービスのレストラン，立食	buffet [bəféi, bu- ǀ búfei]
大衆食堂	cheap restaurant	郷土料理	local food
菜食主義者用レストラン	vegetarian restaurant	軽食堂	snack bar
食べ放題のレストラン	all-you-can-eat restaurant	営業時間	business hours
フランス料理レストラン	French restaurant	窓側の席	window table ／ table by the window
ロシア料理レストラン	Russian restaurant	テラス席	table on the terrace
地中海料理レストラン	Mediterranean [mèditəréiniən] restaurant	屋外の席	outside table
トルコ料理レストラン	Turkish restaurant	予約	reservation [rèzərvéiʃən]
ギリシャ料理レストラン	Greek restaurant	予約をする	make a reservation
ベトナム料理レストラン	Vietnamese restaurant	～時に予約している	have a reservation at ~
タイ料理レストラン	Thai restaurant	二人用の席を予約する	reserve a table for two
中華料理レストラン	Chinese restaurant	予約をキャンセルする	cancel one's reservation
韓国料理レストラン	Korean restaurant	服装の規程はありますか。	Is there a dress code?
日本料理レストラン	Japanese restaurant	夕食は何時からですか。	When do you start serving dinner?
		飲み物だけでもいいですか。	Is it OK to have just drinks?

2

食べる・飲む

4名ですが，席は空いていますか。	We are a party of four. Do you have a table available?
どのくらい待ちますか。	How long is the wait?
（私たち）バーで待ちます。	We'd like to wait in the bar.
予約なし	without a reservation
予約をしてないですが，いいですか。	Is it OK without a reservation?

★注文など

ウエーター	waiter ／ server
ウエートレス	waitress ／ server
（レストランなどの）接客主任	maitre d' [mèitrə díː , mètrə-] ＊ maitre d'hotel の略。
案内係の女性	hostess [hóustəs]
料理長，シェフ，料理人	chef [ʃéf]
料理人，コック	cook [kúk]
メニュー	menu [ménjuː]
日本語のメニュー	menu in Japanese
注文する	order
メニューを見てオーダーする	order from the menu
注文をお願いします。《自分も含めて複数》	Can we order, please?
すぐにできるものはなんですか。	What's fast?

コースはありますか。	Do you have a course menu?
本日の特別メニュー	today's special
店の自慢料理	house's specialty

★食器類など

料理道具	cooking utensils [juː(ː)ténslz]
薬味，香辛料	condiment [kándəmənt] ＊ケチャップ，マスタード，コショウなどが置いてあるコーナーには，CONDIMENTS と掲示。
プレースセッティング	place setting
ディナー皿	dinner plate
パン用バター皿	bread-and-butter plate
サラダ用皿	salad plate
スープ皿	soup bowl
コップ	water glass
ワイングラス	wine glass
カップ	cup
受け皿	saucer
ナプキン	napkin
ステーキナイフ	steak knife
ナイフ	knife [náif]
スープ用スプーン	soup spoon
ティースプーン	teaspoon
サラダ用フォーク	salad fork

夕食用フォーク	dinner fork
箸	chopsticks
フィンガーボウル	finger bowl ＊食事中に卓上で指先を洗うための道具。
パンかご	bread basket
デザートトレー	dessert tray
テーブルクロス	tablecloth [téiblklɔ̀(:)θ]
食事を出す	serve the meal
テーブルをきれいにする	clear the table
食器をさげる	clear the dishes [díʃiz]

★支払い

請求書，勘定書	check
サービス料	service charge
サイン	signature [sígnətʃər]
領収書	receipt [risíːt]
支払う	pay the check
会計をお願いします。	Check, please.
チップ	gratuity [grətjúːəti] ／ tip [típ]
持ち帰り用の袋はありますか。	Do you have a doggy bag?

★ファストフード

これとこれをください。	I will have this one and this one.
ダブルチーズハンバーガー1つとコーラのM をください。	One double cheeseburger and a medium coke, please.

こちらで召し上がりますか，お持ち帰りですか。 ―店内で。	(For) here or to go? —For here please. ＊英国では，Eat-in or take-away?。
テイクアウト，持ち帰り	to go 《米》／ take-away 《英》
大	large
中	medium [míːdiəm]
小	small
相席をする	share the table
炭酸飲料	soda pop
コカコーラ・クラシック	Coca Cola Classic
ダイエット・コーラ	Diet Cola
スプライト	Sprite
ファンタ・オレンジ	Fanta Orange
ジンジャエール	ginger ale
アップルジュース	apple juice [ǽpl dʒùːs]
オレンジジュース	orange juice
グレープジュース	grape juice
ココア《飲み物》	hot chocolate 《米》 ／ cocoa [kóukou] ＊cocoa（ココア〔パウダー〕，カカオの木）
レモネード	lemonade [lèmənéid]
ルートビア	root beer
ドクターペッパー	Dr. Pepper
ミスターピブ	Mr. Pibb ＊ドクターペッパーに似た味の炭酸飲料。

ネスティー	Nestea
シェイク	shake
ミルクシェイク	milkshake
フレンチフライ	French fries
ホット・ファッジ・サンデー	Hot Fudge Sundae
マックフラーリー	McFlurry
バニラ・コーン	Vanilla Cone ＊vanilla extract（バニラエッセンス）
フレッシュ・ベイクド・クッキー	Fresh Baked Cookies
ソフトクリーム	soft serve (ice cream)
アイスキャンディー	popsicle 《米》／ice lolly 《英》

★バーで

バー	bar
パブ，居酒屋	pub
飲みに行く	go drinking
バーテンダー	bartender, barkeep(er) 《米》／barman 《英》
代金引き換え	cash on delivery
（バーやレストランの）アルコール飲料サービスタイム	happy hour
バーカウンター	bar counter
カウンター席	counter [káuntər]

テーブルチャージ	cover charge ＊table charge は和製英語なので×。
スツール，カウンター椅子	stool [stú:l]
はしご酒をする人	bar-hopper ／pub-crawler
トールドリンク	tall drink ＊細長いグラスで飲む軽いカクテル。
ビール	beer [bíər]
生ビール	draft beer
ジョッキ	(beer) mug
発泡酒	low-malt beer ／sparkling liquor
ギネス	Guinness
日本酒	sake
レモネード・シャンディー	lemonade shandy
ウイスキー	whiskey [hwíski] ＊米国、アイルランド以外では whisky と綴る。スコッチは米国でも通例 whisky と綴る。
モルトウイスキー	malt whiskey
ウイスキーの水割り	whiskey and water
ウイスキーのソーダ割り，ハイボール	whiskey and soda
ウイスキー・オンザロック	whiskey on the rocks
ストレートで	neat [ní:t] ＊neat は「酒に水や氷を入れない」《形》。米国では straight ともいう。
シングル	single

ダブル	double
バーボンウイスキー	bourbon [bə́ːrbən]
ジン	gin
ジントニック	gin and tonic
コニャック	cognac [kóunjæk]
ブランデー	brandy [brǽndi]
ワイン	wine
ラム	rum ＊米国では「(一般に) アルコール飲料，酒」の意味もある。
カクテル	cocktail [káktèil]
ホットカクテル	hot cocktail
シューター	shooter ＊ウォッカやテキーラなど，アルコール度の高い酒を使うカクテルのこと。
マティーニ	martini [mɑːrtíːni]

シャンパン	champagne [ʃæmpéin]
ウオッカ	vodka [vádkə]
リキュール	liqueur [likə́ːr]
アルコール度	alcohol content
(アルコール分が) 強い, 濃い	strong
(アルコール分が) 弱い, 薄い	light
(アルコールを含まない) 清涼飲料 (水)	soft drink
ノンアルコール (の)	non-alcoholic
炭酸水	sparkling water
ペットボトルの水	bottled water
水道水	tap water

McSorley's Old Ale House
ニューヨーク最古といわれるパブのひとつ。

トロピカルドリンク	tropical drink
乾杯！	Cheers! ／ Bottoms up!〔グラスの底を上にして飲み干すところから〕
酔っぱらう	get drunk [gét drʌ́ŋk]
私は酒に弱いんです。	I cannot hold my drink. ／ I get drunk easily.
私は酒に強いです。	I can hold my drink. ／ I'm a heavy drinker.

氷入れ	ice pale
氷ばさみ	ice tongs

マドラー，かき混ぜ棒	muddler [mʌ́dlər]
（酒の）つまみ	snacks [snǽks] ／ nibblies [níbəliz]
ガム	gum [gʌ́m]
シュガーレスガム	sugar-free gum
タバコ	cigarette
電子タバコ	e-cigarette ／ vape
間接喫煙	secondhand smoke
灰皿	ash tray [ǽʃ trèi]
禁煙《掲示》	No smoking

3.

住む

1. 住居

★家

（建造物としての）家，一戸建て住宅	house [háus]	タウンハウス，テラスハウス	town house 《米》／ terrace home 《英》 ＊隣家と壁を共有する住宅。
（生活の場としての）家，家庭；わが家へ《副》	home [hóum] ＊家族の生活，団らんのイメージを持つ。	公営住宅	public housing
家を建てる	build a house	プレハブ住宅	prefabricated [prefabbed] house
建て売り住宅	house built for sale	団地	apartment complex ／ housing complex
アパート	apartment 《米》／ flat 《英》	部屋	room ＊enter [go into] a room （部屋へ入る）
アパートを借りる	rent an apartment	インテリア，内装	interior [intíəriər]
家，住宅，邸宅	residence [rézidəns] ＊residence は house, home より形式ばった語。	書斎	study
		子ども部屋	child's room
分譲マンション	condominium [kàndəmíniəm] = condo [kándou] ＊mansion は「豪邸」。	避難所（風雨・危険などを避けるための），シェルター	shelter
賃貸マンション	rental apartment ／ apartment building for rent	地下室	basement [béismənt] ＊「物置きや貯蔵庫にする地下室」は cellar。
ワンルームマンション	studio apartment 《米》／ studio flat 《英》	貯蔵室	storage [stɔ́:riʤ]
		地下倉庫	basement storage
リゾートマンション	resort condominium	モービルホーム，トレーラーハウス	mobile home ／ mobile trailer
マンションを所有する	own a condominium	宿泊設備付きヨット	houseboat
二世帯住宅	duplex [djú:pleks] [two-family] house		

★台所

台所	kitchen [kítʃən]
(台所の) 流し	sink [sínk] * stainless steel sink (ステンレスの流し台)
流しのこし器	sink strainer [stréinər]
三角コーナー	sink-corner strainer
ガス湯沸かし器	gas water heater
蛇口	faucet [fɔ́ːsit] 《米》 / tap [tǽp] 《英》 * turn on [off] the faucet (蛇口を開ける [閉める])
(料理用の) コンロ, ガスレンジ	stove [stóuv] * put the kettle on the stove (やかんを火にかける), turn off the gas at the main cock (ガスの元栓を閉める)
換気扇	(ventilation) fan [(vèntəléiʃən) fǽn]
調理台	kitchen counter
まな板	cutting board
包丁	kitchen knife * sharpen a kitchen knife with a whetstone (砥石で包丁を磨く)
万能包丁	universal knife
菜切り包丁	vegetable knife
出刃包丁	pointed carver
刺身包丁	kitchen knife for sashimi
パン切り包丁	bread knife
果物ナイフ	paring [fruit] knife
(刃物を砥ぐ) やすり棒	honing [sharpening] steel
(パン, 肉など を薄く切る) スライサー	slicer

キッチンバサミ	kitchen shears
スポンジ (で洗う)	sponge [spʌ́ndʒ]
食器用洗剤	dishwashing detergent [ditɔ́ːrdʒənt]
クレンザー	cleanser
スポンジたわし	scrub sponge
金属たわし	scouring pad / scourer / stainless steel scourer
鍋洗い	pot scrubber
水切りかご	dish drainer [dréinər]
(台所用の) ペーパータオル, キッチンペーパー	paper towel [táuəl] 《米》 / kitchen paper [roll] 《英》
(洗った皿を 拭く) ふきん	dish towel / dishcloth / dishrag
台ふきん	kitchen cloth
生ゴミ	(kitchen) garbage 《米》 / (kitchen) rubbish 《英》
生ゴミ処理機	garbage disposal [gáːrbidʒ dispóuzl]
生ゴミ入れ	garbage can 《米》 / garbage bin 《英》, dustbin 《英》
ゴミ箱	trash [garbage] can 《米》 / dustbin 《英》, rubbish bin 《英》
調味料ラック	spice rack
食器棚	cabinet [kǽbənit] / closet [klázət] / cupboard [kʌ́bərd] * take the plates out of the cabinet (食器棚から取り皿を取り出す)

棚	shelf [ʃélf] ＊複数形は shelves [ʃélvz]。
容器	container [kəntéinər]
タッパー	plastic container
蓋付き瓶	preserve jar ＊果物や漬け物を入れるもの。
（缶詰の）缶	can 〈米〉 ／ tin 〈英〉
缶切り	can opener 〈米〉 ／ tin opener 〈英〉
電気缶切り	electric can opener
コルク抜き，ワインオープナー	corkscrew [kɔ́:rkskrù:]
デカンタ	decanter [dikǽntər]
栓抜き	(bottle) opener
キッチンタイマー	cooking timer
計量カップ	measuring cup
計量スプーン	measuring spoons
はかり	scale(s)
ラップ	wrap ／ plastic [cling, food] wrap ／ cellophane ＊Saran Wrap（サランラップ）は商標。
アルミホイル	aluminum foil
盆，トレー	tray [tréi]
エプロン	apron [éiprən]

★台所家電

食器洗い機	dishwasher
トースター	toaster [tóustər]
オーブンミット	oven mitt

オーブン	oven [ʌ́vn] ＊bake ~ in the oven （オーブンで～を焼く）
オーブントースター	toaster oven ＊"オーブントースター"は和製語。
ミキサー（果物，野菜などの）	blender 〈米〉 ／ liquidizer 〈英〉
ジューサー	juicer
（電動）泡立て器	electric mixer
フードプロセッサ	food processor ＊食べ物を切ったり，刻んだり，つぶしたりする電動器具。
電子レンジ	microwave (oven) ＊microwave（電子レンジにかける）
（調理用）レンジ	range [réindʒ] 〈米〉 ／ cooker 〈英〉
レンジ・フード	range hood ＊レンジの上に設置され，蒸気・煙などを外部に排気させるための換気器具。
炊飯器	rice cooker
しゃもじ	rice scoop [skú:p]
魔法瓶	thermos (bottle)
冷蔵庫	refrigerator [rifrídʒərèitər] ／ fridge [frídʒ] ＊take ~ out of refrigerator（冷蔵庫から～を取り出す）
冷蔵庫につけるマグネット	refrigerator magnet
冷凍庫	freezer
コーヒーメーカー	coffee maker
コーヒー豆挽き機	coffee grinder [kɔ́:fi, kɑ́f- gràindər]

★調理器具

鍋，平鍋	pan [pǽn]
フライパン	frying pan ／ skillet 〈米〉
深鍋	pot [pát]
スープ鍋	stockpot [stákpàt]
鉄鍋	iron [áiərn] pot
土鍋	earthen(ware) pot
鍋蓋	pot lid
落とし蓋	drop-lid
鍋つかみ	potholder [páthòuldər]
ミトン	oven mitten(s)
鍋敷き	hot pot stand
中華鍋	wok [wák]
シチュー鍋	saucepan
キャセロール（蒸し焼き鍋）	casserole [kǽsəròul]
ロースター，焼き鍋	roaster
圧力鍋	pressure cooker
焼き網	grid ／ gridiron
蒸し器	steamer
フライ返し	turner
（調理用の）へら	spatula [spǽtʃələ]
おたま	ladle [léidl]
菜箸	kitchen chopsticks
ケーキ焼き皿	cake pan
（パンなどを焼く）耐熱皿	bakeware
クッキーの抜き型	cookie cutter
ブロイラー（肉焼き器）；焼き肉用の若鶏	broiler

バーナー	burner
水切り器	colander [kʌ́ləndər]
茶こし	tea strainer [sieve]
裏ごし器	fine sieve
（竹製の）ざる，籠	bamboo basket
（小麦粉などの）ふるい，ざる	sieve [sív] ／ sifter
水切りざる	strainer [stréinər]
粉挽き器	mill
肉挽き器，ミンサー	mincer [mínsər]
（ミキシング）ボウル	mixing bowl
麺棒	rolling pin
おろし器，おろし金	grater [gréitər]
トング	tongs [tɑ́ŋz]
アイスクリームスクープ	ice cream scooper
（卵・，クリームなどの）泡立て器；（卵，クリームなどを）かき回す	whisk [hwísk]
卵の泡立て器	eggbeater
ガーリックプレス（ニンニク絞り器）	garlic press
皮むき器	peeler
肉たたき器	meat mallet ／ meat tenderizer
すり鉢	grinding bowl
すり粉木	grinding pestle

3
住む

うろこ取り	fish scale remover
巻きす	bamboo rolling mat
串	spit ／ skewer [skjúər]
エッグスライサー（ゆで卵薄切り器）	egg slicer
じょうご	funnel [fʌ́nl]
やかん	kettle [kétl]

★ダイニング・ルーム

ダイニング・ルーム	dining room
ダイニングテーブル	dining (room) table
ダイニングチェア	dining (room) chair
テーブルクロス	tablecloth
ランチョンマット	place mat ＊ひとり分の食器を置く小型のテーブル敷き。
テーブルセンター	centerpiece ＊テーブルの中央に置かれた花などの装飾物。
花瓶	vase [véis, véiz｜《英》vɑ́ːz]
ろうそく	candle ＊ blow out the candles on the cake（ケーキのろうそくを吹き消す）
ろうそく立て	candlestick
食器棚	china cabinet
《集合的に》食器	tableware ／ eating utensils

弁当箱	lunch box ＊ prepare a boxed lunch（弁当を作る）

コップ，グラス	glass ／ tumbler
紙コップ	paper cup
ワイングラス	wineglass
ビールジョッキ	(glass) beer mug ／ (glass) tankard
（コーヒー，紅茶用の）茶わん，カップ	cup [kʌ́p]
ティーカップ	teacup [tíːkʌ̀p]
コーヒーカップ	coffee cup
（コーヒーカップなどの浅い）受け皿	saucer [sɔ́ːsər]
マグカップ	mug
コーヒーポット	coffee pot
ティーポット，急須	teapot [tíːpɑ̀t]
水差し	(water) jug [ʤʌ́g] ／ pitcher [pítʃər]
砂糖入れ	sugar bowl
《コーヒー用の》クリーム（入れ）	creamer
塩入れ	salt shaker 《米》 ／ saltcellar 《英》
こしょう入れ	pepper shaker
回転トレー	turntable ／ Lazy Susan 《米》 ／ dumbwaiter 《英》 ＊食卓の回転盆。またはテーブル中央に置いて料理・調味料を載せて使う回転するトレーのこと。

ナプキン	napkin [nǽpkin]
紙ナプキン	paper napkin
紙皿	paper plate
茶碗	(rice) bowl
陶磁器	china
漆器	japan
銀食器	silverware
スプーン	spoon
（料理を取り分ける）スプーン	tablespoon ＊料理に使う計量用の大さじも意味する。
茶さじ，ティースプーン	teaspoon
スープスプーン	soup spoon
ナイフ	(table) knife
バターナイフ	butter knife [spreader]
フォーク	fork
箸	chopsticks
皿	plate ／ dish
（浅い）皿，取り皿	plate ＊浅く丸い皿で，めいめいよそって食べる皿。
パン皿	bread-and-butter plate
ディナー皿	dinner plate
（深い）皿	dish ＊《米》では dish を plate の意にも用いる。
大皿	platter
スープ皿，スープボウル	soup bowl
サラダボウル	salad bowl [sǽləd bòul]

つまようじ	toothpick
ストロー	straw [strɔ́:]

★リビング

3

住む

リビング，居間	living room 《米》／ siting room 《英》
廊下	corridor [kɔ́(:)rədər] ／ hall 《米》／ passage
通路	aisle [áil]
天井	ceiling [síːliŋ]
壁	wall [wɔ́:l]
床，〜階	floor [flɔ́:r]
じゅうたん，カーペット	carpet [kάːrpit]
（床の一部に敷く）じゅうたん，マット	rug [rʌ́g]
床暖房	floor (panel) heating
絵，絵画	painting
絵	picture
（絵画の）フレーム	(picture) frame
暖炉	fireplace [fáiərplèis]
薪	logs
（暖炉の）火・熱よけのついたて，囲い	fire screen
消火器	fire extinguisher [fáiər ikstìŋgwiʃər]
救急箱	first-aid kit
窓	window

窓ガラス	windowpane
サッシ	metal sash window
カーテン	curtain [kə́ːrtn] ＊draw the curtain（カーテンを引く［開ける／閉める］）, open [close] the curtain（カーテンを開ける［閉める］）
（厚地の）カーテン	drapes [dréips]
ブラインド	blinds ／ (window) shade 〈米〉
観葉植物	house plant
芳香剤	air refresher ／ air freshener

★バスルーム

お手洗い，トイレ；浴室	bathroom 〈米〉／ toilet 〈英〉 ＊〈英〉では bathroom は「浴室」,〈米〉で「浴室」は bath, bathroom。
便器	toilet (bowl) ＊flush the toilet（トイレの水を流す）
便座	toilet seat ＊heated toilet seat（保温便座）
便器のふた	toilet seat lid
トイレットペーパー	bath tissue ／ toilet paper
トイレットペーパーホルダー	bath tissue holder ／ toilet paper holder
トイレ用ブラシ	toilet (bowl) brush
プランジャー（排水管掃除帽）	plunger [plʌ́ndʒər]

消臭スプレー	air freshener ／ deodorizer spray ＊spray air freshener（芳香剤をスプレーする）
シャワーを浴びる	take a shower
シャワーキャップ	shower cap ＊シャワーで髪がぬれないようするもの。
風呂に入る	take a bath
体を洗う	wash oneself
石けんの泡	suds [sʌ́dz]
顔を洗う	wash one's face
（石けんを使わずに）顔をさっと洗う［すすぐ］	rinse one's face
髪を洗う	wash [shampoo] one's hair
タオルで体を拭く	towel off ／ towel oneself dry
浴槽	bathtub
入浴剤	bath oil
泡立て（入浴）剤	bubble bath
タイル	tile
大理石	marble
シャワー・カーテン	shower curtain
シャワー・カーテンロッド	shower curtain rod
シャワー・カーテンリング	shower curtain rings
シャワーヘッド（シャワーの噴水口）	shower head
バスマット	bath mat

（浴室用）滑り止めバスマット	rubber bath mat
排水	drain [dréin]
排水口	drain outlet
（〜を）石鹸（で洗う）	soap [sóup]
石鹸受け［置き］	soap dish
石鹸入れ	soap dispenser
（〜を）シャンプー（で洗う）	shampoo [ʃæmpúː]
リンス	conditioner
浴用タオル	wash cloth
スポンジ	sponge [spΛndʒ]
（ボディー）ブラシ	brush [brΛʃ]
軽石	pumice [pΛmis]
タオルラック	towel rack * towel（タオル：タオルで拭く）
バスタオル	bath towel
ハンドタオル	hand towel
洗面所の（薬入れ）戸棚	medicine cabinet
（バスルームの）洗面台	(bathroom) sink ／ washbowl
鏡	mirror
歯ブラシ立て	toothbrush holder
歯ブラシ	toothbrush
練り歯みがき	toothpaste
歯を磨く	brush one's teeth
デンタルフロス	dental floss
口内洗浄剤	mouthwash
うがいをする	gargle [gáːrgl]
うがい薬	mouthwash ／ gargle

ヘアドライヤー	blow dryer ／ hair dryer
髪を乾かす	dry one's hair
（ひげを）剃る	shave [ʃéiv]
電気シェーバー	electric shaver
かみそり	razor [réizər] * razor burn（かみそり負け）
かみそりの刃	razor blades
シェービングクリーム	shaving cream
アフターシェーブローション	after-shave lotion
オーデコロン	cologne [kəlóun]
毛抜き	tweezers
綿棒	cotton swabs
耳かき	ear pick
爪切り	nail clippers
鼻毛カッター	nose hair trimmer
（体臭を消す）消臭剤	deodorant [dióudərənt]
くずかご	wastebasket
体重計	(bath [bathroom]) scale * get on the scale（体重計に乗る）

★寝具など，睡眠

寝室	bedroom
ベッド	bed
ダブルベッド	double bed
二段ベッド	double-deck bed
二段ベッド（子供用）	bunk bed
（ベッドの頭部の）ヘッドボード	headboard

（ベッドの）ボックススプリング	box spring	寝る，眠る	go to bed ／ go to sleep ＊It's time to go to sleep.（寝る時間だよ）
ベットの骨組	bed frame	目覚ましをかける，アラームを設定する	set one's alarm
ダストラッフル	dust ruffle ＊ベッドの底部外側につけた床まで届く装飾用のひだのついた布。	ぐっすり寝る	sleep tight ＊Sleep tight!（ぐっすりおやすみ！）
ダストスカート（＝ダストラッフル）	dust skirt	寝入る	fall asleep
マットレス	mattress [mǽtrəs]	いびきをかく	snore [snɔ́ːr] ＊snoring（いびき）
ウォーターベッド	waterbed	夢	dream ＊have a dream（夢を見る）
折り畳みベッド	folding bed	寝言を言う	talk in one's sleep
枕	pillow [pílou]	目覚める	wake up
長枕	bolster [bóulstər]	起きる	get up
枕カバー	pillowcase		
（ひだ付きの）枕カバー	pillow sham	**★家具など**	
シーツと枕カバー	bed linen [béd lìnən]	家具	furniture [fɔ́ːrnitʃər] ＊【集合的に；単数扱い】 three pieces of furniture（家具3点）
ベッドカバー	bedspread [béd sprèd]	テーブル	table
シーツ	bed sheet	机	desk
フラットシーツ	flat sheet	椅子	chair
ボックス型のシーツ	fitted sheet	ソファ	sofa [sóufə]
毛布	blanket [blǽŋkit]	（背，ひじかけ付きの）長椅子	settee [setíː]
電気毛布	electric blanket	カウチ，ソファ（ベッド），寝椅子	couch [káutʃ]
掛け布団	comforter [kʌ́mfərtər] ／ quilt [kwílt]		
眠る；睡眠	sleep	ソファベッド	sofa sleeper

二人掛け用ソファ	love seat [lʌ́v sìːt]	扇風機	(electric(al)) fan
ひじ掛け椅子	armchair	暖房器（具），ヒーター	heater
装飾用クッション	throw pillow ＊ベッドやソファに置くクッション。	石油ストーブ	oil [kerosene] heater
（ソファなどのそばに置く）サイドテーブル	end table	（石油）ファンヒーター	(kerosene) fan heater ＊kerosene [kérəsìːn]（灯油）《米》，イギリスではparaffin。
（ソファの前に置く）低いテーブル	coffee [cocktail] table	電気ストーブ	electric heater
（ベッド脇の）ナイトテーブル，サイドテーブル	night table	空気清浄機	air purification / air cleaner
雑誌入れ	magazine holder	加湿器	humidifier
雑誌棚	magazine rack	除湿器	dehumidifier
本箱，書棚	bookcase / bookshelf	オーディオ・システム	audio system
ドレッサー，化粧台，鏡台	dresser	ミニコンポステレオ	minicomponent stereo set
引き出し，たんす	drawer [drɔ́ːr]	ヘッドフォン	headphone / headset
洋服だんす	wardrobe [wɔ́ːrdròub]	液晶テレビ	liquid crystal display TV [television] ＊= LCD TV
クロゼット	closet [klázət]	薄型テレビ	flat-screen TV
整理だんす	chest of drawers	ハイビジョンテレビ	high-definition television set
金庫	safe	4K超解像度テレビ	4K ultra-high-definition television

★電化製品など

家電製品	home electric appliances [əpláiənsiz]	リアプロジェクションテレビ	rear-projection TV
		DVDプレイヤー	DVD player
エアコン	air conditioner	リモコン	remote (control) ＊turn up[down] the volume （ボリュームを上げる［下げる］）
		ホームシアター	home theater 《米》/ home cinema 《英》

タイマー付き ラジオ	clock radio
電気カーペット	electric carpet

★照明・電気

スイッチ（を入 れる［切る］）	switch
明かり	light ＊ switch [put ／ turn] on the light（明かりをつける）
非常灯	emergency light
トラック照明	track lighting ＊レール状のライティン グダクト (track) に沿っ て電灯の位置を自由に変 えられる移動照明。
蛍光灯	fluorescent (light [lamp])
（白熱）電球	light bulb [láit bʌ̀lb]
電灯，スタンド	lamp
電気スタンド	desk lamp ／ desk light
ランプの傘	lampshade
フロアスタンド	floor lamp
寝室用ランプ	night stand
シャンデリア	chandelier [ʃæ̀ndəlíər]
懐中電灯	flashlight《米》／ torch《英》
手提げランプ	lantern [lǽntərn]
燭台	candlestick ／ candlestand
誘蛾灯	light trap

乾電池	(dry-cell) battery ＊ちなみに、「単1」は D (a size D battery)、 「単2」は C (a size C battery)、「単3」は AA (double A と読む - a size AA battery)
充電式電池	rechargeable battery
コンセント	outlet [áutlèt]《米》／ socket [sákət]《英》
延長コード	extension cord
プラグ	plug ＊「プラグをコンセント に差し込む」は put a plug in the outlet。
たこ足配線を する	put too many plugs in one [a single] outlet
ブレーカー	(circuit) breaker ＊「ブレーカーが落ちた！」は The breaker just tripped!。
ヒューズ	fuse ＊「ヒューズが飛んだ！」 は The fuse has blown!。
漏電遮断器	earth leakage circuit breaker ／ ground fault circuit interrupter
配線用遮断器	molded case circuit breaker
電圧	voltage [vóultidʒ]
変圧器	transformer
電流	electric current
説明書	manual [mǽnjuəl]
保証書	guarantee [gæ̀rəntíː]
修理する	repair [ripéər]
部品	part ／ component ＊ spare parts（予備部品）

★正面・裏側

郵便受け；郵便ポスト	mailbox
門	gate
街灯	street light
玄関の前の小道	front walk
庭	yard [jáːrd]
庭；庭いじりをする	garden [gáːrdn] ＊花や野菜の植えてある庭。
前庭	front yard
ステップ（踏み段）	steps
玄関	front door ／ entrance
張り出し玄関	porch [pɔ́ːrtʃ]
防風ドア	storm door
インターフォン	intercom [íntərkàm]
玄関の灯り	porch [front] light
（ドアの）ノブ	knob [náb]
ドアチェーン	door chain
（ドアの）のぞき穴	peephole
玄関マット	doormat
窓	window
窓網戸	(window) screen
（通りから車庫への）私道	driveway [dráivwèi]
車庫	garage [gərάːdʒ│〈英〉gǽraːdʒ]
ガレージの戸	garage door
シャッター，雨戸	shutter(s)
フェンス	fence
屋根	roof

屋根裏	attic [ǽtik]
アンテナ	antenna [ænténə]〈米〉 ／ aerial [éəriəl]〈英〉
パラボラアンテナ	parabolic antenna
ロフト，屋根裏	loft
（屋根）瓦	roof tile
雨漏り	leak (in the roof)
（屋根の）とい［樋］，（道路の排水用）溝	gutter [gʌ́tər]
縦とい	downspout [dáunspàut]〈米〉 ／ drainpipe [dréinpàip]〈英〉
ひさし	eaves [íːvz]
煙突	chimney [tʃímni]
ベランダ	balcony [bǽlkəni] 〈米〉／ veranda [vərǽndə]〈英〉
プール	swimming pool
デッキ	deck [dék]
裏口	back door
網戸	screen door
勝手口	side door
テラス	terrace ／ patio
テラス用家具	patio furniture
物置	tool shed
生け垣（で囲う）	hedge [hédʒ]
ハンモック	hammock
バーベキューグリル	barbecue grill ／ grill

3

住む

3. 家事・育児

★洗濯

家事をする	do the chores [tʃɔ́ːrz] *chore《通例, 複数形で》日常的な仕事 [日常的にやるべきこと], 家事
洗濯 (をすること)	laundry [lɔ́ːndri]《米》/ washing《英》
洗濯する	do the laundry《米》/ do the washing
洗濯する, 洗う	wash
洗濯物	the laundry《米》/ the washing《英》
洗濯機	washing machine *「コインランドリーに行く」は go to the laundromat。
洗濯板	washboard
洗濯かご	laundry [linen] basket / hamper《米》
洗濯物袋	laundry bag
乾燥機	dryer [dráiər] *put the laundry in the dryer [drier] (乾燥機で乾かす)
ドライクリーニングする	dry-clean [drái klíːn]
クリーニング店	laundry
コインランドリー	laundromat [lɔ́ːndrəmæt]《米》/ launderette [lɔ́ːndərét]《英》
～をクリーニングに出す	take [send] ~ to the cleaners / have ~ dry-cleaned

洗濯用洗剤	laundry detergent
柔軟剤	fabric softener [fǽbrik sɔ̀(ː)fnər]
漂白剤	bleach [blíːtʃ]
洗濯のり	starch [stáːrtʃ]
静電気とり	static cling remover
洗える, 洗濯のきく；洗濯のきく衣類	washable
汚れの首輪	dirty neck ring
汚れ, しみ；汚す [汚れる], しみを付ける [が付く]	stain [stéin] *コーヒー, ジュース, 血などがつく汚れ。
泥	mud [mʌ́d]
落ちにくい汚れをとる	remove tough stains
(ベッドの) シーツを取り替える	change the sheets
乾かす, 乾く, 乾燥させる	dry *dry the laundry (洗濯物を乾かす)
物干し台	clothes-drying platform
物干し柱	clothes pole
物干しひも	clothesline [klóu(ð)zlàin]
洗濯バサミ	clothespin
洗濯物を外に干す	hang out the laundry

洗濯物を取り込む	take the laundry down
アイロン（を）かける	iron [áiərn] ＊iron a shirt（シャツにアイロンをかける）
アイロン台	ironing board
アイロンでしわを伸ばす	iron out the wrinkles [ríŋklz]
ズボンに折り目をつける	put a crease in the pants
（服を）たたむ	fold [fóuld] ＊fold and put away the laundry（洗濯物をたたんで片付ける）
ハンガー	hanger
（衣類の）防虫剤	mothball(s) ＊通例，複数形。

★裁縫

裁縫	sewing [sóuiŋ]
裁縫道具	sewing kit
裁縫をする，縫う	sew ＊sew up a rip [hole]（ほころび［穴］を縫う）
ミシン	sewing machine
継ぎ当てする	put a patch
裁縫箱	sewing box
裁縫ばさみ	(a pair of) sewing scissors
裁ちばさみ	shears [ʃíərz]
針	needle [níːdl] ＊thread a needle（針に糸を通す）
まち針	pin
かぎ針	crochet hook [krouʃéi hùk]

針刺し・針山	pincushion [pínkùʃən]
糸	thread [θréd] ＊pass a thread through a needle（針に糸を通す）
糸巻き	spool 《米》／ reel 《英》
糸くず	waste [wéist] thread
指貫	thimble [θímbl]
編む	knit [nít] ＊knit ~ a sweater（〜のためにセーターを編む）
編み棒	knitting needle
編み糸	yarn [jáːrn]
巻尺，メジャー	tape measure

3

住む

★掃除

掃除する，きれいにする	clean ＊clean house（家を掃除する）
掃除機をかける	vacuum [vǽkjuəm] ＊vacuum the floor（床に掃除機をかける）
掃除機	vacuum cleaner 《米》／ hoover [húːvər] 《英》
じゅうたん用掃除機	carpet sweeper [káːrpit swìːpər]
ほうき	broom [brúːm] ＊sweep a room with a broom（ほうきで部屋を掃く）
（柄の短い）小ぼうき，卓上ほうき	whisk broom
ちり取り	dustpan [dʌ́stpæn]
ほこり（を払う）	dust [dʌ́st] ＊「ほこりっぽい」は dusty。dust the furniture（家具のほこりを払う）
はたき	(feather) duster

掃く	sweep [swíːp] ＊sweep the floor（床を掃く）
汚い	dirty [dɔ́ːrti]／filthy [fílθi]
悪臭（を放つ）	stink [stíŋk]
モップする	mop [máp]
磨く；光沢	polish [páliʃ] ＊polish a floor with wax（ワックスで床を磨く）
ゴシゴシ磨く[洗う]，こする	scrub [skrʌ́b]
（こすったりして）汚れを取り除く	scour [skáuər]
（「へら」などを使って表面を）こすり落とす	scrape [skréip]
バスタブから水をぬく	empty the water out of the bathtub
浴槽内部につく汚れ[あか]の輪	bathtub ring
整頓する，片付ける	tidy up [táidi ʌ́p]／clear up [klíər ʌ́p] ＊tidy up a desk（机の上を片付ける[整頓する]）
（元の所へ）しまう，片付ける	put away
並べ替える	rearrange
吊るす，掛ける	hang ＊hang ~ on a wall（壁に~を掛ける）
（ものを）元へ返す	put back ＊put the dictionary back on the shelf（辞書を棚に返す）

散らかっているもの，がらくたの山	clutter [klʌ́tər]
バケツ	bucket [bʌ́kət]
ポリバケツ	plastic bucket
雑巾	dust cloth
ぼろ切れ	rags
ゴム手袋	rubber gloves
拭く，拭き取る	wipe [wáip] ＊wipe off the table（テーブルを拭く）
（不要なものを）捨てる[処分する]	discard [diskáːrd]
灰皿の灰を捨てる	empty an ashtray
ゴミ	garbage [gáːrbiʤ]〈米〉／rubbish [rʌ́biʃ]〈英〉，trash [trǽʃ]〈米〉／litter [lítər] ＊garbageとrubbishは，生ごみや容器類などゴミ類全般を指し，trashは主に紙屑など乾燥したゴミを指す。litterは公共の場や道路などに散乱したゴミ屑等を指す場合が多い。
~をゴミ箱に入れる	put ~ in the wastebasket
ゴミ箱を空にする	empty the wastebasket
ゴミ収集日	garbage collection day
ゴミ集積所	garbage dump〈米〉／rubbish dump〈英〉
ゴミを出す	take out the trash
可燃ごみ	flammable [flǽməbl] garbage／combustible [burnable] garbage

不燃ごみ	non-flammable garbage ／ incombustible [non-burnable] garbage
粗大ゴミ	large garbage [trash] ／ bulk [bulky, big] garbage [trash]
資源ゴミ	recyclable trash
ゴミ袋	trash bag
（半）透明ごみ袋	(semi-)transparent garbage bag
ポリ袋	plastic bag
ペットボトル	plastic bottle
リサイクル用ごみ箱	recycling bin
紙袋	paper bag
ハンディクリーナー	hand vacuum cleaner
（掃除用）洗剤, クレンザー	cleanser [klénzər]
フロアワックス	floor wax
家具つや出し	furniture polish
スクイージー	squeegee [skwíːʤìː] ＊先にゴムがついた窓ふき
銀製品専用クリーナー	silver cleaner
カーペットクリーナー	carpet cleaner
消毒剤	disinfectant ／ sanitizer
水に溶かす [溶ける]	dissolve in water

★育児

3 住む

胎児	a baby in the womb ＊womb [wúːm] は「子宮」。embryo [émbriòu]（妊娠8週までの胎芽）, fetus [fíːtəs]（妊娠9週以後の胎児）
新生児	newborn baby
未熟児	premature baby
赤ちゃん	baby [béibi]
幼児	infant ／ little [small] child
子どもを育てる	bring up a child
スキンシップ, 身体的接触	physical contact
身体の発達	physical development [growth]
発育が早い [遅い]	grow fast [slowly]
母乳	mother's milk ／ breast milk
（赤ん坊に）母乳を飲ませる, 母乳で育てる	breast-feed ＊I'm breast-feeding my baby.（私は赤ちゃんを母乳で育てています）
おっぱいを飲ませる	give *a baby* the breast
（市販の）ベビーフード, 離乳食	baby food ／ weaning food ＊start feeding a baby food（離乳食を始める）
寝返りを打って裏返る	roll over [toss about] in bed
赤ちゃんを仰向けに寝かせる	put a baby flat on his [her] back

赤ちゃんをうつぶせにする	put [place] a baby on his [her] stomach
抱っこする	hold a baby in *one's* arms ＊Carry me, Mom! (ママ，抱っこして！)
赤ちゃんをおんぶする	put [carry] a baby on *one's* back
子守歌を歌って赤ん坊を寝かしつける	sing a baby off to sleep with a lullaby [lʌ́ləbài]
子どもを9時に寝かす［寝かしつける］	put a child to bed [sleep] at nine
泣く子をあやす	pacify a crying child
いないいないばあ	peekaboo [píːkəbùː] 〈米〉／ peepbo [píːpbòu], bopeep [bòupíːp] 〈英〉
息子を肩車する	carry *one's* son on *one's* shoulders

はいはいする	crawl [krɔ́ːl]
つかまり立ちする	pull to stand
よちよち歩く	toddle [tádl]

食べ物の好き嫌いが多い	*be* picky [choosy] about food ＊picky eater（好き嫌いが激しい人）
両親に口答えする	talk back to *one's* parents
いたずら，悪ふざけ	trick

子どもに予防接種をする	vaccinate a child
子どもにポリオ（小児麻痺）のワクチン注射をする	vaccinate a child against polio

★ベビー用品

ベビー用品	baby goods [products]
ベビー服	baby clothes
ベビーベッド	crib 〈米〉／ cot 〈英〉
寝返り防止クッション	sleep positioner
ベッドメリー，モビール	baby mobile ＊ベビーベッドに取り付けるオルゴール付きおもちゃ。
マザーズバッグ，おむつ用バッグ	diaper bag
抱っこ紐，スリング	baby carrier
よだれかけ	baby bib
おくるみ	receiving blanket

哺乳瓶	baby bottle 〈米〉／ feeding bottle 〈英〉
哺乳瓶の乳首	nipple 〈米〉／ teat 〈英〉
粉ミルク	(baby) formula 〈米〉／ baby milk 〈英〉
おしゃぶり	pacifier [pǽsəfàiər] 〈米〉／ dummy 〈英〉
搾乳機	breast pump
授乳用クッション	nursing cushion

ベビーバス	baby bathtub
湯温計	bath thermometer
体温計	thermometer
（赤ちゃん用熱冷まし薬）タイレノール	Infants' Tylenol 《商品名》
ベビー石鹸	baby wash
ベビー用シャンプー	baby shampoo
おむつ	diaper [dáiəpər] 《米》 / nappy [nǽpi] 《英》 *change a baby's diaper（おむつを替える）, disposable diaper（紙おむつ）
おむつ交換台	changing pad / changing [dressing] table
ウェットティッシュ（ベビー用）	baby wipes *おしりふき。「（通常の）ウェットティッシュ」は wet wipes。
おむつ用ゴミ箱	diaper pail
おむつかぶれ用クリーム	diaper rash cream *diaper rash（おむつかぶれ）
使い捨ておむつ交換シート	disposable changing pad
おしり拭きウォーマー	wipe warmer
洗浄綿	cleansing wipes
消毒綿	alcohol swab
蒸気滅菌器	steam sterilizer
綿棒	cotton swab / Q-tip *Q-tip は商標。clean one's ears with a Q-tip（綿棒で耳あかを取る）

おまる	potty (chair) / pot *sit on a potty（おまるに座る）
ゆりかご	cradle [kréidl] *rock a baby in a cradle（赤ちゃんをゆりかごに入れてゆする）
歩行器	walker *toddle along on a walker（歩行器にすがってよちよち歩く）
ベビーカー	stroller [stróulər] 《米》 / pushchair, buggy [bʌ́gi] 《英》
チャイルドシート	child [baby] car seat / child safety seat
（カーシート用）ヘッドサポート	head support
積み木	block 《米》 / brick 《英》
ぬいぐるみ人形	rag doll
（動物の）ぬいぐるみ	stuffed animal 《米》 / soft toy 《英》 *stuffed dog（犬のぬいぐるみ）
がらがら	rattle [rǽtl]
ままごとをする	play house
びっくり箱	jack-in-the-box
おもちゃ箱	toy box [chest] *put ~ back into the toy box（～をおもちゃ箱に戻す）
滑り台で遊ぶ	play on the slide
砂場で遊ぶ	play in the sandbox [《英》 sandpit]
鬼ごっこをする	play tag
かくれんぼうをする[して遊ぶ]	play hide-and-seek

3

住む

★庭仕事

庭仕事	yard work ＊do yard work（庭仕事をする）
軍手	work gloves
雑草（を取り除く）	weed [wíːd]
水をかける [まく／入れる]	water
（植物・草木を）植える	plant [plǽnt] ＊名詞は、「植物、（樹木に対して）草花, 苗木」「（製造）工場」。
種子（をまく）	seed
肥料	fertilizer [fɔ́ːrtəlàizər]
肥料を与える	fertilize [fɔ́ːrtəlàiz]
刈り込んで整える [手入れする]	trim [trím]
熊手（で掃除する）	rake [réik]
（土砂などを運ぶ）手押し車	wheelbarrow [hwíːlbæ̀rou]
じょうろ	watering can [pot]
ノズル	nozzle [názl]
ホース（で洗う）	hose [hóuz]
スプリンクラー	sprinkler
リーフブロワー	leaf blower ＊葉っぱを風圧で掃除する機械。
シャベル, スコップ	shovel [ʃʌ́vl]
ツルハシ	pickax [píkæks]

鍬（くわ）	hoe [hóu]
鋤（すき）	spade [spéid]
（園芸用の）移植ごて	trowel [tráuəl] ＊片手で持つ小さい「シャベル」。
鉢	pot [pá(ː)t	pɔ́t]
はしご	ladder [lǽdər]
脚立	stepladder [stéplæ̀dər]
高枝切りバサミ	high pruning shears
刈り込みばさみ	hedge clippers
芝刈りをする	mow the lawn
芝刈り機	lawn mower
（草刈り用の）鎌	sickle [síkl]
草を刈る	cut the grass
虫よけスプレー	bug spray
殺虫剤	bug killer ／ insecticide [inséktəsàid] ／ vermicide [vɔ́ːrməsàid] ／ pesticide [péstəsàid]
除草剤	weed killer

★日曜大工

日曜大工	do-it-yourself ＝ DIY
（部屋、家具などを）修理 [修繕／改装／改修／リフォーム] する	renovate [rénəvèit]

修理［修繕］する	fix ／ repair
ハンマー（で打つ），ハンマーで〜を打つ	hammer [hǽmər] ＊hammer nails into the board（板にハンマーで釘を打ち込む）
釘	nail [néil] ＊pull out a nail（釘を抜く），drive a nail into a pillar（釘を柱に打ちつける）
くさび（をいれる）	shim [ʃím]
道具［工具］箱	toolbox
ドライバー	screwdriver
プラスのドライバー	Phillips screwdriver
マイナスのドライバー	slotted screwdriver ／ flat-head screwdriver ／ flat-blade screwdriver
ペンチ	pliers [pláiərz]
カッターナイフ	utility knife
レンチ，スパナ	wrench 《米》／ spanner 《英》 ＊hexagonal wrench（六角レンチ）
モンキースパナ	monkey wrench
ねじ	screw [skrú:]
ワッシャー	washer
ボルト	bolt [bóult] ＊tighten [táitn] a bolt（ボルトを締める［留める］），remove a bolt（ボルトをはずす）
ナット，留めネジ	nut [nʌ́t]
ワイヤー，針金	wire [wáiər]
ちょうつがい	hinge [híndʒ]

のこぎり（でひく）	saw [sɔ́:]
（金属などを切る）弓のこ，かなのこ	hacksaw [hǽksɔ̀:]
きり，ドリル	drill [dríl]
（らせん）きり	auger [ɔ́:gər]
のみ（で彫る）《大工道具》	chisel [tʃízl]
かんな（をかける）	plane [pléin] ＊plane a surface smooth（かんなをかけて表面をなめらかにする）
バール	claw bar [klɔ́: bɑ̀:r] ／ wrecking bar
万力	vise 《米》[váis] ／ vice 《英》
水準器	level
発電機	generator
ハンドドリル	hand drill
ハンドドリルの曲がり柄	brace [bréis]
電気ドリル	electric drill ／ power drill
ドリルの刃	drill bit
電動糸のこぎり（で切る）	jigsaw [dʒígsɔ̀:]
電動のこぎり	power saw
チェーンソー	chain saw
ガソリン入れ	gas can
機械油	oil
塗料皿	paint pan
ペイントローラー	paint roller
（ペイント用の）刷毛	paintbrush [péintbrʌ̀ʃ]

3

住む

87

ペンキ，塗料	paint
ペンキを塗る	paint ／ apply paint ＊apply two coats of paint（ペンキを2度塗りする）
ニス（を塗る）	varnish [vάːrniʃ]
塗りむら	uneven coating
塗料用シンナー	paint thinner [θínər]
（液体などの濃さを）薄くする；薄い	thin ＊thin paint with paint thinner（〔塗料用〕シンナーで塗料を薄める）
油性の	oil-based ＊oil-based ink（油性インキ）
水性の	water-based ＊water-based paint（水性塗料）
さび止めペンキ	rust-resistant paint
（ペンキを削り落とす）へら，（玄関などの）靴の泥落とし	scraper [skréipər]
《掲》ペンキ塗り立て	FRESH PAINT ／ WET PAINT
防水［防護］シート	tarp ＊= tarpaulin [tɑːrpɔ́ːlən]。
ヤスリ（をかける）	file ＊file one's nails smooth（爪にヤスリをかけてなめらかにする）
紙ヤスリ	sandpaper
紙ヤスリで磨く	sand [sǽnd]
砥石（といし）	whetstone ／ sharpening stone ＊sharpen a knife on a whetstone（砥石でナイフを研ぐ）

接着剤，のり	glue [glúː]
木工用ボンド	wood glue
瞬間接着剤	instant glue ／ superglue
ダクトテープ	duct tape ＊配管などの補修用に使われる。
壁紙（を貼る）	wallpaper
断熱材	insulation
漆喰（しっくい）	plaster
ひび	crack [krǽk]
パテ（を塗る［でふさぐ］）	putty [pʌ́ti]
砂利（じゃり）	gravel [grǽvl]
金網（かなあみ）	wire netting
ベニヤ版	plywood [pláiwùd]
材木	lumber [lʌ́mbər] ＊板材や角材に製材された挽き材。
材木の切りくず	wood chip
木目	grain(ing) [gréin(iŋ)]
（木の）節（ふし）	knot [nάt]
角材	square timber
小角材（こがくざい）	scantling [skǽntliŋ] ＊約13センチ角未満の角材。
コンクリートブロック	concrete block
レンガ	brick [brík]
セメント	cement [səmént]
ロープ	rope [róup]
はんだ	solder [sάdər, sɔ́ː-]
はんだごて	soldering iron [sάdəriŋ àiərn]

★リフォーム・収納など

家を改修［改築］する	renovate [rénəvèit] a house
改築	home renovation
改築，リフォーム	remodel [rìːmá(ː)dəl | -mɔ́dəl]
部屋をリフォーム［改装］する	remodel a room
家の見取り図	house plan
家の大きさ	house size
間取り	room layout
建築期間	building time
土地代	land cost
建築費	building [construction] cost
建築方式	construction system
部屋の改装	room makeover
部屋のデザイン	room design
室内装飾	home decor [hóum deikɔ̀ːr]
台所の改築	kitchen remodeling

棚の張り替え	cabinet refacing
窓の交換	window replacement
害虫駆除	pest control
芝生の手入れ	lawn treatment
フローリング（の床）	wooden floor ／ flooring
石灰石のフローリング	limestone flooring
大理石のフローリング	marble flooring
床下暖房	underfloor heating
室内扉	internal doors
（DVD/CD 等の）収納庫	media storage
（DVD/CD 等の）収納棚	media cabinet
オーディオ用棚	audio cabinetremodel
マルチメディア用棚	multimedia cabinet

3
住む

5. 不動産

★不動産広告，案内表記

不動産業者	real estate agent
家	House 《HSE》
共同	Share 《SHR》
独身者のみ	Single Only 《SGL ONLY》
即時入居可	Immediate Occupancy 《IMM OCC》
居住中	Occupied 《OCC》
家具付き	Furnished《FURN》 ＊ furnish（〔家具などを〕備えつける）
洗濯機・乾燥機付き	Washer & Drier 《W/D》
バルコニー付き	With Balcony 《W/BALC》
ファミリールーム	Family Room《FR》
寝室3，浴室2，ファミリールーム	3 Bedroom, 2 Bath & Family room 《3+2+FR》
高級，豪華	Luxury 《LUX》
新装	Newly Decorated 《NUDEC》
改築	Remodel 《REMOD》
修繕済み	Renovated 《RENO》
清潔	Immaculate《IMMAC》
大きい，広い	Large 《LG, LRG》
平方フィート	sq.ft. 《square feet》 ＊ = square foot ／ 1 平方メートル= 10.763 sq.ft.
場所	Location 《LOC》

眺めがいい	View 《VW》
交通機関	Transportation 《TRANS》
近い	Near 《NR》
別々	Separate 《SEP》
朝食のコーナー《台所の小テーブルのある所》	Breakfast nook
ガスレンジ,（料理用の）コンロ	Stove 《STV》
(家の) テラス	Deck [dék]
床	Floor 《FLR》
堅木張りの床	Hardwood Floor 《HDWD, HWFL》
温水プール	Heated Pool 《HTD Pool》
ジャグジー	Jacuzzi 《JACZ》
ランドリー	Laundry 《LDRY》
リビングルーム	Living Room 《LIV, LIVRM, LR》
ウォークインクローゼット	Walk-in Closet
天窓	Skylight 《SKYLT》
ガレージ	Garage 《GAR, GARG》
収納庫	Storage 《STOR》
庭	Garden 《GRDN》 ＊花，野菜，芝などが植えてある庭。

庭	Yard 《YD, YRD》 ＊むき出しの庭や作業を する庭。
駐車場	Parking 《PRG, PRGK》
電気・ガス・ 水道など	Utility 《UTL》
家賃，賃貸する	rent
家賃，賃借料	(house) rent
月	Month 《MO》
光熱費込み	Utility Included [Paid] 《UTL INC [PD]》
セキュリティ ービル	Security Building 《SEC BLDG》
セキュリティー	Security 《SEC, SECUR》
要保証人	References Required 《REFS REQ'D》
礼金，権利金	key money
敷金	deposit [dipázət]
更新料	renewal fee
20万ドル	$200,000 《200K》 ＊200K と略される。K = 1000
照会（先）	References 《REFS》
建物管理会社	property management company

★不動産用語

不動産	real estate
家主，家の持 ち主	landlord 〈男性〉, landlady 〈女性〉／the owner of a house

下宿人，寄宿生	boarder
宿泊人，間借り人	roomer 〈米〉／ lodger 〈英〉
賃貸物件	leasehold property
売り家	house for [on] sale
貸家	house for rent ／ rental house ／ rent house
住宅ローン	housing [house] loan
住宅ローンの 金利	mortgage interest rate
住宅ローン減 税	home buyers' tax break
住宅地域	residential area
抵当(に入れる)	mortgage
抵当権取得	mortgage acquisition
抵当契約	mortgage agreement
抵当の委任	mortgage assignment
抵当証券	mortgage certificate
不動産担保証 券	mortgage-backed securities 《MBS》
商業用不動産 担保証券	commercial mortgage-backed securities 《CMBS》
不動産登記	immovable property registration
不動産鑑定士	real estate appraiser
不動産取得税	real estate acquisition tax
不動産譲渡	transfer of real estate
不動産売却益	profit on the sale of real estate
担保物件	collateral

3

住む

担保付きローン	collateral loan
モーゲージ担保債務証書	collateralized mortgage obligation
住宅税	housing tax
年利	annual rate
融資，ローン	financing ／ loan
融資額	loan amount
借り換え融資	refinanced loan
利息	interest
固定金利	fixed interest rate
固定資産	fixed assets
固定資産税	fixed property tax
変動金利	variable interest rate
前金，頭金	down payment
月払い	monthly payments
返済	repayment
返済期日	repayment date
返済期限	repayment deadline
据え置き期間中	repayment grace period
全額返済	repayment in full
分割返済	repayment in installments
建築費見積もり	invoice for construction cost
火災保険	fire insurance
地震保険	earthquake insurance
競売	auction

競りで売る	sell at auction
入札	bid
建ぺい率	building coverage ／ building-to-land ratio
容積率	floor-area ratio
固定資産税評価額	assessed value of fixed assets
固定資産の内容	classes of fixed assets
固定資産処分	disposal of fixed assets
債権者	creditor
債務者	debtor [détər]
地盤調査	soil exploration
設計仕様書	specifications
費用	costs
所有，所有権	ownership
所有者	owner
所有権移転登記	ownership transfer registration
連帯保証人	cosigner [kòusáinər]
地代	ground rent ／ land rent
借地	leased land
借地人	(land) leaseholder
借地権	(land) leasehold
借地契約	leasehold contract
借地抵当権	leasehold mortgage
売買契約書	purchase and sales contract
不法入居者	squatter

4.

街角を歩く

1. 道を尋ねる

★基本単語&表現

最寄りの駅	the nearest station	この方角でいいのでしょうか。	Am I going in the right direction?
この道は〜へ行きますか。	Does this road lead to ~?	これは〜へ行く道ですか。	Is this the right way to ~?
〜はどこにありますか。	Can I ask you where ~ is?	地図だと, どこですか。	Where is it on the map?
すみません, 駅はどちら(の方向)ですか。	Excuse me, which way is the station?	地図だと, どこにいるのでしょうか。	Where am I on the map?
この辺りに郵便局はありますでしょうか。	Can I ask you if there's a post office around here?	地図を書いていただけますか。	Could you please draw a map?
〜への道	the way to ~	道なりに行く	follow the road
〜への行き方を教えていただけますか。	Could you tell me the way to ~?	通りを真っすぐ進む	go along the street
ここから近いですか。	Is it near here?	左に曲がる	turn (to the) left
ここから遠いですか。	Is it far from here?	右に曲がる	turn (to the) right
歩いていける距離ですか。	Is it within walking distance?	《車の運転で》左に曲がる《米口》	hang a left *運転手に指示して言う。
ここからどれくらいの距離ですか。	How far is it from here?	《車の運転で》右に曲がる《米口》	hang a right *運転手に指示して言う。
どれくらい時間がかかりますか。	How long does it take to get there?	〜を通り過ぎる	go past ~
徒歩で	on foot	道の向こう側に	across the street
バスで	by bus	道の反対側に	on the other side of the street
地下鉄で	on the subway *「地下鉄」は, イギリス英語では underground, tube〈口語〉。	道の同じ側に	on the same side of the street
		真っすぐに行く, 直進する	go straight ahead
		私は方向音痴なんです。	I have no sense of direction.

2. 通りと交差点，建物・公共施設

★通りと交差点

メトロポリス，主要都市	metropolis [mɔtrápəlis]		街灯	street light
大通り，～街	avenue [ǽvənju] 《Av., Ave.》 ＊Fifth Av. (5番街)。New York 市では，南北に走る縦の通りを指す。		歩道	sidewalk
			(歩道の) 縁石	curb [kə́ːrb] 《米》／ kerb 《英》
			歩道，小道	pathway
通り，～通り	street 《St.》 ＊New York 市では，東西に走る通りを指す。		(建物の間の，裏庭や車庫に通じる) 横道，路地	alley [ǽli]
メインストリート，大通り，表通り	main street		横断歩道	crosswalk 《米》／ (pedestrian) crossing 《英》 ＊cross at the crosswalk (横断歩道を渡る)
裏通り	back street			
交差点	intersection／crossing		歩行者 (用) の	pedestrian [pədéstriən]
T字路	T intersection			
三叉路	junction of three roads／three-forked road		通りがかりの人，通行人	passer-by／《複》 passers-by
			消火栓	fire hydrant／fireplug
袋小路	dead end ＊「(行動・政策などの) 行き詰り」の意味もある。		ゴミ箱	trash can
			自動販売機	vending machine
ロータリー	rotary [róutəri]		公衆電話ボックス	phone booth／telephone booth ＊telephone box 《英》
歩行者天国	car-free mall／holiday promenade			
バス専用レーン	busway 《米》／bus lane 《英》		駐車場	parking garage／parking lot
			パーキングメーター	parking meter ＊feed the parking meter (パーキングメーターにコインを入れる)
信号	traffic light [signal]／light／stoplight			
道の曲がり角，街角	street corner		地下鉄の入口	subway entrance
交通渋滞	traffic jam		地下鉄改札口	subway ticket gate

4 街角を歩く

（駅の）ホーム	track 《米》／ platform 《英》
新聞雑誌売場	newsstand
バス停	bus stop
歩道橋	pedestrian overpass [bridge] ＊ cross over the pedestrian overpass （横断歩道橋を渡る）
立入禁止区域	OFF LIMITS

★建物

スカイライン，（高層ビル等の）空を背景とした輪郭	skyline
摩天楼，超高層ビル	skyscraper [skáiskrèirpər]
オフィスビル	office building 《米》／ office block 《英》
雑居ビル	building with many small tenants ／ multi-tenant building
アパート，共同住宅	apartment building
貸しビル	building for rent
工場	factory [fæktəri]
ショッピング・モール，ショッピングセンター	shopping mall
小規模ショッピングセンター	strip mall
倉庫（に入れる）	warehouse

★公共施設など

空港	airport
駅，停留所	station
消防署	fire station
警察署	police station
市庁舎，市役所	city government office ／ city hall 《米》
郵便局	post office
教会	church
モスク	mosque
ユダヤ教の礼拝堂	synagogue [sínəgàg]
裁判所の庁舎，郡庁舎 《米》	courthouse
市場	market
ホテル	hotel
（劇場・ホテル・マンションの）ロビー	foyer [fɔ́iər]
モーテル	motel [moutél]
銀行	bank [bǽŋk]
病院	hospital [háspitl]
老人ホーム，高齢者福祉施設	nursing home [nɔ́ːrsiŋ hòum]
劇場	theater
映画館	movie theater
図書館	library [láibrèri]
ヘルスクラブ	health club
学校	school
公園	park
公衆トイレ	public lavatory
噴水	fountain
彫像	statue
遊園地	amusement park

★交通規則・標識など

交通規則	traffic rules ／ regulations
交通違反	traffic violation
交通違反呼び出し状	traffic ticket
駐車違反	parking violation
スピード違反切符	speeding ticket
飲酒運転	drinking and driving
飲酒および麻薬の影響下の運転	driving under the influence
罰金	fine
道路標識	road sign ／ traffic sign
歩行表示（信号等）	walk sign
一方通行のサイン	one-way sign
道路規則	rules of the road
看板	signboard
歩行者優先	YIELD TO PEDESTRIANS [pədéstriənz]
タイヤチェーン・スタッド等の滑り止め装着車通行禁止	NO VEHICLES WITH LUGS ＊ vehicles [víːəklz], lugs [lʌ́gz]
許可車両以外の通行禁止	AUTHORIZED VEHICLES ONLY

最低制限速度	minimum speed limit
夜間制限速度	nighttime speed limit
牽引車制限速度	towed vehicles speed limit
一時停止道路	stop street
全方向一時停止の場所（交差点）	all-way stop
歩行者専用	Pedestrians only
バス専用	BUSES ONLY
駐車禁止	NO PARKING
駐車ゾーン	PARKING ZONE
牽引地帯	TOW-AWAY ZONE
道路閉鎖	ROAD CLOSED
車両進入禁止	NO ENTRY FOR VEHICLES
Uターン禁止	NO U-TURN
追い越し禁止	NO PASSING
追い越し禁止区域	NO-OVERTAKING ZONE
制限速度	SPEED LIMIT
スピード違反	speeding (offense)
一方通行	ONE WAY
行き止まり	NO OUTLET ／ DEAD END
一時停止の道路標識	stop sign

4

街角を歩く

徐行の標識, 譲れの標識	yield sign
先方優先道路, 譲れの標識《英》	GIVE WAY
優先道路	right-of-way ／ through street
高速車専用車線	express lane
中央線	center line
本線	thru traffic ＊thru = through
停止線	stop line
学童横断路	school crossing
通学地域	school zone
踏切	railroad crossing
サービスエリア	service area
この先交差点 有り	INTERSECTION AHEAD
対面通行	TWO WAY TRAFFIC
通行禁止	NO ENTRY ZONE
車線指示	lane direction
縦列駐車	parallel parking
長方形の駐車 スペース	rectangular parking ＊rectangular [rektǽŋɡjələr]
片側駐車規制	alternate side parking regulations
横断禁止	NO PEDESTRIANS CROSSING
信号を堂々と無視 して道路を渡る, 横断歩道のないと ころを横切る	jaywalk
通行止め,封鎖	closure

青信号	green light
黄色信号	yellow light
赤信号	red light ＊jump a red light（信 号を無視する）
曲がっていい 青信号	green turn light
点滅黄色信号	flashing yellow light
点滅赤信号	flashing red light
坂の標識	hill sign
降雨時スリッ プ注意	slippery when wet sign
右折禁止標識	no right turn sign
左折禁止標識	no left turn sign

★道路

道路	road, roadway
舗装されてい ない道路	dirt road
幹線道路	highway
高速道路	expressway ／ freeway, motorway〈英〉
有料高速道路	turnpike
立体交差	overpass
地下道	underpass〈米〉／ subway〈英〉
破線（道路中 央の）	broken line
実線（道路中 央の）	solid line
車の追い越し禁 止を示す黄色い 中央線《米》	yellow line

路肩	shoulder
中央分離帯	divider
左側車線	left lane
中央車線	middle lane
右の車線	right lane
追い越し車線	passing lane
低速車線	slow lane
バス優先	priority lane for buses
料金所	tollgate
通行料金支払所	tollbooth
通行料を支払う	pay a toll
橋	bridge
カーブ標識	curve sign
岩の道路	rock road
州道路	state road
裏道, 脇道 (を進む)	backroad
トラックサービスエリア (長距離トラック運転手を対象)	truck stop

★建設現場

工事	construction [kənstrʌ́kʃən]
工事中	UNDER CONSTRUCTION
設計士	architect
現場監督者	foreman
建設労働者	construction worker
大工	carpenter

石工	mason
溶接工	welder
設計図	blueprint
大梁 (おおばり)	girder [gɔ́ːrdər]
はしご	ladder [lǽdər]
安全帽, 安全ヘルメット	hard hat
留め金, フック	hook
ツールベルト	tool belt ＊工具を入れるベルト。
足場	scaffold [skǽfəld]
クレーン	crane [kréin]
クレーン車	crane truck
蒸気ローラー車	steamroller
掘削現場	excavation site
ダンプカー	dump truck
フロントエンド・ローダー	front-end loader ＊土木作業用車
ショベルカー	power shovel ／ excavator ／ digger
ブルドーザー	bulldozer
掘削機	backhoe [bǽkhòu]
防爆マット	blasting mat
セメント	cement
コンクリートミキサー	cement mixer
コンクリート (製の)	concrete
レンガ	brick
手押し車	wheelbarrow
ジャックハンマー, (手で持つ) 削岩機	jack hammer

4

街角を歩く

シャベル	shovel [ʃʌ́vl]		ニューイングランド地方	New England
大ハンマー	sledgehammer		東海岸	The East Coast
つるはし（で掘る）	pickax [píkæks]		中央大西洋沿岸諸州	Middle Atlantic States

★地図・方角・北米地域

地図	map		南部諸州	Southern States
地図帳	atlas		南部	The South
道路地図	road map		南西部諸州	Southwestern States
方角	direction			
道を教える	give directions		南西部	The Southwest
反対方向	(the) opposite direction		米国中西部諸州	Midwestern States
間違った方向	(the) wrong direction		中西部	The Midwest
			ロッキー山脈諸州	Rocky Mountain States
方位磁石	compass			
北／北の	north ／ northern		太平洋側諸州	Pacific Coast States
南／南の	south ／ southern			
東／東の	east ／ eastern		西海岸	The West Coast
西／西の	west ／ western		北カナダ	Northern Canada
北東	northeast		西カナダ	Western Canada
北西	northwest		ブリティッシュコロンビア（カナダ西部）	British Columbia
南東	southeast			
南西	southwest			
北に進む［行く・向かう］，北上する	go north		プレーリー諸州（カナダ中部）	The Prairie Provinces
			オンタリオ（カナダ南東部の州）	Ontario
～は…の南にあります。	be in the south of ...			
			ケベック（カナダ東部の州）	Quebec
～は…の東部にあります。	be in the eastern part of ...		大西洋諸州（カナダ東部）	The Atlantic Provinces
			沿海州（カナダ南東部）	The Maritime Provinces

5.

乗り物に乗る

1. 乗り物

★乗り物

（陸上の）乗り物，車，車両	vehicle [víːəkl]	キャンピングカー	recreational vehicle《RV》（日本でのRV車とは少し異なる）／ camper　＊camping car は和製語。
交通機関	transportation [trænspərtéiʃən]		
交通手段	a means of transportation	デューンバギー（砂丘走行用自動車）	dune buggy
車	car ／ automobile	ダンプカー	dump truck
小型乗用車	compact car	引っ越しトラック	moving van《米》／ removal van《英》
中型の乗用車	mid-sized car		
大型乗用車	full-sized car	フラットな荷台のトラック	flatbed truck
オープンカー	convertible [kənvə́ːrtəbl]　＊open car は和製語。		
		ケータリングトラック	catering [kéitəriŋ] truck
軽自動車	light automobile	トレーラー	trailer　＊「（映画の）予告編」の意味もある。
ジープ	jeep		
リムジン	limousine [líməzìːn]	コンクリートミキサー車	concrete (cement) mixer
電気自動車	electric car [vehicle]		
セダン	sedan [sidǽn]	タンクローリー	tanker truck《米》／ tanker lorry《英》
ハッチバック	hatchback [hǽtʃbæk]		
クーペ《2ドア》	coupe [kuːpéi]	レッカー車	wrecker ／ tow truck
小型トラック	pickup truck	パトカー《警察》	police car
		パトカー《保安》	sheriff car
ステーションワゴン	station wagon	救急車	ambulance [ǽmbjələns]
SUV（スポーツ用多目的車）	SUV (= Sports Utility Vehicle)	消防車	fire truck ／ fire engine
ミニバン	minivan [mínivæn]	はしご車	ladder vehicle ／ hook-and-ladder truck ／ ladder truck
モーターホーム（居住空間のある大型自動車）	motor home		

除雪車	snowplow [snóuplàu]
ゴミ収集車	garbage truck 〈米〉／ dust cart 〈英〉
トラクター	tractor
コンバイン	combine (harvester)
フォークリフト	forklift (truck)

オートバイ	motorcycle
小型オートバイ，原付	motorbike
自転車	bicycle ／ bike
三輪車	tricycle
一輪車	unicycle
スノーモービル	snowmobile [snóuməbì:l]

折畳式のベビーカー	stroller 〈米〉／ pushchair 〈英〉 ＊baby car とはいわないので注意。
ベビーカー	baby carriage [buggy] 〈米〉／ pram 〈英〉
車椅子	wheelchair
人力車	ricksha ／ rickshaw ＊日本語の jinrikisha から派生した。
犬ぞり	dog sled ／ dog sledge

電車，列車	train
路面電車	streetcar 〈米〉／ tram 〈英〉

モノレール	monorail [mánərèil	mónourèil]
ケーブルカー	cable car
ロープウェイ	ropeway
蒸気機関車	steam train [locomotive]

船舶	vessel [vésl]
フェリー	ferry [féri]
船	ship
水陸両用車	amphibious vehicle
いかだ	raft [ræft	rá:ft]
ヨット	yacht [ját]
モーターボート	motorboat
クルーザー	cruiser [kru:zər]
潜水艦	submarine [sʌ́bmərì:n]
蒸気船	steamboat ／ steamship
帆船 (はんせん)	sailing ship

航空機	aircraft
飛行機	airplane
貨物機	cargo airplane
飛行船	airship
ヘリコプター	helicopter
グライダー	glider
宇宙船	spaceship ／ spacecraft

5 乗り物に乗る

2. 地下鉄・電車に乗る

★駅・構内

鉄道	railroad
地下鉄	subway 《米》／ underground, tube 《英》
ステーションビル	station building
鉄道の駅	train station
地下鉄の駅	subway station
発券カウンター	ticket counter
切符売り場	ticket office
券売機	ticket (vending) machine ＊Where are the ticket machines? （券売機はどこですか）
自動改札機	automatic ticket checker
運賃	fare ＊fare chart （運賃表）／ What's the fare to Chicago? （シカゴまで料金はいくらですか）
チケット	ticket
片道切符	one-way ticket 《米》／ single ticket 《英》
往復切符	round-trip ticket 《米》／ return ticket 《英》 ＊How much is a round-trip ticket to Boston? （ボストンまで往復でいくらですか）
定期券	commuter pass
クーポン	coupon [kúːpɑn]

列車の時刻表	train schedule
時刻表	timetable
ラッシュアワー	rush hour
始発駅	starting station
停車する駅	stop
終点	last stop
乗り換え駅	transfer station
プラットホーム	platform [plǽtfɔːrm] ＊Which platform does the train leave from? （列車は何番ホームから出ますか）
改札口	ticket gate
改札口（戸の下半分が開閉するドア形式のもの）	wicket [wíkit]
回転式改札口	turnstile [tə́ːrnstàil]
入口	entrance [éntrəns]
出口	exit [éɡzit, éɡsit]
キオスク	kiosk [kíːɑsk]
待合室	waiting room
手荷物一時預かり所	baggage room
コインロッカー	(coin-operated) locker
駅長	stationmaster／ station manager
駅員	station attendant
客車，車両	car 《米》／ carriage 《英》

104

★電車

普通列車	local (train)
急行列車	express (train)
臨時急行列車	special express (train)
特急列車	limited express (train)
超特急列車	super-express (train)
夜行列車	night [overnight] train
食堂車	dining car
ビュッフェ	buffet [bəféi, bu-]
寝台車	sleeping car / sleeper
荷物置き場	baggage rack / luggage rack
個室	compartment
通勤	commute [kəmjúːt]
通勤者，通学者	commuter
通勤列車	commuter train
車掌 (列車の)	conductor 《米》/ guard 《英》
運転士	motorman
操車係	train dispatcher
列車乗務員	train crew
始発列車	the first train
終列車	the last train
直通列車	through train
長距離列車	long-distance train
コンテナ貨物列車	freight train [fréit tréin]
新幹線	bullet train [búlit tréin]

痴漢	groper / molester
すり	pickpocket
無賃乗車	free ride
乗る	get on / ride / take
降りる	get off
～行き	bound for ~
優先席	priority seats
列車を使う，列車に乗る	take the train
列車で行く	go by train
列車に乗り遅れる	miss the train
列車に間に合う	catch the train
次のシカゴ行きの列車は何時ですか。	When is the next train for Chicago?
どこで乗り換えればいいですか。	Where should I transfer [change] trains?
電車は何分おきに出ていますか。	How often do the trains run?
すみません，ヤンキースタジアムに行く一番よい方法を教えていただけますか。	Excuse me, but could you tell me the best way to get to Yankee Stadium? *stadium の発音は [stéidiəm]。
～に行くのにどれくらい時間がかかりますか。	How long does it take to go to ~?
約50分ほどかかります。	It takes about 50 minutes.

乗り物に乗る

3. タクシー・バスに乗る

★タクシー

タクシー	taxi ／ cab [kǽb]
タクシー料金	taxi fare [tǽksi fèɚr]
初乗り料金	initial [starting] fare
空車	empty taxi
空車《表示》	VACANT [véikənt] ／ FOR HIRE
回送《表示》	OFF DUTY
タクシー乗り場	taxi stand ／ taxi rank
手を挙げてタクシーを止める	hail [héil] a taxi
タクシーで行く, タクシーに乗る	take a taxi
タクシーを拾う	pick up a taxi
タクシーを呼ぶ	call me a taxi
料金メーター	(taxi)meter
料金メーターを回したままにする	leave the meter running
乗務員証	taxi license
目的地／行き先	destination
タクシーに乗る	get in the taxi
タクシーを降りる	get out of the taxi
どちらまで？	Where to?
～までお願いします。	~, please.
道順を教える	give directions
急いでください。	Hurry up, please.
（車を道路の片側に寄せて）止めてください。	Pull over.

～で降ろしてください。	Drop me off at ~.
ここで降ろしてください。	Let me off here, please.
ここで止めてください。	Stop here, please.
ここで結構です。	Here's fine.
チップ	tip [típ]
お釣りはいりません。	Keep the change.

★バス

バス	bus
通路	aisle [áil]
吊革	strap
バスの停留所	bus stop
バス乗車料金	bus fare
ルート，系統	route
バス路線図	bus route map
バスの運転手	bus driver
乗客	passenger
～行きのバスにはどこから乗るのですか。	Where can I catch a bus to ~?
料金はいくらですか。	What's the fare?
バス停はどこですか。	Where's the bus stop?
このバスは～に止まりますか。	Does this bus stop at ~?

4. 車を運転する

★車を運転する

運転免許	driver's license 《米》／ driver's licence《英》
シートベルトを締める	buckle *one's* seat belt
椅子の位置を調整する	adjust the seat
キーをイグニッションに差し込む	put the key into the ignition
車を始動する	start the car
エンスト（する）	stall ＊I stalled my car.／ My car is stalled. （エンストしちゃった）
ギアを入れ替える	shift gears ＊shift into high gear《米》／ change into top《英》（ギアをトップに入れる）
スピードを落とす	slow down
スピードを上げる	speed up
真っ直ぐ行く	go straight
車をバックさせる	back up *one's* car
制限速度を守る	obey the speed limit
高速道路に乗る	get on the expressway
前の車を追い抜く	pass the car in front
高速道路を降りる	get off the expressway
スピード違反で捕まる	get a speeding ticket

ウインカーを出す	use [give] a turn signal [a blinker] 《米》／ use [give] an indicator 《英》
右にウインカーを出す	hit the right-turn signal
車線を変える	change lanes
左折 [右折] する	turn left [right]
Uターンする	make a U-turn
迂回（する）／回り道（をさせる[する]）	detour [díːtuər] ＊make a detour （遠回りする）
近道をする	take a short cut
交通渋滞に巻き込まれる	get stuck in a traffic jam
信号	traffic light [signal] ＊ignore a red light （赤信号無視する）
信号を守る	obey the traffic lights
歩行者に道を譲る	yield to pedestrians [pədéstriənz]
発煙筒	flare [smoke] pot
発煙筒を焚く	light a flare [fléər]
ガソリン	gas 《米》／ petrol 《英》
ガス欠になりそう！	We're running out of gas!
ガソリンスタンド	gas station ＊go to the gas station （ガソリンスタンドに入る）
給油ポンプ	pump [pʌmp]

5 乗り物に乗る

ガソリンを満タンにする	fill up the tank ＊Fill it up, please.（満タンにしてください）
駐車する	park ＊park on the street（路上駐車する）
駐車場	parking lot ＊pull a car into a parking lot（駐車場に車を入れる）
私はペーパードライバーです。	I have a license but I rarely drive.

★車のパーツ

運転席	driver's seat
アクセル	accelerator, gas pedal 《米》 ＊depress [step on] the gas pedal（アクセルを踏む）
ブレーキ	brake [bréik] ＊put on the brake.（ブレーキをかける）
サイドブレーキ	parking brake 《米》／ hand brake 《英》 ＊yank [release] the parking brake（サイドブレーキを引く [解除する]）
クラッチ	clutch ＊engage [disengage] the clutch（クラッチを繋ぐ，切る）
イグニッション	ignition
変速レバー	gearshift
バックギア	reverse (gear)
ハンドル	steering wheel ＊「ハンドルを切り損なう」は，lose control of one's car。
エアバッグ	airbag

クラクション	horn ＊blow [sound] the (car) horn（クラクションを鳴らす）
ウインカー	turn signals, blinkers 《米》／ indicators 《英》
ダッシュボード	dashboard
カーナビ	car GPS ／ sat nav ＊satellite navigation（衛星ナビゲーション）の略。
オイルゲージ	oil gauge [géidʒ]
速度計，スピードメーター	speedometer [spidámətər, spi:dámətər] ＊スペル，発音に注意。
走行距離計	odometer [oudámətər]
ガスゲージ	gas gauge
温度ゲージ	temperature gauge
自動車の小物入れ	glove compartment
助手席	front seat
後部座席	back seat
チャイルドシート	child safety seat ／ (child) car seat
バックミラー	rear-view mirror ＊back mirror は和製語。
サイドミラー	side-view mirror 《米》／ wing mirror 《英》
フロントガラス	windshield [wíndʃiːld] 《米》／ windscreen 《英》 ＊front glass は和製語。
フロントガラスワイパー	windshield wipers
ヘッドライト	headlight
フード，ボンネット	hood [húd] 《米》／ bonnet [bánit] 《英》

バンパー	fender 《米》／ bumper 《英》
タイヤ	tire 《米》／ tyre 《英》 ＊発音は [táiər]。
タイヤの溝	tread [tréd]
スパイクタイヤ	studded tire
車輪	wheel
ホイールキャップ	wheel cover, hubcap
パンク	flat tire ＊I've got a flat tire. (パンクした)
マフラー	muffler
ガスタンク	gas tank

ブレーキライト	brake light
テールランプ	taillight
トランク	trunk 《米》／ boot 《英》 ＊boot は米英語では「車輪止め」意味がある。
ナンバー・プレート	license plate [láisəns plèit] ＊《英》では名詞は licence で，動詞は license。

5 乗り物に乗る

5. 飛行機に乗る

★空港・出入国

空港	airport ＊rush to the airport（急いで空港に行く），exchange money at the airport（空港で換金する）
飛行機	airplane
滑走路	runway
（飛行場の）誘導路	taxiway
航空管制塔	air traffic control tower ＊《略》ATCT
管制官	air traffic controller
空港バス	airport limousine
航空会社	airlines／airways（英）
空港ターミナル	airline terminal
到着ターミナル	arrival terminal
出発ターミナル	departure terminal
国内線	domestic flight
国際線	international flight
搭乗時間	boarding time
搭乗案内	boarding announcement
フライト案内板	flight information display [screen]
発着表示モニター	arrival and departure monitor
旅客降機《表示》	IN TERMINAL
通関中《表示》	CUSTOMS
到着済み《表示》	ARRIVED
到着《表示》	ARRIVING
定刻《表示》	ON TIME
遅延《表示》	DELAYED
直行便	direct flight ＊direct [nonstop] flight to ~（～への直行便）
乗り継ぎ便	connecting flight
乗り継ぎ客	transfer passenger
到着時刻	arrival time
出発時刻	departure time
飛行時間	flight time
搭乗手続き	check-in
搭乗手続きカウンター	check-in counter
航空券	airline ticket
航空券取扱人	ticket agent
搭乗券	boarding pass [card]
空港税	airport tax
ゲート	gate [géit] ＊What's the gate number?（何番ゲートですか）
搭乗待合室	boarding area
機内持ち込みの手荷物	carry-on baggage [luggage]
預け荷物	check-in baggage [luggage]
身の回り品	personal belongings ＊Please remember to take all your personal belongings with you.（お手荷物のお忘れ物がないようにご注意ください）

手荷物検査所	security checkpoint
ボディチェック	body search
手荷物引取所	baggage claim area
回転台	carousel [kæʳəsél]
荷物カート	cart
ポーター	porter
配送サービス	delivery service
税関	customs ＊clear [go through] customs（税関を通る）
税関申告書	customs declaration form
関税検査官	customs officer
入国審査	immigration
パスポート	passport [pǽspɔ̀ːrt | páːs-] ＊apply for a passport（パスポートを申請する）
国籍	Nationality
発行国	Issuing country
有効期間満了日	Date of expiry
職業	Occupation
滞在目的	Purpose of visit
申告用紙	declaration form
出国カード	embarkation card
入国カード	disembarkation card ＊fill out the disembarkation card（入国カードに記入する）
トランジット［乗り継ぎ］カード	transit card

★飛行機内

コックピット	cockpit [kákpìt]
パイロット	pilot
客室乗務員	flight attendant
通路側の席	aisle seat [áil sìːt]
窓側の座席	window seat
窓のブラインド	shade
（頭上の）荷物入れ	overhead compartment
酸素マスク	oxygen mask
飛行機酔いの袋,エチケット袋	airsickness bag, disposal bag, barf bag, sick bag
救命胴衣	life vest
トレーテーブル	tray table
飲料カート	beverage cart
化粧室	lavatory [lǽvətɔ̀ːri] ＊If you need to use the lavatory, please do so now.（化粧室をご利用になられる方は今のうちにお済ませください）
（トイレなどの）使用中	occupied [ákjəpàid]
（トイレなどの）使用可, 空き	vacant [véikənt]
緊急ボタン	emergency button
呼び出しボタン	call button

搭乗する	board the plane
搭乗券を見せる	show one's boarding pass
座席を見つける	find one's seat

5

乗り物に乗る

機内持ち込みの手荷物を収納する	stow *one's* carry-on bag	機内娯楽サービス（映画上映・音楽鑑賞等）	in-flight entertainment
席の上にある荷物棚	overhead bins ＊ put [place] *one's* baggage in the overhead bins（頭上の荷物棚に置く［入れる］）	機内誌	in-flight magazine
		免税品カタログ	duty free booklet
シートベルト着用指示	seat belt sign	乱気流	(air) turbulence [éər tə̀ːrbjələns] ＊ We are expecting some turbulence.（当機は〔機体の〕揺れが予想されます）
シートベルトを締める	fasten [fǽsn] *one's* seat belt ＊ Please fasten your seat belt tight and low around your hips.（シートベルトを腰の低い位置でしっかりとお締めください）		
		背もたれを元の位置に戻す	return *one's* seat back to the upright position ＊ Please return your seat backs and tray tables to their full upright position.（座席の背もたれとテーブルを元の位置にお戻しください）
シートベルトをはずす	take off *one's* seat belt		
席についたままでいる	stay [remain] in *one's* seat		
離陸する	take off ＊ We will be taking off shortly.（間もなく離陸いたします）	降下	descent [disént]
		着陸する	land ＊ We will be landing at Narita International Airport in about 15 minutes.（当機はおよそ15分で成田国際空港に着陸いたします），We will be on the ground shortly.（当機は間もなく着陸いたします）
ブランケット	blanket [blǽŋkit] ＊ Excuse me. Can I have a blanket?（すみません。毛布をもらえますか）		
		時差ボケ	jet lag ＊ get [suffer from] jet lag（時差ボケになる［苦しむ］）

Brooklyn Bridge and Airports street signs in New York City

6.

公共の場所で・電話

★郵便

郵便局	post office [póust à:fəs, - ɔ́:fəs]
郵便局員	postal clerk
郵便配達員	mail carrier, mailman 《米》／ postman 《英》 [póus(t)mən]
郵便	mail
手紙を書く	write a letter
～に手紙を出す	send a letter to ～
手紙を受け取る	receive a letter
返事を書く	write back ＊ write back to someone 「(人) に返信する」，write back to do「～するために返信する」。
～の手紙に返事を書く［出す］	answer one's letter ／ send an answer to one's letter
切手	stamp ＊ put a stamp「切手を貼る」。
切手自動販売機	stamp machine
記念切手	memorial stamp
切手シート	sheet of stamps
封筒	envelope [énvəlòup]
便箋	letter paper
社用箋	company letter paper
はがき	postcard

小包	package 《米》／ parcel 《英》 ＊ send a package to ～ (～に小包を送る)
段ボール箱	cardboard box
梱包用テープ，ガムテープ	packing tape
発泡スチロール	Styrofoam 《米商標》／ expanded polystyrene
エアキャップ，プチプチ	bubble wrap ／ AirCap 《米商標》
身の回りの物，私物	personal belongings
取り扱い注意！《注意書き》	Fragile!
印刷物在中《注意書き》	Printed Matter
親展《注意書き》	PRIVATE & CONFIDENTIAL
郵便番号	zip code
宛名，住所	address
差出人住所，返送先	return address
～様方	c.o. 《care of》
私書箱	P.O. Box 《Post Office Box》
消印	postmark [póustmà:rk]
郵便料金，郵送料	postage [póustidʒ]
はかり	scale [skéil]

日本へ送りたいのですが。	I want to send this to Japan.
送料着払い，代引き	cash-on-delivery (COD)
元払い	prepaid shipping
航空便	airmail ＊sea mail「船便」，surface mail「船便／陸便」。
速達郵便	express mail ＊send ~ a letter by express「～に速達で手紙を送る」。
書留	registered mail
国際速達郵便	Express Mail Service（EMS）
書留郵便物受領通知	return receipt
局留め郵便	general delivery〈米〉／ poste restante〈英〉[pòust restáːnt │ réstɔnt]
郵便為替	money order〈米〉（MO）／ postal order〈英〉（PO）
当日配達	same day delivery
翌日配達	next-day delivery／ overnight delivery
（投函用の）郵便ポスト	mailbox〈米〉／ post〈英〉
郵便ポストの投入口	mail slot
郵便袋	mailbag

ユナイテッド・パーシャル・サービス株式会社	UPS ／ United Parcel Service
配送	delivery
郵便トラック	mail truck
配達証明郵便	certified mail
郵送先名簿；メーリングリスト	mailing list
ダイレクトメール	direct mail
迷惑メール	junk mail ＊勝手に送られてくる広告・勧誘などの郵便物・電子メールなど。
配達不能郵便物	dead letter
ファンレター	fan mail
ラブレター	love letter
航空貨物運送状	Air Waybill（AWB） ＊航空運送契約の証拠書類。
送り主	sender
送り主の名前	sender's name
受取人	recipient
受取人の名前	recipient's name
関税	custom duties
第三者	third party
土曜日の配送	Saturday delivery
問い合わせ番号	tracking number
荷物追跡（サービス）	package tracking

★銀行

銀行	bank [bǽŋk]
口座を開く	open an account ＊I would like to open a new account. 「口座を新規開設したいのですが」。
最低預金残高	minimum deposit
口座を解約する	close an account
身分証明	identification 《ID》
預金（する）	deposit [dipázət] ＊have ~ yen on deposit（~円の預金がある）
銀行に預金する	deposit money in a bank
銀行からお金を引き出す	withdraw [draw] money from an account
金額，額	amount
残高	balance [bǽləns]
残高照会する	check the balances ／ make a balance inquiry
残高不足	insufficient funds
～の口座にお金を振り込む	pay money into someone's bank account
口座振替	bank transfer
～に送金する	transfer money to ~
自動引き落し	automatic debit [deduction]
預金通帳	bankbook ／ passbook

口座の種類	account type
普通預金口座	savings account 《米》／ deposit account 《英》
定期預金口座	(fixed-)term deposit account ／ savings account 《英》
金利	interest rate
固定金利	fixed interest rate
変動金利	floating interest rate
普通預金の利率はどのくらいですか。	What is the interest rate for the savings account?
当座預金口座	checking account 《米》／ current account 《英》
口座名義人	account holder
口座番号	account number
暗証番号	personal identification number 《PIN》／ secret code
預金	savings
外貨預金	foreign currency deposit
貯蓄する	save
預金者	depositor
ATM	automatic teller machine 《ATM》
キャッシュカード	ATM card 《米》／ cash card 《主に英》

お引き出し《ATM機画面表示》	Withdrawal	為替レート	exchange rate
お預入れ《ATM機画面表示》	Deposit	今日の為替レートはいくらですか。	What's the exchange rate today?
残高照会《表示》	Balance Inquiry	手数料はいくらですか。	How much is the commission?
送金 & 支払い振込み《表示》	Transfers & Payments	どのように(両替えを)しましょうか。	How would you like it? *どのようにしたらいいか、どんな風にしたらいいかを尋ねる丁寧な表現。
取引手数料	Transaction Fee		
クレジットカード	credit card	10 ドル札でお願いします。	In ten-dollar bills, please.
デビットカード	debit card	この 100 ドル札を 20 ドル札 2 枚, 10 ドル札 5 枚, 1 ドル札 10 枚にくずしたいのですが。	I'd like to change this 100-dollar bill into two 20s, five 10s and ten singles.
電子マネー	electronic money		
小切手	check 《米》／cheque 《英》		
小切手帳	checkbook 《米》／chequebook 《英》	小銭をもらえますか。	Can I have some small change?
銀行取引明細書	bank statement	トラベラーズチェックを現金に換えたいのですが。	I'd like to cash this traveler's check.
為替手形	draft ／ a bill (of exchange)		
約束手形	promissory note		
通貨	currency	担保, 抵当	mortgage [mɔ́ːrɡidʒ]
紙幣	bill 《米》／ note 《英》	貸付	loan [lóun]
硬貨	coin	借入金	borrowed money ／ loan
にせ札	counterfeit bill	返済	repayment ／ refund

★両替

両替をお願いします。	Exchange, please.
円をドルに両替していただけますか。	Could you give me dollars for yen?

借金	debt [dét] *発音注意。
借金する	get [go] into debt ／ borrow money

3. 書店で

★書店

書店	bookstore 《米》／ bookshop 《英》
オンライン書店, ネット書店	online bookstore
古本屋	used bookstore ／ second-hand bookstore
新刊書	new books
古本	used book ／ secondhand book
古書	old book ／ antiquarian book
図書券, 図書カード	book coupon 《米》／ book token 《英》
出版社	publisher [pʌ́bliʃər]／ publishing company
出版する	publish
書評	book review
ブックフェア	book fair

本を読む	read a book
本を斜め読みする	skim through a book
本の虫, 読書家	bookworm ＊＝「本をむしばむ虫《シミなど》」
活字離れ	aliteracy [eilítərəsi]
書名	book title
ブックカバー	book jacket
袖（カバーの）	flap
背表紙	spine

表紙	cover
裏表紙	back cover
見返し	flyleaf
奥付	imprint [ímprint]

ペーパーバック	paperback
ハードカバー	hardcover
ジャンル	genre [ʒɑ́:nrə]
小説, 長編小説	novel
中編小説	novella [nouvélə]
短編小説	short story
ベストセラー	bestseller
ベストセラー小説	bestselling novel ／ top-selling novel
フィクション	fiction ＊Truth is stranger than fiction.（事実は小説よりも奇なり）《ことわざ》
ノンフィクション	nonfiction ＊nonfiction writer（ノンフィクション作家）
詩（ジャンルとしての）	poetry [póuətri] 《集合名詞》
詩（一編一編の）	poem [póuəm, -em]
冒険小説	adventure novel [story ／ fiction]
ファンタジー小説	fantasy novel [story ／ fiction]
ホラー小説	horror novel [story ／ fiction]

サスペンス小説	suspense novel [story / fiction]	定期刊行物	periodical
推理小説, ミステリー小説	mystery novel [story / fiction]	新聞・雑誌の総称	journal
		雑誌	magazine
SF 小説	science-fiction novel [story]	写真雑誌	photography magazine
歴史小説	historical novel [story / fiction]	週刊誌	weekly journal [magazine]
恋愛小説	romance novel [story / fiction]	月刊誌	monthly journal [magazine]
大河小説	saga novel / roman-fleuve	季刊誌	quarterly journal [magazine]
風俗小説	novel of manners	フリーペーパー	free newspaper

マンガ	comic [ká(:)mik, kɔ́m-]	作家, ライター	writer [ráitər]
絵本	picture book	小説家	novelist / fictionist
旅行案内書	guidebook (for travel(l)ers)	エッセイスト	essayist
		翻訳家	translator
ファッション誌	fashion magazine	翻訳する	translate
学習参考書	study-aid book	詩人	poet [póuət]
実用書	how-to (book) / practical book	読者	reader
エッセイ, 随筆	essay	作者, 著者, 作家	author [ɔ́:θər]
評論	critical essay	ペンネーム	pen name
伝記	biography	仮名, 偽名	pseudonym [sjú:dənim]
自伝	autobiography		
百科事典	encyclopedia	著作権	copyright
おとぎ話	fairy story [tale]	著作権を侵害する	infringe a copyright
寓話	allegory [ǽləgɔ̀ri]		
伝説	legend	印税	royalty [rɔ́iəlti]
神話	mythological story	読書をして過ごす	spend one's time reading

119

★基本表現

もしもし。スミスさんのお宅ですか。	Hello. Is this the Smith's residence?
田中ですが、リサさんに代わってもらえますか。	This is Tanaka calling. I'd like to speak to Lisa, please.
ナオミですが、スーザンはいますか。	This is Naomi speaking. Is Susan there?
ABC社です。	This is ABC Company.
ABC社の山田一郎です。	This is Ichiro Yamada of ABC.
グリーンさんをお願いしたいのですが。	May I speak to Mr. Green? ＊Mike, it's for you.（マイク、きみに電話だよ）
私です。	This is he [she]. ／ It's me.《カジュアル》 ／ Speaking.
どちら様でしょうか。	May I ask who's calling? ／ May I ask your name, please?
どなたですか。	Who's calling?
ジョンです。	John speaking. ／ It's John here.
どのようなご用件でしょうか。	How may I help you?
申し訳ございませんが、彼は今、会議中です。	I'm sorry, he is in a meeting right now.
彼は今、外出中です。	He is out now.
彼は本日はもう社には戻れません。	He has left for the day.
彼は今席を外しています。	He is not at his desk right now.
彼は別の電話に出ています。	He is on another line right now. ＊on another line は、on the other line でも OK。
このままお待ちになりますか。	Would you like to hold?
彼はもう帰宅いたしました。	He has already left for home today.
また明日、おかけ直しいただけないでしょうか。	Could you call again tomorrow?
今日はお休みをいただいております。	He [She] is off today.
ただ今、出張中です。	He [She] is on a business trip.
いつ電話を差し上げたらよいでしょうか。	When is a good time to call?
10月1日に戻る予定です。	He [She] will be back here on October 1st.
彼は月曜日に戻ります。	He'll be back in the office on Monday.

営業部におつなぎいたします。	I'll put you through the Sales Department.
ご用件はどんなことでしょうか。	What are you calling about?
〜の件で電話をしています。	I'm calling about ~.
担当者に代わります。	I'll put you through to the person in charge.
英語を話す者に代わります。	I'll get someone who speaks English.
田中に代わります。	I'll get Mr. [Ms.] Tanaka for you.
少々お待ちください。	Just a moment, please. ／ Hold the line, please.
伝言なさいますか。	May I take your message? ／ Would you like to leave a message?
折り返しお電話するように伝えましょうか。	Shall I tell him [her] to call you back later?
後ほど私に電話をするよう彼に伝えていただけますか。	Could you ask him to call me?
電話番号をうかがえますか。	May I have your number?
お名前と電話番号をいただけますか。	Could I take your name and number, please?

お名前はどのようなつづりですか。	How do you spell your name? ／ Could you spell your name, please?
伝言をお伝えます。	I'll give him [her] a message.
伝言をお願いしてもいいですか。	May I leave a message?
もう少しゆっくりお話いただけますか。	Could you speak a little more slowly?
（話に）ついていけません。	I can't follow you.
もう一度言っていただけますか。	Excuse me? ／ Could you repeat that?
もう少し大きな声でお話いただけますか。	Could you speak a little louder, please?
電波が悪いようです。	I think we have bad connection.
バッテリーが切れそうです。	My battery's about to run out.
あまりよく聞こえません。	I can't hear you very well.
あとでメッセージを送ります。	I'll text you later.
後ほど折り返してもよろしいですか。	Can I call you back?
後ほど折り返します。	I'll call back later.
今，話をしても大丈夫ですか。	Is it convenient to talk at the moment?

お電話ありが とうございま した。	Thank you for your call. ／ Thank you for calling.

★基本単語

電話	(tele)phone
コードレス電話	cordless phone
親機	base [main] phone
子機	cordless handset
携帯電話	cellular phone, cellphone, cell 〈口語〉《米》／ mobile phone, mobile 〈英〉
プッシュホン	push-button telephone, touch-tone telephone
国際電話	international call
市内通話	local call
市外通話	long distance call
電話ボックス	telephone booth
（携帯電話の） 電話帳，住所録	address book
電話番号	(tele)phone number
フリーダイアル	toll-free number
市外局番	area code

（電話の）発 信音	dial tone
話し中の音	busy signal [tone]
（携帯電話の） 着信音	ringtone
電話に出る	get [answer ／ pick up] the phone

電話をかける	make a phone call
～に電話をか ける	call ~ (up), give ~ a call [buzz] 《米》／ ring ~ (up), give ~ a ring 〈英〉 ＊ Give me a call when you get home. （家に着いたら電話してね）
～に何度か電 話をかける	make some calls to ~
ダイヤル（する）	dial [dáiəl]
電話を切る	hang up 《米》／ ring off 〈英〉
電話が切れる	get disconnected

登録された電 話番号	preprogrammed number ／ number saved on one's phone
短縮ダイヤル	speed dial
再ダイヤル （する）	redial
（電話の）自 動転送	call forwarding
ファクス	fax, facsimile

留守番電話	answering machine
留守電にメッ セージを残す	leave a message on someone's phone
留守電をチェ ックする	check a phone message ／ check one's voice mail

7.

オシャレをする

1. 衣類など

★衣類全般

流行，ファッション	fashion [fǽʃən] ＊follow [keep up with] the fashion（流行を追う），be in [out of] fashion（流行して [すたれて] いる）
身につけている，着て [履いて／かぶって／はめて] いる；服，衣服	wear [wéər] ＊wear a T-shirt（Tシャツを着る [着ている]），wear high heels（ハイヒールを履いている），wear a hat（帽子をかぶる）
（服などを）身につける，着る，（化粧品を）つける	put on [pùt án] ＊put on one's coat（コートを着る）
（衣服，メガネなどを）脱ぐ，はずす，取る	take off [tèik ɔ́ːf] ＊take off one's jacket（ジャケットを脱ぐ）
カジュアルな [ラフな] 格好をしている [する]，普段着を着る	dress down ＊He dresses down in jeans and a T-shirt.（彼はジーンズとTシャツでラフな格好をしている），dress-down（普段着の）。
着飾る，洋服を着る	dress up ／ doll up
おしゃれする，おめかしする，着飾る	get dressed up
（女性が）美しく着飾っている	be dolled up ＊She was dolled up in a pink dress.（彼女はピンクのドレスで着飾っていた）
着飾りすぎる，かしこまりすぎた服装をする	overdress
薄着 [厚着] している	be lightly [heavily, thickly] dressed

こぎれいな服装をしている	be neat in one's dress ＊neat は「（服装などが）こぎれいな，小ざっぱりした」。wear neat clothes（こぎれいな服を着ている）
（異性の気をひくために）派手な服装をしている，ばっちりめかしこんでいる	be dressed (up) to kill
着替える；着替え	change ＊change into [out of]（〜に [を] 着替える）
試着する	try on [trài án] ＊May I try this on?（試着してもいいですか）
《集合的に》服，衣服	clothes [klóu(ð)z]
《集合的に》衣類，衣料品	clothing [klóuðiŋ]
（1着の）衣類	garment ＊woolen garments（ウールの衣類）
ペアルック	matching outfits [clothing / clothes]
（特に商品としての）衣服，衣料（品）	apparel [əpǽrəl]
（職業，時代，民族などを表す）服装，衣装	garb [gáːrb]
（ある国民，階級，時代，地方などに特有の）服装，衣装	costume [kástjuːm] ＊装飾品や髪型なども含む。

（特別な場合に着る）服装一式	outfit ＊a wedding outfit（結婚式の礼服一式），a fishing outfit（釣り用の服装）
ドレス，衣服，ワンピース；服を着せる［着る］	dress ＊be dressed in blue（ブルーの服を着ている）
服を脱ぐ［脱がせる］；裸（同然）の状態	undress
カジュアルな衣服，普段着	casual clothes [wear]
お下がり	hand-me-downs〈米〉／ reach-me-downs〈英〉
古着	cast-offs ／ used clothing
作業着	work clothes
洋服をたくさん持っている人	clotheshorse
男性服，紳士服	menswear ／ men's clothing
女性服，婦人服	womenswear ／ women's clothing
子供服	children's wear [clothes]
ベビー服	baby wear [clothes]
制服	uniform
マタニティドレス	maternity dress
ユニセックスの衣服	unisex clothing
礼装	formal dress
タキシード	tuxedo [tʌksíːdou]
スーツ	suit [súːt]
三つ揃いのスーツ	three-piece suit

（男性用の）ワイシャツ，シャツ	shirt [ʃɔ́ːrt]
ドレスシャツ，礼装用ワイシャツ	dress shirt [drès ʃɔ́ːrt]
半袖シャツ	short-sleeved shirt
長袖シャツ	long-sleeved shirt
ブラウス	blouse [bláus]
Tシャツ	T-shirt
タンクトップ	tank top
スポーツウェア	sportswear
スポーツシャツ	sport shirt
ポロシャツ	polo shirt
ラガーシャツ	rugby shirt
襟	collar [kálər]
襟の折り返し	lapel
袖	sleeve
ボタン（を留める）	button [bátn] ＊fasten [undo] a button（ボタンをかける［はずす］）。fasten の発音は [fǽsn]。
ボタンをはずす	unbutton
チャック，ファスナー	zipper〈米〉／ zip〈英〉
（ズボンの）前開きチャック	fly〈米〉／ flies〈英〉 ＊Your fly is open.（前のチャックが開いてるよ）〈米〉
（背中の）ジッパーを上げてくれる？	Will you zip me up, please?
ポケット	pocket [pákət] ＊search one's pockets（ポケットの中を探す）
ネクタイ	necktie ／ tie ＊tie a necktie（ネクタイを結ぶ），put on [remove] a tie（ネクタイをする［はずす］）
蝶ネクタイ	bow tie [bóu tái]

7 オシャレをする

ベスト，チョッキ	vest 〈米〉／waistcoat 〈英〉	チノパン	chinos [tʃíːnouz]
ジャケット，上着	jacket [dʒǽkit]	ジーンズ	jeans 〈複数扱い〉
ブレザー	blazer [bléizər]	デザイナーブランドのジーンズ	designer jeans
コート	coat [kóut]	オーバーオール	overalls 〈複数扱い〉
毛皮のコート	fur coat [fə́ːr kóut]	ベルボトム	bell-bottoms 〈複数扱い〉＊裾が広がったズボン。
オーバーコート	overcoat	コーデュロイ	corduroys
トレンチコート	trench coat	デニム（のスボン）	denims＊デニム生地で作られた，ジーンズ。denim は形容詞的に「デニム（地）の」。
ウインドブレーカー	windbreaker		
パーカ	parka [páːrkə] 〈米〉／anorak [ǽnəræk] 〈英〉		
ダウンジャケット	down jacket	半ズボン，（運動用の）短パン	shorts＊米では「男性用下着のパンツ」の意味もある。
セーター	sweater [swétər] 〈米〉／jumper 〈英〉＊knit a sweater（セーターを編む）	スカート	skirt
		キュロットスカート	culottes [kúːlɑts | kjulɔ́ts]／divided skirt
クルーネック（のセーター[シャツ]）	crew neck＊襟のない丸首のもの。crew-neck sweater（丸首のセーター）	ジャンパースカート	jumper 〈米〉／pinafore (dress) 〈英〉
		スウェットパンツ	sweatpants
タートルネック	turtleneck 〈米〉／polo-neck 〈英〉	トレーナー	sweatshirt
		水着	swimsuit
V ネック	V-neck [víːnèk]＊V-necked sweater（V ネックのセーター）	トランクス《男性用》	swimming trunks
		レオタード	leotard [líːətàːrd]
カーディガン	cardigan [káːrdigən]	靴下類	hosiery [hóuʒəri]
ズボン	pants [pǽnts] 〈米〉〈複数扱い〉／trousers [tráuzərz] 〈英〉〈複数扱い〉＊a pair of pants（ズボン1着），two pairs of pants（ズボン2着）。〈英〉では pants は「下着のパンツ」を指すので要注意。	ストッキング	stockings [stákiŋz]
		（ストッキングの）伝線	run 〈米〉／ladder 〈英〉＊have a run in one's stocking（ストッキングが伝線している）
		靴下，ソックス	socks
		ハイソックス	knee socks, knee-highs
スラックス	slacks [slǽks] 〈複数扱い〉＊baggy slacks（だぶだぶのスラックス）	バスローブ	bathrobe [bǽθròub | báːθròub]

パジャマ	pajamas [pədʒáːməz]
寝巻	nightwear ＊パジャマなど。
ネグリジェ	nightie ／ nightgown
仕立屋，テーラー；(服を)仕立てる	tailor [téilər] ＊主に紳士服を仕立てる。
ドレスメーカー	dressmaker ＊女性服・子供服を仕立てる仕立屋。
既製服	ready-made clothes, off-the-rack clothes 《米》／ off-the-peg clothes 《英》
(服，帽子，靴などの) サイズ	size ＊What is your size? (サイズは何番ですか)
きつい	tight ＊This is too tight. (《試着してみて》ちょっときつすぎます)
ゆるい	loose [lúːs] ＊These slacks are a little loose at the waist. (このスラックスはウエストのところが少しゆるい)
(サイズや型などが) ぴったり合う，似合う	fit ＊These shoes fit me perfectly. (この靴，ピッタリ)
フリーサイズ (の)	one-size-fits-all

★下着

下着	underwear
(女性用の)肌着類	lingerie [làːnʒəréi, -ríː]
コルセット	corset [kɔ́ːrsət]
パンティストッキング	pantyhose《複数扱い》 [pǽntihòuz]

ガードル	girdle
ガーターベルト	garter belt
ブラジャー	brassiere [brəzíər] ／ bra [bráː] 《略》 ＊braless (ノーブラ)
キャミソール	camisole
下着のパンツ	underpants 《米・男女両方》／ pants 《英・男女両方》
下着のパンツ《女性用》	panties 《米》／ knickers [níkərz] 《英》
スリップ	full slip
ハーフスリップ，ペチコート	half slip
タイツ	tights
レギンス，スパッツ	leggings [légiŋz]
Tバック	thong [θɔ́(ː)ŋ] ／ G-string ＊T-back は和製英語。
(男性用の) パンツ	underpants
ブリーフ	briefs [bríːfs]
トランクス	boxer shorts
アンダーシャツ	undershirt 《米》／ vest 《英》 ＊vest は《英》では通例, 「袖なしの男性用肌着」。

★履き物

履き物	footwear
靴屋	shoemaker
靴	shoes [ʃúːz] ＊a pair of shoes (靴1足), put on [take off] one's shoes (靴をはく [脱ぐ])
革靴	leather shoes

7 オシャレをする

ローファー	loafers ＊tassel loafers（房のついたローファー）
ハイヒール	high heels
パンプス	pumps
スニーカー	sneakers《米》／ trainers《英》
運動靴	sports shoes／ athletic shoes
サンダル	sandals
ゴム草履	(rubber) flip-flops
厚底の靴	platform shoes
（かかとのついた）スリッパ	slippers
（かかとのない）スリッパ	scuffs [skʌ́fs]《米》 ／mule [mjúːl]《英》
テニスシューズ	tennis shoes
ブーツ	boots
登山用ブーツ	mountain-climbing boots／ mountaineering boots
かかと	heel ＊the heel [instep] of a shoe（靴のかかと[甲]）
靴底；足の裏	sole [sóul]
靴ひも	shoestring《米》／ shoelace《英》
靴ブラシ	shoebrush [ʃúːbrʌ̀ʃ]
靴磨きのクリーム	shoe polish
靴を磨く	shine shoes《米》／ polish shoes《英》
靴べら	shoehorn ＊use a shoehorn（靴 べらを使う）

靴擦れしました。	I've got a blister on my foot. ＊blister（水ぶくれ，〔足 の〕まめ）

★小物

帽子	hat [hǽt] ＊縁のある帽子。straw hat（麦わら帽子）
キャップ	cap [kǽp] ＊野球帽のような縁のな い帽子。
ヘアバンド	headband
リボン	ribbon [ríbn] ＊wear a ribbon in one's hair（髪にリボンを 着ける[着けている]）
マフラー	scarf [skɑ́ːrf] ＊put on [wear] a scarf around one's neck（マ フラーを首に巻く[巻いて いる]）。《米》で muffler は車の「マフラー」をイ メージする。
耳あて	earmuffs [íərmʌ̀fs]
手袋	gloves [glʌ́vz] ＊wear gloves（手袋を はめる[する]）
ミトン	mitten [mítn] ＊親指だけ離れたふたま た手袋。
ベール	veil [véil]
ベルト	belt ＊fasten [loosen] a belt （ベルトを締める[緩める]）
ベルト通し	belt loop
ベルトの留め金	belt buckle
サスペンダー	suspenders《米》／ braces《英》

《汗止め用の》リストバンド	wristband [rístbænd]
（挟むタイプの）ネクタイピン	tie clip [clasp]
（刺すタイプの）ネクタイピン	tiepin
カフスボタン	cuff links 《米》／ sleeve links 《英》 * cuff（袖口）
腕時計	watch * = wristwatch。put one's watch right（時計を合わせる）
メガネ	glasses * put on [take off] glasses（メガネをかける [はずす]）
メガネケース	glasses case
コンタクトレンズ	contact lens
サングラス	sunglasses ／ dark glasses
遠近両用メガネ	bifocals [bàifouklz]
書類かばん	briefcase
ハンドバッグ	purse 《米》／ handbag 《英》 * carry a purse（ハンドバッグを持ち歩く）
《男性用の》財布，札入れ	wallet
《女性用の》財布，札入れ	wallet 《米》／ purse 《英》
名刺入れ	business card wallet ／ business card case ／ business card holder
《リング状の》キーホルダー	key chain [ring] * キーホルダーとは言わない。

《ケース状の》キーホルダー	key case
《首にかける》ストラップ	neck strap
ウエストポーチ	waist [fanny] pack 《米》／ waist [bum] bag 《英》 * ウエストポーチは和製英語。
ショルダーバッグ	sliding bag
ハンカチ	handkerchief
バンダナ	bandanna [bændǽnə]
ウエットティッシュ	wet wipes ／ moist towelette(s) * wet tissue とは言わない。

★雨具など

傘	umbrella [ʌmbrélə]
長傘	stick umbrella
折りたたみ傘	folding [collapsible] umbrella
ワンタッチ傘	self-opening umbrella
ビニール傘	plastic umbrella
傘を差している	hold an umbrella
傘を差す	open [raise / spread / put up] an umbrella
傘を閉じる	close [fold] an umbrella
日傘	(UV) parasol
レインコート	raincoat
雨用の帽子	rain hat
雨靴	rain boots

2. アクセサリー・宝石, 化粧

★アクセサリー

アクセサリー	accessory [əksésəri]
ペンダント	pendant ＊wear a pendant（ペンダントをつけている）
ブローチ	brooch [bróutʃ] ＊wear [put on] a brooch on *one's* dress（ドレスにブローチをつけている [つける]）
ブレスレット	bracelet [bréislət] ＊fasten [put on] a bracelet（ブレスレットをはめる）, remove [take off] a bracelet（ブレスレットをはずす）
イヤリング	earrings ＊put on [take off] *one's* earrings（イヤリングをつける [はずす]）
ピアス	pierced earrings ＊wear pierced earrings（ピアスをつけている）
鼻ピアス	nose ring
ネックレス	necklace [nékləs]
磁気ネックレス	magnetic necklace
指輪	ring
ダイヤモンドリング	diamond ring
婚約指輪	engagement ring
結婚指輪	wedding ring ／ wedding band《米》
プラチナ	platinum [plǽtinəm]
金	gold [góuld]
18金	18-karat gold
純金	pure [solid] gold

イミテーションの金, 人造金	artificial [à:rtifíʃl] gold
銀	silver ＊silver necklace（銀のネックレス）

★宝石

宝石類	jewelry [dʒú:əlri] ＊gems [dʒémz]（〔カットして磨いた〕宝石）
宝石	jewel [dʒú:əl]
誕生石	birthstone
《1月の誕生石》ガーネット	garnet [gá:rnit]
《2月の誕生石》アメジスト, 紫水晶	amethyst [ǽməθist]
《3月の誕生石》アクアマリン	aquamarine [æ̀kwəmərí:n]
《4月の誕生石》ダイアモンド	diamond [dáimənd]
《5月の誕生石》エメラルド	emerald [émərəld]
《6月の誕生石》パール, 真珠	pearl [pə́:rl] ＊pearls（真珠の首飾り）
《7月の誕生石》ルビー	ruby [rú:bi]
《8月の誕生石》ペリドット	peridot [pérədàt]
《9月の誕生石》サファイア	sapphire [sǽfaiər]

《10月の誕生石》オパール	opal [óupl]		泥パック	mudpack
《11月の誕生石》トパーズ	topaz [tóupæz]		あぶらとり	cleansing pad
《12月の誕生石》トルコ石，ターコイズ	turquoise [tə́ːrkɔiz]		バニシングクリーム	vanishing cream
翡翠	jade [dʒéid]		ホワイトニングクリーム	whitening cream
ブラック・オパール	black opal		日焼け止めクリーム	sunblock [sʌ́nblὰk]
キャッツアイ	cat's eye		健康で美しい肌を保つ	maintain one's healthy and beautiful skin
ムーンストーン	moonstone		潤いのある肌	moist skin

★化粧

化粧	makeup [méikὰp]		すべすべした肌	smooth skin
化粧をする	put on makeup ＊put on heavy makeup（厚化粧をする），take off one's makeup（化粧を落とす）		肌荒れ，ガサガサ肌	rough skin
			乾燥肌	dry skin
			脂性 [オイリー] 肌	oily skin
			くすんだ肌	dull skin
化粧台	dresser, vanity table 〈米〉／dressing table 〈英〉		しみ	spot(s)
			そばかす，しみ	freckle(s)
化粧品	cosmetics [kɑzmétiks]		吹き出物	rash
スキンケア，肌の手入れ	skin care		化粧下地	makeup base
			ファンデーション	foundation ＊wear heavy foundation（ファンデーションが濃い）
クレンジングクリーム	cleansing cream			
化粧水，ローション	toner／toning lotion ＊apply a toning lotion to the face and neck（顔と首に化粧水をつける）		口紅	lipstick ＊apply [put on] lipstick（口紅をつける），wipe off lipstick（口紅を拭き取る）
			リップグロス	lip gloss
乳液	milky lotion		リップクリーム	lip chap, lip balm [líp bὰːm]
保湿クリーム	moisturizing cream			
コールドクリーム	cold cream		頬紅をつける	apply [put on] blusher

マスカラ；〜にマスカラをつける	mascara [mæskǽrə | -káːrə] * apply [put on] mascara （マスカラをつける）	マニキュアの除光液	nail-polish remover
つけまつげをしている [する]	wear false [fɔ́ːls] eyelashes	爪やすり	nail file
アイシャドー	eye shadow * apply [wear] eye shadow （アイシャドーをつける [つけている]）	（マニキュア，ペディキュア用の）爪やすり	emery board
		爪切り	nail clippers
（ペンシル型の）アイブロウ	eyebrow pencil * use an eyebrow pencil / pencil one's eyebrows （眉を書く）	毛抜き，ピンセット	tweezers [twíːzərz] * pull out a thorn with tweezers （ピンセットで棘を抜く）
アイラインを引く	put on eyeliner	むだ毛	unwanted hair * remove [shave] unwanted hair （むだ毛を処理する）
ラメ	glitter [ɡlítər]	脱毛する	remove hair
メーク落とし	makeup remover		
化粧を落とす	remove one's makeup	脱毛剤	depilatory [dipílətɔ̀ːri]
コンパクト《携帯用のおしろい・鏡・パフ入れ》	compact	《女性に対して》とても魅力的にみえる	look (like) a million dollars 《米》 * She looks like a million dollars. （彼女，素敵だね）
香水（をつける）	perfume [pə́ːrfjuːm] * put perfume on one's neck （首に香水をつける）	美形の，とても魅力のある	gorgeous [ɡɔ́ːrdʒəs] * 男女共に使う。She is gorgeous. （彼女，魅力的だね）
化粧ポーチ	vanity case [bag] / makeup pouch	《女性が》顔立ちのよい [美しい]	comely [kʌ́mli] 《形》 / good-looking [ɡúdlúkiŋ]
マニキュア液	nail polish 《主に米》 / nail varnish 《主に英》	《女性が》非常に美しい，うっとりさせる	ravishing [rǽviʃiŋ]
マニキュアをする	put on nail polish		
マニキュア；（手・爪の）手入れをする，〜にマニキュアを塗る	manicure [mǽnikjùər] * get [have] a manicure （マニキュアをしてもらう）		

3. 美容院・理容院，美容・ダイエット

★美容院・理容院

美容院	beauty parlor [salon]　＊go to the beauty parlor（美容院に行く）	ヘアスプレー	hair spray　＊spray one's hair with hair spray（髪にヘアスプレーをかける）
美容師，ヘアドレッサー	hairdresser ／ hairstylist	ハサミ	scissors [sízərz]
理容院，床屋	barber's ／ barber	すきバサミ	thinning scissors
髪	hair　＊bind one's hair at the back（髪を後ろで束ねる）	髪をすく	thin one's hair
		バリカン	hair clippers
散髪，髪型	haircut	（刈り取って）きれいに整える；（髪型を変えない）手入れ	trim　＊have one's hair trimmed（髪を整えてもらう），trim one's nails（爪を切る）
髪型	hairstyle, hairdo		
ヘアブラシ	hairbrush [héərbrʌʃ]		
髪をブラッシングする	brush one's hair	枝毛	split ends
		くせ毛	unruly hair
くし；くしでとかす	comb [kóum]　＊comb one's hair（髪をくしでとかす）	縮れ毛	frizzy hair
		襟足	neckline ／ hairline along the neck ／ nape of one's neck
バレッタ，《板状の》ヘアクリップ	barrette [bərét]《米》／ hair slide《英》		

前髪	bangs [bǽŋz] 《米》/ fringe [fríndʒ] 《英》 ＊Take about two centimeters off my bangs. (前髪を2センチほど切ってください), Leave the bangs just long enough to reach my eyebrows. (前髪を眉毛にかかるくらいにしてください)
あまり短くしないでください。	Don't cut it too short.
後ろ髪を3センチほど切ってください。	Shorten it in the back by about three centimeters.
ワンレンにしてください。	I want a one-length cut.

もみあげ	sideburns ＊leave [trim] the sideburns (もみあげを残す [整える])
あごひげ	beard [bíərd] ＊shave off one's beard (あごひげを剃り落とす)
口ひげ	mustache [mʌ́stæʃ] ＊have [wear] mustaches (口ひげを生やしている)
ほおひげ	whiskers [hwískərz] ＊shave off one's whiskers (ほおひげをそり落とす)
ボブ	bob [báb]
《女性の》シングルカット	shingle [ʃíŋgl] ＊刈り上げのショートボブ。先端が次第にとがる形。
フェザーカット	feathercut [féðərkʌ̀t]
三つ編み，おさげ（髪）	braid [bréid] 《米》《通例 ～s》/ plait 《英》《通例 ～s》 ＊wear one's hair in braids (髪を三つ編みにする)

ポニーテール	ponytail [póuniteìl] ＊wear one's hair in a ponytail (髪をポニーテールにしている)
刈り上げる	have close [cropped] hair at the back
ツーブロック	undercut / shaved sides ＊I want a undercut.(ツーブロックにしてください)
丸刈り	close crop / buzz-cut ＊have a close crop (haircut) (丸刈りにする)
スポーツ刈り	crew cut ＊get a crew cut (スポーツ刈りにする)
モヒカン刈り	mohawk [móuhɔ̀ːk]
横分け	side part
髪を左側で[真ん中から]分ける	part one's hair on the left [in the middle]
（髪の）ボリュームを落とす	reduce the volume of one's hair
（髪の）トップにボリュームを出す	add volume on the top
パーマ（をかける）	perm ＊have one's hair permed (髪にパーマをかける), A soft permanent, please. (軽くパーマしてください)
髪を染める	dye one's hair / change one's hair color
髪を染めてもらう	have one's hair dyed ＊have one's hair dyed light brown (明るい茶色に髪を染めてもらう)
自分で髪を染める	color one's hair oneself

縮毛矯正してもらう	**have** *one's* **hair relaxed** ＊ **hair straightening**（縮毛矯正）
（髪などを）乾かす（こと），乾かしながらセットする(こと)	**blow-dry** ＊ **blow-dry** *one's* **hair**（ドライヤーで髪を乾かす）
（化粧・髪形・服装など）イメージチェンジする	**get a makeover** ／ **change** *one's* **look**
髪をアップにする	**put** *one's* **hair up**
髪をお団子にする	**put** *one's* **hair up in a bun**
ウィッグ，付け毛	**wig** [wíg] ＊ **wear a wig**（ウィッグ[付け毛]を着ける）
ヘアーエクステンション，付け毛	**hair extension**
整髪剤，整髪料	**hairstyling product**
頭皮	**scalp** [skǽlp]
ヘアトニック，養毛剤	**hair tonic**
ヘアローション，ヘアリキッド	**hair lotion**
ヘアクリーム	**hair cream**
ムース	**mousse** [múːs]
ヘアワックス	**hair wax**
（整髪用）ジェル	**gel** [dʒél]

★美容・ダイエット

7 オシャレをする

（顔のしわをとる）美容整形手術	**face(-)lift(ing)** ＊ **have a facelift**（しわとり整形する）
形成外科	**plastic surgery**
腹部の脂肪を取る手術	**tummy tuck** [tʌ́mi tʌ̀k]
日常の食べ物，食事療法，規定食，ダイエット	**diet** [dáiət] ＊ *be* [go] **on a diet**（ダイエットをしている[始める]）
ダイエット，食事療法をすること	**dieting**
断食（期間）；《宗教的あるいは健康上の理由で，または抗議のため》断食する	**fast** [fǽst] ＊ **go on a fast**（断食に入る）
カロリー	**calorie** [kǽləri] ＊ **reduce** (*one's*) **calorie intake**（カロリー摂取量を減らす），**be high [low] in calories**（カロリーが高い[低い]）
カロリーチャート	**calorie chart**
カロリーカウンター	**calorie counter**
咀嚼（そしゃく）する	**chew** [tʃúː] ＊ **chew** *one's* **food well**（食べ物をよくかんで食べる）
（体内)消費(量)	**consumption** [kənsʌ́mpʃən] ＊ **alcohol consumption**（アルコール摂取量）

食事の規定量, 規定食;食事の, 食餌療法の	dietary [dáiətèri]
ダイエットの反 動で太る	rebound from dieting
減量するために 間食をやめる	stop eating between meals to lose weight
高蛋白の食事	high-protein diet
高ビタミン食事	high-vitamin diet ＊vitamin の発音は,〈米〉 [váitəmin],〈英〉[vítə-]

減塩食	low-salt diet
無塩食	salt-free diet
長寿食	macrobiotic diet
絶食療法,断 食療法	hunger cure
摂生,食事療法	regimen [rédʒəmən]
完全な菜食主 義者	vegan [víːgn]
グレープフルー ツ・ダイエット	grapefruit diet

8.

観光地を訪ねる

1. 旅行の準備をする

★旅行・携帯品

旅行（する）	travel [trǽvl]
旅行者	traveler 《米》／ traveller 《英》
旅行代理店	travel agency [trǽvl èidʒənsi]
旅行案内業者	travel agent ＊I have a great travel agent. (素晴らしい旅行案内業者についてもらっています)
旅程（表）	itinerary [aitínərèri]
旅行保険	travel insurance [trǽvl inʃùərəns] ＊buy traveler's insurance (旅行保険に加入する)
パスポート	passport ＊renew a passport (パスポートを更新する)
パスポートの有効期限を確認する	check one's passport expiration [èkspəréiʃən]
ビザ	visa [víːzə]
トラベラーズチェック	traveler's check 《米》／ traveller's cheque 《英》
クレジットカード	credit card [krédit kàːrd]
換金する	exchange money
自動外貨両替機	automatic foreign currency exchange machine
グループ旅行	group travel
出張	business trip ＊go [be] on a business trip to ~ (~に出張に行く[出張中である])

出張旅費	travel expenses
旅行用品	travel goods
手荷物，旅行用かばん類	baggage [bǽgidʒ] 《主に米》／ luggage [lʌ́gidʒ] 《主に英》
スーツケース	suitcase [súːtkèis]
スーツケースベルト	luggage strap
キャリーバッグ	roller bag ＊「キャリーバッグ」(和製語)は一般的にビニール製や布製で底に車輪がついたものを指す。
バックパック；バックパックを背負って旅行[ハイキング]する	backpack ＊backpacker (バックパッカー〔バックパックで旅行する人〕)
トートバッグ	tote bag [tóut bæ̀g]
ブリーフ・ケース	brief case
ダッフルバッグ	duffle bag
ボストンバッグ	traveling bag
コンピュータバッグ	computer bag

旅行用具一式	trip kit
旅行用枕	travel pillow
アイマスク	eye mask
耳栓	earplugs
靴を入れるバッグ	shoe sack
キャビンバッグ	cabin bag
三つ折りの衣類用バッグ	tri-fold garment bag

衣類カバー	garment cover		飛行機酔いする	get airsick
搭乗券ホルダー	boarding pass holder		乗り物酔いする	get travel-sick ＊I got travel-sick. (〔乗 り物に〕酔いしました)
ポーチ，小袋	pouch [páuʧ]			
セキュリティ ポーチ	security pouch		船酔いする	get seasick
化粧品袋	cosmetic bag		日帰り旅行	one-day trip ／ day trip 〈主に英〉
エコバッグ	reusable bag			
財布	wallet [wάlət]		現地調査旅行	field trip
化粧ポーチ	cosmetic pouch ／ vanity [beauty] case		《通例，団体の》 小旅行，遠足	excursion [ikskə́ːrʒən]
洗濯洗剤	laundry detergent		世界一周の旅行	round-the-world trip
ガイドブック	guide book		周遊旅行	round trip
電子辞書	electronic dictionary		社員旅行	company trip
筆記用具	writing implements [materials]		よい旅を！	Bon voyage!
メモ帳	notepad		宿泊先を決める	choose a hotel
身分証明写真	identification photo ／ ID photo		ホテルの予約 を取る	make a hotel reservation
着替え(余分の衣服)	extra clothes		旅の前に天候 を調べる	check the weather before the trip
(旅行用の) 洗面道具	travel toiletries		荷物をスーツケ ースに詰める	pack one's suitcase
化粧品	cosmetics			
薬	medicine [médəsn]		大事な旅行関 係の書類をコ ピーする	make copies of important travel documents
睡眠薬	sleeping pill [tablet]			
腕時計	wristwatch		貴重品リスト を作成する	make a list of valuables
水着	swimwear			
生理用品	sanitary items		飛行機を予約する	book a flight
折りたたみ傘	collapsible umbrella		予防接種を受 ける	get vaccinated [væksənèitid]
変換プラグ	conversion plug			
乗り物酔い	motion sickness ／ travel-sickness		国際運転免許 証を取得する	obtain an international driving permit
乗り物酔い止 め薬	motion sickness drug			

8

観光地を訪ねる

★設備・サービス

リゾートホテル	resort hotel
ビジネスホテル	commercial hotel, no-frills hotel (for business people), economy hotel／budget hotel〈英〉 ＊business hotel は和製語。no-frills は「余計なサービス抜きの」。
朝食付きのホテル	B & B (Bed and Breakfast)〈主に英〉
フロント，受付	reception [risépʃən]／front desk
会計係	cashier [kæʃíər]
シングルルーム	single room
ツインルーム	twin room
ダブルルーム	double room
スイート	suite [swíːt]
ペット不可のベッドルーム	pet-free bedroom
眺めのいい部屋	room with a nice view
静かな部屋	quiet room
喫煙ルーム	smoking room
禁煙ルーム	non-smoking room
ホテルの設備	hotel amenities
無料の朝食	free breakfast
駐車	parking
無料駐車サービス	complimentary parking
（ホテルやレストランの）駐車係	valet [væléi]
ベルボーイ	bellboy

ポーター	porter
接客係，コンシェルジュ（観劇や旅の手配を行うサービス）	concierge [kànsiéərʒ]
ルームメイド	room maid
新聞	newspaper [nyúːzpèipər]
スパ	spa [spáː]
サウナ（風呂）（に入る）	sauna [sɔ́ːnə]
ジャグジー	Jacuzzi [dʒəkúːzi]〈商標〉
バー	bar
カクテル・ラウンジ	cocktail lounge
ランドリーサービス	laundry service
同日仕上げランドリーサービス	same-day laundry service
モーニングコール	wake-up call
ビジネスセンター	business center
ジム	gym [dʒím]
ヘルスクラブ（運動器具を備えたジムのような施設）	health club
プール	pool

屋内プール	indoor swimming pool		バスローブ	bathrobe
ミーティングルーム	meeting room		ヘアドライヤー	hair dryer
レストラン	restaurant		アメニティグッズ	bath amenities ＊「アメニティグッズ」は和製語。
ギフトショップ	gift shop			
空港行きシャトルバス	airport shuttle bus		ミニバー（客室にある酒類を入れた小型冷蔵庫）	mini bar
レンタカー予約デスク	rental car desk			
航空券予約デスク	airline desk		ドリップ式コーヒーメーカー	drip coffee machine
ツアー予約デスク	tour desk		エアコン	air conditioner
外貨交換所	foreign money exchange		ラジオ	radio [réidiou]
			テレビ	television
美容院	beauty salon		テレビゲーム	video game
マッサージと美容術	massages and beauty treatments		ペイパービュー方式（の）	pay-per-view ＊ユーザーが視聴した分だけ料金を払う方式。
製氷機	ice machine			
靴磨きの店	shoeshine shop		室内電話	(hotel) room telephone
アーケード街	shopping arcade		館内電話	house phone
ベビーベッド	crib 〈米〉／ cot 〈英〉		金庫	safety deposit box
ベビーシッター	babysitter, sitter 〈米〉／ childminder 〈英〉		アイロン	iron [áiərn]
			ズボンプレッサー	pants press 〈米〉／ trouser press 〈英〉
手荷物一時預かり所	short-term luggage storage		簡易キッチン（スペース）	kitchenet(te) [kìtʃənát]
			目覚まし時計	alarm (clock)

★客室

客室の設備	guest room amenities
共用バスルーム	shared bathroom
専用の浴室［トイレ］	private bathroom

留守電のメッセージ	voice-mail message
24 時間ルームサービス	24-hour room service

8

観光地を訪ねる

★部屋の予約

今晩の部屋を予約したいのですが。	I'd like to reserve a room for tonight.
今晩空いている部屋はありますか。	Do you have a room available for tonight? / Do you have a vacant room for tonight? ＊ vacant [véikənt]（〔部屋・座席などが〕空いている）
3月6日に予約をしたいのですが。	I'd like to make a reservation for March 6.
あいにく満室でございます。	I'm afraid we are fully booked.
あいにく今晩は満室です。	I'm sorry, but we have no vacancies tonight.
何泊なさいますか。	How long will you be staying? / How many nights are you staying for?
2泊します。	I'm staying for two nights.
何名様のご予約ですか。	How many people is it for?
どのタイプの部屋がよろしいですか。	What type of room would you like?
1泊いくらですか。	How much is it per night? / How much do you charge for a night?
シングルルームは1泊いくらですか。	How much is a single room per night?
1泊、税金・サービス料別で120ドルでございます。	The room rate is 120 dollars per night, excluding tax and service charge.
もっと安い部屋はありますか。	Do you have any less expensive rooms?
海に面した部屋はありますか。	Do you have a room with an ocean view?
朝食はついていますか。	Is breakfast included?
お支払いはいかがなさいますか。現金ですか、クレジットカードですか。	How would you like to pay? Cash or credit card? ＊クレジットカード以外の支払いは one-night deposit（1泊分料金の前払い金）が必要になることがある。

★チェックイン

チェックインカウンター	check-in counter
チェックイン[チェックアウト]タイム	check-in [check-out] time ＊ Could you keep my baggage until the check-in time?（チェックインの時間まで荷物を預かっていただけますか）
宿泊者カード	registration form ＊ Could you fill out this (registration) form, please?（こちらの宿泊者カードにご記入ください）

ホテル・バウチャー, ホテル利用券	hotel voucher ＊ホテルの手配を旅行会社に依頼すると，ホテルバウチャーを渡される。
宿泊予約確認書	confirmation slip ＊ Here is my confirmation slip.（これが宿泊予約確認書です）
チェックイン，お願いします。	I'd like to check in, please.
小林太郎です。予約してあります。	My name is Taro Kobayashi. I have a reservation.
お名前をうかがってもよろしいでしょうか。	May I have your name, please?
予約している田中です。	I have a reservation under Tanaka.
予約なさっていますか。	Do you have a reservation?
ウェブ予約しました	I made a reservation online.
チェックアウトは何時までですか。	What time should I check out by?
この荷物は自分で持ちます。他の荷物を運んでください。	I'll carry this bag. Can you bring the other bags to my room?
貴重品	valuables [vǽljəblz, -ljuə-] ＊ Can you keep my valuables?（貴重品を預かってもらえますか）
宿泊を延長する	extend one's stay

追加料金	extra charge ／ additional charge
部屋のタイプ	type of room
宿泊数	number of nights
定刻より早いチェックイン	early check-in
定刻より遅いチェックアウト	late check-out

★チェックアウト

チェックアウト，お願いします。	I'd like to check out, please.
精算書	bill ＊ Bill, please.（請求書をお願いします）
請求明細書	invoice [ínvɔis]
もう１泊したいのですが。	I'd like to stay one more night.
１日早くチェックアウトしたいのですが。	I'd like to leave one night earlier.

8 観光地を訪ねる

3. 観光地に行く

★観光

観光案内所	tourist information center
ツアーに参加する	join a tour
観光地	sightseeing spots
観光ツアー	sightseeing tour
ツアーガイド, 観光ガイド	tour guide [conductor] ＊hire a tour guide（ツアーガイドを雇う）
日本語を話すガイド	Japanese-speaking guide
旅行案内書, 旅行ガイド	travel guide ／ guidebook
観光小冊子	sightseeing brochure [brouʃúər]
旅行者地図	tourist map
無料の地図	free map
バスツアー	bus tour
パッケージツアー	package tour
市内観光ツアー	city sightseeing tour
オプショナルツアー	optional tour
ガイド付きツアー	guided tour
博物館	museum [mjuːzíəm]
水族館	aquarium [əkwéəriəm]
動物園	zoo
植物園	botanical garden
庭園	garden
入場料	admission (fee)
学割	student discount
団体割引	group discount

開館時間	the opening time
閉館時間	the closing time
休館日	closed days
宮殿	palace [pǽləs]
城	castle
天守閣	castle tower ／ main keep
寺	temple
神社，神殿	shrine [ʃráin]
塔，タワー	tower
劇場	theater [θíətər] ／ theatre 《英》
遊園地	amusement park
滝	waterfalls
渓谷	valley [vǽli]
ビーチ	beach
名所	scenic spot [síːnik spát]
歴史的な名所，史跡，旧跡	historic spot ＊historic（歴史上有名な）
遺跡	remains [riméinz] ／ ruins [rúː)inz]
国立公園	National park
オアシス	oasis [ouéisis]《発音注意》
風景	landscape
歓楽街，夜の街	nightlife district
カジノ	casino [kəsíːnou]《発音注意》
服装の規程，ドレスコード	dress code
どのような服装をすればいいですか。	How should I dress?

世界遺産	World Heritage [hérətidʒ] site
世界自然遺産	World Natural Heritage site
世界文化遺産	World Cultural Heritage site
世界遺産活動（ユネスコの取り組み）	World Heritage Activity《WHA》

★レンタカーを借りる

レンタカー	rental car
車を借りる	rent a car ＊I'd like to rent a car.（車を借りたいのですが）
レンタカーの予約を取る	make a rental car reservation
料金表	price list
クーポン券	voucher [váutʃər]
特別割引	special discount
保証金［前金］を払う	pay a deposit [dipázət] ＊Do you need a deposit?（保証金が必要ですか）
車を返す	return the car
国際免許証	international driving permit
どんな車種がありますか。	What kind of cars do you have?
6日間，中型車を借りたいのですが。	I'd like to rent a mid-size car for six days.
シカゴで乗り捨ててもいいですか。	Can I drop off the car in Chicago?

8

観光地を訪ねる

行き先で乗り捨てはできますか。	Can I drop the car off at my destination?	交通違反歴	traffic violation record ／ bad driving record
車を返す場所は同じですか。	Should I return the car to the same place?	違反歴なし（無違反）	a clean driving record ＊店によって，無違反のドライバーでないと車を借りられない場合もある。
1日延長をお願いします。	I'd like to extend the rental for one more day.		
返すときに満タンにしなくてはいけませんか。	Do I need to fill up the tank when I return it?	遅延損害金	late charge
		（ホテル・乗り物などを）予約しながら来ない客	no-show
保険	insurance [inʃúərəns] ＊I want to get an insurance.（保険をかけたいのですが）	乗り捨てレンタル	one-way rental
対人	bodily injury	追加料金	surcharge
対物	property damage	アップグレードする	get an upgrade ＊予約した車種以外の車種を勧められることがある。追加料金を請求されるので，注意。
賠償責任	liability [làiəbíləti] ＊《複数形で》負債，債務		
対人無保険車	uninsured motorist bodily injury		
無過失保険	no-fault insurance	アップグレードしてもらう	ask for an upgrade
確認［予約］番号	confirmation number／reservation number		

4. 旅のトラブル

★盗難・紛失など

窃盗	theft [θéft]
強盗，盗難	robbery [rábəri]
泥棒，こそどろ	thief [θíːf]
建物に侵入する 押し入り強盗 [泥棒]	burglar [bə́ːrglər] ＊A burglar broke into my room.（部屋に泥棒が押 し入った［侵入した］）
スリ（を働く）	pickpocket ＊Someone pickpocketed my wallet.（誰かに財布をすら れました）
カメラを盗ま れました。	My camera was stolen. ／ I had my bag stolen.
かばん［ハン ドバッグ］を ひったくられ ました。	Someone snatched my bag 〈米〉[purse 〈米〉 ／ handbag 〈英〉].
置き引き《人》	baggage thief
置き引き《行為》	baggage stealing
～で置き引き にあった	I had my baggage stolen at ...
警察を呼ぶ	call the police
警察に届ける	report it to the police
盗難証明書	theft report

助けて！	Help! ／ Someone, help me!
泥棒！　捕ま えて！	Thief! Stop him!
お巡りさん！	Police!
放して！	Let me go!
手を放して！	Let go of your hand!

出て行け！	Get out of here!
一緒に警察に 来なさい。	Come with me to the police.
財布を失くし ました。	I lost my wallet [purse 〈英〉].
遺失物取扱所	lost and found ／ lost property (office) 〈英〉
クレジットカー ドを無効にする	cancel one's credit card
再発行（する）	reissue ＊Can I have my passport reissued?（パ スポートを再発行してもら えますか）
日本大使館	Japanese Embassy ＊Please call the Japanese Embassy.（日本大使館に連絡し てください）
～が見つかり ました。	I found ....
荷物の紛失	lost baggage
荷物の損傷	damaged baggage
航空会社に～ を届け出る	report ... to the airline
英語がよく話 せません。	I can't speak English very well.
日本語の話せ る人を呼んで ください。	Call for a Japanese- speaking staff member, please. ／ Please call someone who can speak Japanese.

8 観光地を訪ねる

147

便を取り消される（航空会社のオーバーブッキングが原因）	get bumped off a flight
席割りをリクエストする	request a seat assignment
クレジット会社の電話番号を携行する	carry *one's* credit card company's telephone number

★事故

事故	accident
交通事故	traffic accident ／ car accident
道路交通法	traffic laws
交通違反	traffic violation
目撃者	witness
場所	location
ナンバープレートの番号	license number
保険番号	insurance policy number
運転免許証番号	driver's license number
（警官の）バッジ番号	badge number
（警官の）分隊	squad [skwád]
自動車事故報告書	motor vehicle accident report
過失	fault [fɔ́:lt] ＊It's not my fault.（自分の過失ではありません）
けが	injury [índʒəri]
けが人	injured person

衝突事故	collision [kəlíʒən] accident
むち打ち症	whiplash injury
打撲（傷）	bruise [brúːz] ＊get a bruise（あざ［打撲傷］ができる）
腕［手首，足，親指］にひびが入る	fracture [frǽktʃər] *one's* arm [wrist / leg / thumb]
足を骨折する	break *one's* leg
痛み	pain ＊kill [relieve/remove] the pain with drugs（薬で痛みを止める）
（多量の）出血	hemorrhage [héməridʒ]《米》／ haemorrhage《英》
出血（している）	bleeding ＊control bleeding from a wound（傷口からの出血を抑える）
鼻血（が出ること）	nosebleed ＊have a nosebleed（鼻血が出る［を出す］）
応急手当	first aid ＊give *someone* first aid（〔人〕に応急手当てをする）
パトカー	police [patrol] car ＊an unmarked police car（覆面パトカー）
救急車	ambulance [ǽmbjələns]
救急車を呼ぶ	call an ambulance
救急隊員	rescue personnel
急いでください。	Please hurry.
こっちです。	This way.

（自然の名所一覧）

【アメリカ編】

state park	州立公園
U.S. National Park	米国国立公園
Great Smoky Mountains	グレートスモーキー山脈
Rocky Mountain	ロッキー山脈
Hawaii Volcanoes	ハワイ火山
Mesa Verde [méisə vớːrd] National Park	メサ・ヴェルデ国立公園（コロラド州）
Crater Lake National Park	カルデラ湖クレーター・レイク国立公園（オレゴン州）
Yosemite [jousémэti] National Park	ヨセミテ国立公園（カリフォルニア州）
Death Valley [déθ væli]	デスヴァレー（カリフォルニア州）
Everglades [évərglèidz] National Park	エバーグレーズ国立公園（フロリダ州）
Grand Canyon	グランドキャニオン（アリゾナ州）
Antelope Canyon	アンテロープキャニオン（アリゾナ州）
Monument Valley Navajo [nævəhòu] Tribal Park	モニュメントバレーナバホトライバルパーク（ユタ州南部とアリゾナ北部）
Bryce Canyon National Park	ブライスキャニオン国立公園（ユタ州）
Horseshoe Bend	ホースシューベンド（アリゾナ州）
Niagara Falls [naiǽgərə fɔ́ːlz]	ナイアガラの滝（ニューヨーク州とカナダのオンタリオ州の境）
Zion National Park	ザイオン国立公園（ユタ州）
Cathedral [kəθíːdrl] Rock	カセドラルロック（アリゾナ州）
Charles River	チャールズ川（マサチューセッツ州）
Hoover Dam [húːvər dǽm]	フーバーダム（アリゾナ州とネバダ州の境にあるコロラド川）
White Sands National Monument	ホワイトサンズ国定記念物（ニューメキシコ州）
Multnomah Falls [məltnóumə fɔ́ːlz]	マルトノマ滝（オレゴン州）
Grand Teton [tíːtn] National Park	グランドティトン国立公園（ワイオミング州）
Joshua Tree National Park	ジャシュアツリー国立公園（カリフォルニア州）

8

観光地を訪ねる

Mount Rainier [máunt rəníər]	レーニア山（ワシントン州）
Redwood [rédwùd] **National Park**	レッドウッド国立公園（カリフォルニア州）
Yellowstone [jéloustòun] **National Park**	イエローストーン国立公園（アイダホ州，モンタナ州，及びワイオミング州にまたがる）

【イギリス・オセアニア編】

Hyde Park	ハイドパーク（ロンドン）
Cotswolds	コッツウォルズ（イギリス中央部複数の州にまたがる地域）
Kensington Gardens	ケンジントンガーデンズ（ロンドン）
River Thames	テムズ川（ロンドン）
Seven Sisters Country Park	セブンシスターズカントリーパーク（イーストサセックス）
Lake Windermere	ウィンダーミア湖（イギリス湖水地方）
Carlton Hill	カールトンヒル（エジンバラ）
Kew Garden	キューガーデンズ（ロンドン）
Regent's Park	リージェンツパーク（ロンドン）
Green Park	グリーンパーク（ロンドン）
Giant's Causeway	ジャイアンツコーズウェー（北アイルランド）
Lake Grasmere	グラスミア湖（湖水地方）
Hidcote Manor Garden	ヒドコットマナーガーデン（コッツウォルズ地方）
Queen Mary Rose Garden	クイーンメアリーローズガーデン（ウェストエンド）
Dartmoor National Park	ダートムーア国立公園（エクセター）
Little Venice	リトルヴェニス（ロンドン）
Glastonbury Tor	トールの丘（グラストンベリートー）
Snowshill Lavender Farm	スノーズヒルラベンダーファーム（コッツウォルズ地方）
Glencoe [glenkóu]	グレンコー（スコットランド）
Ironbridge Gorge [gɔ́ːrdʒ]	アイアンブリッジ峡谷（シュロップシャー州）

The White Cliffs of Dover	ホワイトクリフ（ドーヴァー）
Castlerigg Stone Circle	キャッスルリッグストーンサークル（湖水地方）
Coniston Water	コニストン湖（湖水地方）
Wimbledon Park Lake	ウィンブルドンパーク（ウィンブルドン）
Primrose Hill	プリムローズヒル（ロンドン）
Skomer Island	スコーマー島（イギリス）
The Carlton Gardens	カールトンガーデン（豪／ビクトリア州）
Lord Howe Island	ロード・ハウ島群（豪）
Kakadu National Park	カカドゥ国立公園（豪／ノーザンテリトリー）
Great Barrier Reef	グレート・バリア・リーフ（豪／北東岸）
Willandra Lakes Region	ウィランドラ湖群地域（豪）
Tasmanian Wilderness	タスマニア原生地域（豪／タスマニア州）
Wet Tropics of Queensland	クイーンズランドの湿潤熱帯地域（豪）
Ayers Rock [éərz rák], Uluru [úːlurù]	エアーズ・ロック，ウルルはアボリジニによる呼び名（豪／ノーザンテリトリー）
Mount Augustus	マウント・オーガスタス（豪／カーナボン）
Fraser Island [fréizər áilənd]	フレーザー島（豪／クイーンズランド）
Te Wahipounamu-South West New Zealand	テ・ワヒポウナム－南西ニュージーランド（新／南島）
Tongariro National Park	トンガリロ国立公園（ニュージーランド／北島）
Aoraki / Mount Cook National Park	アオラキ／マウント・クック国立公園（ニュージーランド／南島）

8

観光地を訪ねる

Waikiki beach in Honolulu, Hawaii

Monument Valley Navajo Tribal Park

9.

買い物をする

1. 買い物

★お店

チェーン店	chain store 〈米〉／ multiple shop 〈英〉	菓子店	confectionery shop ＊confectionery（菓子類）は pastry, sweets, cakes, jelly, chocolates, pies, ice cream などの総称。
食料品店チェーン	food-store chain		
大手スーパーチェーン	major grocery store chain	（調剤）薬局，病院内の薬局	pharmacy [fáːrməsi] ＊薬剤師が医師の処方箋をもとに薬を調剤する薬局。
スーパーマーケット	supermarket ＊supermarket flyer（スーパーのチラシ）	ドラッグストア，薬局	drugstore 〈米〉 ＊市販されている薬を販売し，ほかに，日用品や化粧品も置いている。
コンビニ	convenience store [kənvíːniəns stɔ́ːr]		
		薬局	chemist's (shop) 〈英〉
ショッピングセンター	(shopping) mall 〈米〉／ shopping centre 〈英〉	酒屋《販売店》，酒店	liquor shop [store] 〈米〉／ off-license 〈英〉 ＊liquor の発音は，[líkər]。
アウトレット店	outlet store	ディスカウントショップ，安売り店	discount shop
オンラインショップ，インターネット上の店	online shop [store]		
		ホームセンター	hardware store／ DIY store
商店街	shopping promenade	電器店	electric appliance store
地下街	underground mall ／ underground shopping arcade	楽器店	musical instruments store
		玩具店	toy store
食料品店	grocery store	工芸品店，細工物店	craftwork shop
パン屋	bakery		
精肉店，肉屋	butcher shop	陶器店	pottery shop
魚屋	fish store 〈米〉 ／ fishmonger's (shop) 〈英〉	食器店	tableware shop
		衣料品店	clothing store
八百屋	vegetable shop	洋服店	tailor shop 〈米〉／ tailor's (shop) 〈英〉
青果店	fruit and vegetable shop		
		ブティック	boutique [buːtíːk]
果物店	fruit shop	クリーニング店	laundry [lɔ́ːndri, lάːn-]

花屋，生花店	florist / flower shop
靴店	shoe store
書店	bookstore 《主に米》／ bookshop 《主に英》
眼鏡店	glasses shop
宝石店	jewelry shop
アクセサリーショップ	accessory shop ＊accessory の発音は, [əksésəri, æk-]。
高級ブランド店	luxury brand store
化粧品店	cosmetic store
両替店	exchange shop ＊「空港などの両替所」は, money exchange counter。
免税店	duty free shop
土産物店	souvenir shop
オークション	auction [ɔ́:kʃən]

青空市	street market
骨董市	antique market
ノミの市，フリーマーケット	flea market ＊free market は「自由市場 (じゆうしじょう)《経済用語》」。
(慈善) バザー	rummage sale 《米》／ jumble sale 《英》
ガレージセール	garage [yard] sale
質屋，質店	pawnshop [pɔ́:nʃɑ̀p]
リサイクルショップ	secondhand store / thrift shop ＊recycle shop は和製語で×。

★ショッピング

営業時間	business hours
開店中《掲示》	OPEN / WE'RE OPEN.
10時開店《掲示》	OPEN 10 A.M.
閉店しました《掲示》	CLOSED / WE'RE CLOSED.
本日休業《掲示》	CLOSED TODAY
(お店の) 店員	salesclerk [séilzklə̀:rk, -klɑ̀:k] 《米》 / sales [shop] assistant 《英》
ウィンドウショッピングをする	do some window-shopping
フリーサイズの	one-size-fits-all ＊free size は和製語なので×。a one-size-fits-all T-shirt (フリーサイズのTシャツ)
買い物ガイド	shopping guide
ショッピングカート	(shopping) cart《米》 / trolley [trɔ́li] 《英》
値札	price tag
(値段が) 高い, 高価な	expensive [ikspénsiv, eks-] ＊expensive bag (高級バッグ)
(値段が) 安い, 安価な	cheap ＊be cheap in price (値段が安い)
手頃な価格で	at a reasonable [moderate] price
通常価格	regular price
セール価格	sale price
厳選商品	select goods
品揃え, 製品構成	product lineup

在庫 (品)	stock [sták | stɔ́k] ＊I'm looking for a book called "The President is Missing". Do you have it in stock? (『大統領失踪』という本を探しています。在庫はありますか)
品切れ	out of stock ＊be out of stock (在庫が切れている), Temporarily Out Of Stock 《掲示》ただいま品切れ中)
取り置きする	put ... on hold ＊Can you put it on hold for me? (取り置きしてもらえますか)
中古の 《形》, 中古で 《副》	secondhand [sèkəndhǽnd] ＊a secondhand car (中古車), secondhand books (古本)。「～を中古で手に入れる [買う]」は, get [buy] ... secondhand。
人気のある	popular [《米》pápjələr, 《英》pɔ́pjələr] ＊a popular product (人気 [ヒット] 商品)
最新流行の, 流行を追う 《形》	trendy ＊a trendy hairstyle (いまはやりの髪型)。
お買い得品, 特価品	bargain [bá:rgin] ＊This coat was a real bargain. (このコートはすごくお買い得でした)。real は, 「《名詞の前で；強意的に》まったくの, すごい」。
3つで2つ分の値段《掲示》	3 FOR 2
2つ買うと1つ無料《掲示》	Buy 2 get 1 free / Buy one Get one
1つ買うともう1つが半額《掲示》	Buy 1 Get 2nd 50% off / Buy one Get one 50% off

期間限定特売品	limited-time special offer
(バーゲン) セール, 大売出し	sale ＊bargain sale は和製語で×。
発売中, 特価で	on sale
オンラインで販売されている	be for sale online
非売品《掲示》	Not For Sale
在庫一掃セール	clearance sale [klíərəns sèil]
新学期セール	back-to-school sale
開店5周年記念セール	5th anniversary sale
10%引きセール	10% off sale
クーポン券, 優待券, 割引券	coupon [kúːpàn] ＊expired coupon（期限切れのクーポン）
(分割払いの) 頭金, 手付金	down payment [dáun péimənt]
(分割払いの) 1回分の支払い	installment ＊pay by [in] installments（分割で支払う）
6回払いで	in 6 installments
ポイントカード	rewards card
保証書	guarantee [gæ̀rəntíː] / warranty [wɔ́(ː)rənti, wɑ́r-] ＊be under guarantee [warranty]（〔商品が〕保証期間内である）
請求明細書, 送り状	invoice [ínvɔis]
通信販売, 通販	mail order ＊mail-order《形》通販の：《副》通販で
～をオンライン [インターネット (上)]で買う	buy ... online ＊online「《副》オンラインで, 《形》オンラインの, 《名》オンライン」。

ネット販売限定	online exclusive ＊be available exclusively online（オンラインでのみ入手可能である）
配送に関する情報	shipping information
配送規定	shipping policy
商品追跡番号	order tracking number
ファッション・ウィーク品揃え	fashion week lineup
新着（商品）	new arrivals
カスタマーサービス	customer service

★デパートで～階数

デパート	department store
地上階／1階に [で]	on the first floor《米》／ on the ground floor《英》
2階に [で]	on the second floor《米》／ on the first floor《英》 ＊イギリス英語では the second floor は「3階」。
地下に [で]	in the basement ＊in the first basement（地下1階に [で]）
最上階に [で]	on the top floor
屋上に [で]	on the rooftop
《エレベーター内で》何階ですか。――7階をお願いします。	What [Which] floor?— Seven, please. / Seventh floor, please.
《エレベーター内で, 混雑時に》9階を押してください。	Push nine, please. / Push ninth floor, please.

どうぞお先に。《乗り降りするとき》	After you.
すみません，降ります。	Excuse me, I have to get off.

★デパートで〜売場の表示

台所用品	Kitchen items [stuff]
家庭用品（コーナー）	Housewares 《米》
婦人用品	Women's items
紳士用品	Men's items
子供用品	Children's items
宝石	Jewelry
腕時計	Watches
化粧品	Cosmetics [kɑzmétiks]
家具	Furniture [fə́ːrnitʃər] *集合名詞。three pieces of furniture（家具3点）
衣服	Clothing [klóuðiŋ]
靴	Shoes [ʃúːz]
寝具	Bedding
おもちゃ	Toys
学習用おもちゃ	Learning toys
テレビゲーム	Video games
スポーツとレジャー用品	Sports & Leisure
フィットネス用品	Fitness
テーブルゲーム	Table games
写真センター	Photo center
贈り物と花	Gift & Flowers
本	Books

映画	Movies
家電製品と音楽	Electronics & Music
ガーデン＆パティオ用品	Garden & Patio
パティオ用家具	Patio furniture

★店員との会話

何かお探しですか。／いらっしゃいませ。	Can [May] I help you?
ちょっと見ているだけです。	(I'm) just looking [browsing].
すみません。オーガニック製品はありますか。	Excuse me? Do you carry [have] organic products? *carry には，「〜《商品など》を置いている，扱っている」の意味もある。
靴売場はどこにありますか。	Where can I find the shoe department?
台所用品はどこで買えますか。	Where can I buy kitchen stuff?
婦人服売り場は何階ですか。	Which floor is women's clothing on? *What floor is women's clothing on? でも OK。文末の on は文頭にも置ける。
3階にあります。	It's on 3rd floor.
（これを）試着してもいいですか。	Can I try this on?
試着室はどこですか。	Where is the fitting room?
試着してみますか。《店員》	Would you like to try it on?

こちらのデザインも試着してみますか。《店員》	Would you like to try this design?
いかがですか。——ちょうどいいです。	How does it fit? — It fits me.
このドレス，ピッタリです。	This dress is a perfect fit.
この靴，私にピッタリです。	These shoes fit me like a glove [glʌ́v]. 《発音注意》 ＊fit ... like a glove（〔人〕にピッタリ合う）
私には少し短［長／小さ／大き］すぎます。	It's a little too short [long / small / large] for me.
袖が短すぎます。	The sleeves are too short.
このパンツはウエストがゆるすぎ［きつすぎ］ます。	These pants are too loose [tight] around the waist [wéist]. 《発音注意》
このドレス，似合いますか。	Does this dress suit me?
似合いますか。	How do I look?
あなたにとてもよく似合っていますよ。《店員》	It looks very good on you.
どちらが（私に）似合うと思いますか。	Which do you think suits me better?
このネクタイはこのシャツに合いますか。	Does this tie match [go with] this shirt?
ほかに何色がありますか。	What colors does it come in? ＊come in（〜の色〔種類，サイズ〕がある［売られている］）

これの赤いものはありますか。	Do you have a red one? ＊Do you have this in red? ともいえる。
私には派手すぎます。	It's too flashy [showy] for me.
これの色違いはありますか。	Do you have this in other colors?
ほかの色もありますよ。《店員》	It comes in different colors too.
このシャツのLサイズはありますか。	Does this shirt come in size large?
あいにく今在庫がないんです。《店員》	Unfortunately, it's out of stock at the moment.
来週の火曜日に入荷する予定です。《店員》	It's scheduled to arrive next Tuesday.
お取り置きいたしましょうか。《店員》	Would you like us to keep one for you?
寸法を直してもらえますか。	Can you alter this?
裾を上げてもらえますか。	Can you take up the hem? ＊take up「（衣類の丈を）短くする，上げる」。hem「裾」。
いつ出来上がりますか。	When will it be ready?
手にとって(見て)もいいですか。	Can I hold it?
どうやって使うのですか。	How do you use it?
これより小さい［大きい］サイズはありますか。	Do you have a smaller [larger] size?

9

買い物をする

159

これは何でできていますか。／素材は何ですか。	What is this made of? ＊be made of は，ギターなど，何からできているか見た目でわかるもの，制作工程を経ても材質が変わっていないものについて使う。
それは何でできていますか。／素材は何ですか。	What is it made from? ＊be made from は，日本酒など，元の素材の原形を留めていないものについて使う。
値段はいくらですか。	How much is it?
これは値引きしてありますか。	Is this marked down?
もう少しいいものはありますか。	Do you have anything less expensive?
少しまけてもらえないでしょうか。	Can you give me a little discount?
少し安くしてもらえますか。	Could you come down a little? ＊come down（値段を下げる，まける）
少し値引きしてもらえますか。	Could you cut the price a little?
100 ドルぐらいのものがいいんですが。	Somewhere around $100.
高すぎて買えません。	I can't afford it. ＊afford は「（～を買う）余裕がある」。

これください。	I'll take this.
ちょっと考えてみます。	I'll think about it.
これを5個ください。	Can I have five of these, please? ／ I'd like five of these.

★レジで

(店の) レジ係	cashier [kǽʃiər]
(店の) レジ	(cash) register 《米》／ till 《英》
セルフレジ	self-checkout
レジはどこですか。	Where do I pay?
ビニール袋，それとも紙袋？《レジで，店員》	Plastic or paper?
紙袋をもう1枚余分にもらえますか。	Can I have an extra paper bag?
現金ですか，カードですか。《店員》	Cash or charge?
現金［カード］で支払います。	I'll pay in cash [by card].
クレジットカードは使えますか。	Do you accept credit cards?
カードで支払えますか。	Can I pay by credit card?
こちらにサインしていただけますか。	Could you sign here?
一括払いにいたしますか。	Would you like to pay in full?
暗証番号を押していただけますか。	Could you enter your pin? ＊pin = personal identification number（暗証番号）
カードとレシートです。	Here is your card and receipt.

申し訳ありませんが，有効期限切れでカードが使えません。	I'm afraid your card has been rejected because it's expired.
お釣りが間違っています。	I think you gave me the wrong change.
まだお釣りをもらっていません。	I haven't got my change yet.

★送料・配達・頭金

（配）送料	shipping (cost [fee / charge / expense]) ＊「送料込みで 500 ドル」は，500 dollars including shipping fee。
（配）送料	delivery charge
送料及び手数料	shipping and handling (charge) ＊略して S&H。
送料と手数料を含めて総額は 2,540 円です。	The total with shipping and handling is 2,540 yen.
これは送料込みですか。	Does this include the shipping (fee)?

送料はかかりますか。	Do you charge for shipping?
送料無料《掲》	FREE shipping
プレゼント用に包装してもらえますか。	Can you gift-wrap it?
別々に包んでもらえますか。	Could you wrap this separately, please?
宿泊先のホテルに配送してもらえますか。	Can you deliver it to my hotel?
現金前払い	advance payment in cash
頭金なし	100% loan / zero down payment
このギターの頭金として 20 万円払います。	I'll pay 200,000 yen down on this guitar. ＊ pay 〜 down on ... は「…の頭金として〜（金額）を支払う」。

2. 交換・返品，カードの紛失

★交換・返品

こちらを交換してもらいたいのですが。	I'd like to exchange this.
（これを）大きい[小さい]サイズのものと交換してもらえますか。	Can I exchange this for a larger [smaller] size?
注文したものと色が違います。	It's a different color from what I ordered. ＊「思っていたのと違いました」なら，It was different from what I had expected.。
（これを）返品したいのですが。	I'd like to return this.
こちらは返品できますか。	Can I return this?
こちらがレシートです。	Here's the receipt. ＊receipt [risíːt]《語末 -pt の p は発音しない》
これは私が買ったものではありません。	This isn't what I bought.
ここが壊れています。	It's broken here.
製品の一部が壊れていました。	Some of the items were damaged.
不良品	defective product [merchandise] ＊defective [diféktiv]「不良品の」〈形〉．merchandise [máːrtʃəndàiz]「集合名詞で」商品」。
不良品のようです。	It seems to be defective.

この製品は不良品のように思うのですが。	I'm afraid that the product is defective.
購入日は10月頃でした。	The date of purchase was around October.
返金と交換のどちらでしょうか。《店員》	Would you like a refund or an exchange?
返金をお願いしたいのですが。	I'd like a refund, please.
2週間前に注文した製品がまだ届いていないのですが。	The order I placed two weeks ago hasn't arrived yet. ＊order は「注文（品）」。place an order（注文する）

★クレジット・カードの紛失

クレジットカードをなくしました。	I lost my credit card.
財布を置き忘れました。	I misplaced my wallet.
クレジットカード番号	credit card number
口座番号	account number
カードを無効にする	cancel the card
今日現在で，本日付けで	as of today
新しいカードを発行する	issue a new card ＊How long will it take to issue my new card?（新しいカードの発行にはどのくらいかかりますか）

10.

病気と健康

1. 症状

★受付

総合受付	Reception 〈掲〉／ front office
受付窓口	reception desk
外来受付	outpatient reception
総合案内	general information
入院受付	Admissions Office〈掲〉
初診	first visit
再診	return visit
初診問診票	first visit questionnaire [kwèstʃənéər]

★症状を伝える基本表現

病院へ連れて行ってください。	Can you take me to a hospital?
救急車を呼んでください。	Call an ambulance, please.
お腹が痛いです。	I have a stomachache. ／ I have a bellyache. ＊stomachache [stʌ́məkèik] (胃痛, 腹痛, 腹部の痛み)。
どこが痛みますか。──《手で示して》このあたりです。	Where does it hurt? ─ Around here. ＊hurt [hə́ːrt] (〔身体の一部が〕痛む)。
痛い場所を指でさしていただけますか。──ここが痛いです。	Could you point with your finger to the location of the pain? ─ I have a pain here.

胃がキリキリ痛みます。	I have a sharp pain in my stomach.
胃が差し込むように痛いです。	I have a stabbing pain in my stomach.
（ひどい）頭痛がします。	I have a (terrible [bad]) headache. ＊headache [hédèik] (頭痛)
歯が痛いです。	I have a toothache.
右上［右下］の奥歯が痛みます。	My upper [lower] right back tooth hurts.
《触診して》痛いですか。──痛い！	Does it hurt? ─ It hurts!
左膝の関節に痛みがあります。	I have joint pain in my left knee.
筋肉痛がします。	I have sore muscles. ／ My muscles ache. ＊sore [sɔ́ːr], muscle [mʌ́sl]。sore muscle (筋肉痛)
足を骨折しました。	I broke my leg.
足首を捻挫したようです。	I think I sprained [twisted] my ankle. ＊sprain [spréin] (〔足首, 手首など〕をくじく, 捻挫〔する〕)。ついでに,「階段を踏み外しました」は, I missed a step on the stairs.。
足首が腫れています。	My ankle is swollen. ＊swollen [swóulən] (ふくれた, 腫れ上がった)。

風邪を引きました。	I caught a cold. ／ I came down with a cold. ＊catch a cold（風邪を引く）。come down with は，「（病気に）かかる，（病気で）倒れる」。「インフルエンザにかかる」は come down with the flu. I caught the flu. ／ I had the flu. は「インフルエンザにかかりました」。
ここ数日，体調不良です。	I've been under the weather for a few days. ＊under the weather（〔やや〕体調が悪い，元気がない）
風邪を引いたかもしれません。	I might've caught a cold.
38度の熱があります。	I have a fever [temperature] of 38 degrees.
微熱があります。	I have a low [slight] fever.
熱が高いです。	I have a high fever.
少し熱っぽいです。	I feel a little feverish.
熱が下がりません。	My fever won't go down.
熱は下がりました。	My fever went down.
寒気がします。	I feel cold [chilly].

喉が痛みます。	I have a sore throat. ＊sore throat（喉の痛み）。have a frog in one's throat（喉ががらがらで声が出にくい）
喉がぜいぜいします。	I'm wheezing [hwíːziŋ].

咳が出ます。	I have a cough. ＊cough の発音は，[kɔ́(ː)f]。
咳でよく痰が出ます。	I cough up a lot of phlegm. ＊phlegm（痰）の発音は [flém]。get phlegm in one's throat（痰がのどにからむ）
風邪を引いて声が出ません。	I caught a cold and lost my voice.
鼻水が出ます。	I have a running [runny] nose.
鼻が詰まっています。	My nose is stuffed up. ／ I have a stuffed-up [stuffy] nose. ＊nasal congestion（鼻詰まり）

気分がよくありません。	I'm not feeling well.
耳鳴りがします。	My ears are ringing.
めまいがします。	I feel dizzy. ／ I have vertigo. ＊dizzy [dízi]（めまいがする，立ちくらみがする）《形》，dizziness（〔ふらふらする〕めまい）《名》，vertigo [vɚ́ːtigòu]（回転性めまい）。
食欲がありません。	I have no appetite. ＊appetite [ǽpitàit]（食欲）。
吐き気がします。	I feel throwing up. ／ I feel nauseated. ＊nauseated [nɔ́ːzièitid]（吐き気がする，気分が悪い）
嘔吐しました。	I vomited. ／ I threw up.

10

病気と健康

私は小麦アレルギーです。	I'm allergic to wheat. ＊allergic [əlɔ́ːrdʒik]（アレルギー〔体質〕の)《形》。wheat [(h)wíːt]。
私は花粉症です。	I have hay fever. ／ I have a pollen allergy. ／ I'm allergic to pollen. ＊hay fever [héi fìːvər]（花粉症)、pollen [pálən	pɔ́lən]（花粉)、allergy [ǽlərdʒi]（アレルギー)《名》。
私はほこりアレルギーです。	I have a dust allergy.
アスピリンアレルギーがあります。	I'm allergic to aspirin. ／ I have an allergy to aspirin.
お腹が緩いです。／下痢をしています。	I have loose bowels [stools]. ＊I have (explosive) diarrhea.（〔激しい〕下痢をしています)の遠回しな言い方。diarrhea [dàiəríːə]（下痢)《医》、stools [stúːlz]（〔遠回しに〕大便)。
下痢をしています。	I have the runs. ＊have the runs（下痢をしている)
《「下痢」を遠回しに》お腹[腸]の調子が悪いんです。	I have intestinal trouble. ＊intestinal [intéstənl]（腸の)。
5日間ほど便秘です。	I have constipation for about five days. ＊constipation [kànstəpéiʃən]（便秘)
血便が出ました。	There was blood in my stools. ＊「血便」はほかにbloody stool。

生理中です。	I'm having my period. ＊have one's period(s)（生理がある〔中である〕)
生理痛があります。	I have cramps. ＊cramps [kræmps]（激しい腹痛〔胃痛〕、腹部のけいれん；生理痛；〔筋肉の〕けいれん)
生理不順です。	I have irregular periods. ／ My periods are irregular.

★痛み

痛み	ache [éik] ／ pain [péin] ＊pain《名》は、ache《名》よりも痛みの度合いが強かったり、急性のもの、また心の痛みにも使われる。ache は、断続的な痛みのニュアンス。
急性の痛み	acute pain
鋭い痛み	sharp pain
鈍い痛み、鈍痛	dull pain [dʌ́l péin]
強い痛み、激痛	severe [strong] pain
圧痛	pressing pain
断続的に痛みがあります。	It hurts intermittently. ＊intermittently（途切れ途切れに、断続的に)
胸が痛い、胸痛がする	have a pain in one's chest
ぎゅっと締めつけられるような痛み／圧迫するような痛み	squeezing [tightening] pain ＊squeezing [skwíːziŋ]（締めつけられるような)、tightening [táitniŋ]（締めつけるような)
ズキズキする痛み	throbbing pain ／ pounding pain

胸の中央が圧迫される感じがします。	I feel pressure in the middle of my chest.

★検査

検査室	laboratory
処置室	treatment room
検査	examination
身体検査	physical examination
血液検査	blood test * blood sugar level [blʌ́d ʃúgər lévl] (血糖値)
血圧検査	blood pressure test
検尿	urine test
検便	stool test
胸部 X 線検査	chest X-ray
胃部 X 線検査	gastric X-ray examination
胃部内視鏡検査	gastrofiberscope examination
心電図	ECG = electrocardiogram
MRI 検査	MRI examination
眼底検査	funduscopic examination
超音波検査	ultrasound examination
体温計	(clinical) thermometer * take one's temperature (体温を計る)
体重計	(weight) scale * health meter は和製語なので×。 get on the scale (体重計に乗る)

★医療関係者

病院長	director of a hospital
医師	(medical) doctor
内科医	internist 〈米〉／ doctor 〈英〉
外科医	surgeon [sə́:rdʒən]
インターン (の身分)	internship ／ intern * work on an internship (インターンとして働く)
専門研修医	resident (physician) 〈米〉／ specialist trainee 〈英〉 * インターンの上の地位。
看護師	nurse
正看護師	registered nurse 〈略：RN〉
准看護師	(licensed) practical nurse
オペ室看護師	surgical nurse
器械出し看護師	scrub nurse
外回り看護師	circulating [circulation] nurse
歯科医	dentist ／ tooth doctor 〈口語〉／ dental surgeon
歯科衛生士	dental hygienist 〈米〉 ／ hygienist 〈英〉
歯科技工士	dental technician
産婦人科医	obstetrician and gynecologist [gàinəkáledʒist] ／ obstetrician-gynecologist ／ ob-gyn [ábgain]

10
病気と健康

助産師	midwife ／ obstetric nurse
眼科医	eye doctor [specialist]
精神科医	psychiatrist [səkáiətrəst, sai-] ／ mental specialist ／ shrink 《口語》
小児科医	pediatrician ／ paediatrician 〈英〉
監察医，検死官	medical examiner
獣医	veterinary ／ vet 《口語》／ veterinarian 〈主に米〉／ veterinary surgeon 〈英〉
放射線科医(師)，X線技師	radiologist ／ radiation technologist
薬剤師	pharmacist ／ chemist 〈英〉
臨床検査技師	clinical laboratory technician ／ laboratory medical technologist
臨床工学技士	biomedical equipment technician
救急救命士	paramedic ／ emergency life-saving technician
救急隊員	ambulance attendant [technician]
保健師	(public) health nurse
管理栄養士	managerial dietician
社会福祉士	certified social worker
精神保健福祉士	psychiatric social worker
理学療法士	physical therapist

作業療法士	occupational therapist
義肢装具士	prosthetist
言語聴覚士	speech-language pathologist
視能訓練士	orthoptist

★診療

症状	symptom [símptəm] ＊ have cold symptoms （風邪の症状がある）
（人の）体調，調子	condition [kəndíʃən] ＊ be in (a) good [in (a) bad ／ out of] condition （調子がよい［悪い］）
患者	patient [péiʃənt]
病歴	clinical history
既往歴	personal medical history ／ past medical history
（介護を要する）病弱な人，病人	invalid [ínvələd | ínvəlìːd]
身体障害者	disabled person ／ disabled people
診断時の年齢	diagnosis age
家族の病歴；家族の歴史	family history
体温	(body) temperature
血圧	blood pressure ＊ My blood pressure is 124 over 80 （血圧は上が 124 で下が 80 です）
心拍数	heart [ventricular] rate
脈拍数	pulse rate

脈拍を測る	take *someone's* pulse
呼吸数	breathing [respiratory / respiration] rate
聴診器	stethoscope [stéθəskòup]
血圧計	sphygmomanometer [sfìgmoumənámətər]
酸素マスク	oxygen mask [ɑ́ksidʒən mæ̀sk | - mὰːsk]
ストレス	stress [strés] ＊ have been under a lot of stress（ストレスがたまっている）
治療，手当て	treatment《不可算名詞》

（病気，けがなどを）治療する，手当する	treat [tríːt] ＊ treat a patient（患者を治療［手当て］する）
（病気，痛みに対する）治療薬，療法；（病気などを）治療する，治す	remedy [rémədi] ＊ baldness remedy（脱毛治療），chemical remedies（化学療法）
（病気などの）治療，治療薬［法］；（医者，薬などが）（病気，けがを）治療する	cure [kjúər] ＊ effective cures for ...（〜に対する有効な治療法）
応急処置を受ける	get [receive] first aid
〜に応急手当を施す	give [provide] first aid to ...

消毒（傷口など）	disinfection [dìsənfékʃən] ＊ disinfect / sterilize（消毒する）
解毒剤	antidote [ǽntidòut]
注射	injection ／ shot
点滴	drip ／ intravenous [IV] drip infusion ＊ *be* put on a drip（点滴を受ける），put ... on a drip（〜に点滴をする），IV pole（点滴台）
黄疸	jaundice [dʒɔ́ːndəs, dʒɑ́ːn-] ＊ develop the symptoms of jaundice（黄疸の症状が出る）
入院（治療）	hospitalization
特効薬	miracle cure [drug]
抗血小板剤	anti-platelet agents
抗がん剤治療	anti-cancer therapy
化学療法	chemotherapy ＊ anticancer chemotherapy（抗がん化学療法）
マイトマイシン	mitomycin
ペニシリン	penicillin [pènəsílin]
テトラサイクリン	tetracycline
インフルエンザの予防接種を受ける	get a flu shot
〜の予防接種を受ける	get a vaccine (shot) against ...

10 病気と健康

2. 主な病名など

★内科

風邪，感冒	(a) cold ＊head cold（鼻風邪）
(普通の) 風邪	the common cold
インフルエンザ，流行性感冒	influenza [ìnfluénzə] ＊アクセントの位置に注意。
インフルエンザ	(the) flu [flúː] ＊influenza の短縮語。 「インフルエンザにかかっている [かかる]」は，have [get] the flu。
咳	cough [kɔ́(ː)f] ／ coughing ＊I can't stop coughing.（咳が止まりません）。「咳をする [が出る]」《動》は，cough。
くしゃみ (をする [が出る])	sneeze [sníːz] ＊I'm going to sneeze.（くしゃみが出そう）。くしゃみの音「ハクション」は ahchoo [ɑːtʃúː]，atchoo [ətʃúː] ／ achoo [ətʃúː]《米》，atishoo [ətíʃuː]《英》などで表す。
風邪でくしゃみをする [が出る]	sneeze from a cold
炎症を起こす，腫れる	become inflamed
(鼻風邪で) 鼻が詰まる [ぐずぐずする]	have the sniffles
寒気がする	feel [have] a chill
寒気, 悪寒(おかん)	the shivers
冷や汗をかく [かいている]	break into [be in] a cold sweat
発熱	fever [fíːvər]
汗，発汗	sweat ／ perspiration
寝汗をかく	sweat in one's sleep ／ sweat at night
疲労 (感)，疲れ，だるさ	fatigue [fətíːg] ／ tiredness [táiərdnəs] ＊physical [mental] fatigue（肉体的 [精神的] 疲労）
疲労を感じる	feel fatigued
疲れやすい	easily fatigued
吐き気	nausea [nɔ́ːziə｜-siə]
嘔吐 (おうと)	vomiting
貧血 (症)	anemia ／ anaemia 《英》[əníːmiə]
しこり，こぶ	lump [lʌ́mp] ＊develop a lump in one's breast（胸にしこりができる）
太る	gain weight ／ put on weight ＊I've been putting on weight.（最近, 太ってきました）
痩せる	lose weight
脂質異常症	hyperlipemia [hàipərlaipíːmiə]
動脈硬化	hardening of the arteries ／ arteriosclerosis
高血圧 (症)	hypertension ／ high blood pressure
低血圧 (症)	hypotension ／ low blood pressure
心臓病	heart [cardiac] disease ＊cardiac ventricle（心室），cardiac atrium（心房），heart valves（心臓の弁膜）

動悸がする	have palpitations
不整脈	irregular pulse ／ irregular heartbeats
狭心症	angina [ænʤáinə] (pectoris)
心臓発作	heart attack ＊have a heart attack（心臓発作を起こす）, heart [cardiac] failure（心臓麻痺）, valvular disease of the heart（心臓弁膜症）
心筋梗塞	myocardial infarction
心不全	heart failure
心停止	cardiac arrest
足のむくみ	swelling of feet
熱中症	heatstroke ＊get heatstroke（熱中症になる）
日射病	sunstroke
急性	acute [əkjúːt] ＊acute alcoholic poisoning（急性アルコール中毒）
慢性	chronic [kránik] ＊have a chronic disease（持病［慢性的な疾患］がある）
腫瘍（しゅよう）	tumor [tjúːmər] ／ tumour（英） ＊benign [bənáin] tumor（良性腫瘍）, malignant tumor（悪性腫瘍）
癌（がん），悪性腫瘍	cancer [kǽnsər] ＊get [develop] cancer（癌になる）, have stomach cancer（胃癌にかかっている）
肺がん	lung cancer
潰瘍（かいよう）	ulcer [ʌ́lsər]

胃潰瘍	stomach [gastric] ulcer [ʌ́lsər] ＊have [get ／ develop] stomach ulcer（胃潰瘍ができている）, duodenal ulcer（十二指腸潰瘍）
胃炎	gastritis [gæstráitəs]
肝臓病，肝不全	liver ailment ／ liver trouble
肝硬変	hepatic cirrhosis
脂肪肝	fatty liver
肝臓がん	liver cancer
胆石	gallstone [gɔ́ːlstòun]
大腸炎	colitis [kəláitəs]
糖尿病	diabetes (mellitus)
痛風	gout [gáut] ＊suffer from gout ／ have an attack of gout（痛風を患う）, uric acid level（尿酸値）
ビタミン欠乏症	vitamin deficiency disease
（病気などで突然）倒れる，卒倒する，意識を失う	collapse [kəlǽps] ＊collapse from overwork [cerebral infarction]（過労［脳梗塞］で倒れる）
意識を失う	lose consciousness ／ fall [become] unconscious
意識を回復する［取り戻す］	recover [regain] consciousness ／ come to oneself
胃［お腹］の調子が悪い［おかしい］	have an upset stomach
乗り物酔い	motion sickness

10

病気と健康

船酔い	sea sickness
飛行機酔い	air sickness
車酔い	car sickness
アレルギー	allergy [ǽlərdʒi]
アナフィラキシーショック	anaphylactic shock

息切れがする	*be* short of breath
息苦しいです。	I have difficulty breathing. ＊「息（が）苦しい，呼吸困難を起こす」は，have difficulty (in) breathing／have breathing difficulties／*be* hard to breathe。
息を吸う［吐く］	breathe in [out] [brìːð ín [áut]]
痰	phlegm [flém]
血痰	bloody phlegm
ゼーゼーいう音，喘鳴	wheezing [hwíːziŋ]
気管支炎	bronchitis [brɑŋkáitis] ＊ chronic bronchitis （慢性気管支炎），acute bronchitis （急性気管支炎）
気管支喘息	bronchial asthma [ǽzmə	ǽs-]
肺炎	pneumonia [njuːmóuniə] ＊ get pneumonia from the flu （インフルエンザから肺炎になる）
肺気腫	emphysema [èmfəsíːmə]

血友病	hemophilia [hìːməfíliə]
白血病	leukemia [luːkíːmiə]

★眼科

眼精疲労／目の疲れ	eyestrain [áistrèin]
充血した目	inflamed [bloodshot] eyes ／ red-eye ＊ I have inflamed eyes. ／ My eyes are bloodshot. （目が充血しています）
目がかすむ	get blurred [bláːrd] vision
目やに	eye mucus
結膜炎	conjunctivitis [kənʤʌ̀ŋktəváitis]
（流行性）結膜炎	pink-eye
白内障	cataract [kǽtərækt]
緑内障	glaucoma [glɔːkóumə, glau-]
網膜剥離	retinal detachment
視覚障害がある	have impaired sight [vision]
色覚異常	color-defective vision
目がいい［悪い］	have good [poor] eyesight
検眼，視力測定（法）	optometry ＊ eyesight [áisàit] （視力）
視力検査を受ける	have an eye test

★耳鼻咽喉科

中耳炎になる	develop otitis media
耳垂れが出る	have runny ears

耳鳴り	ringing／tinnitus [tənáitəs, tínə-]
聴力障害	hearing loss
副鼻腔炎	sinusitis [sàinəsáitəs]
鼻が詰まっている	have a stuffy nose
アレルギー性鼻炎	allergic rhinitis [raináitəs]
鼻血が出る	get a bloody nose／get [have] a nosebleed
花粉症	hay fever [héi fìːvər]
喉頭炎	laryngitis [lærəndʒáitəs]
扁桃炎 (へんとうえん)	tonsillitis [tùnsəláitəs]

★皮膚科

発疹 (ほっしん)，吹出物	rash [ræʃ]
発疹が出る	break [come] out in a rash
湿疹	eczema [éksəmə]
じんましん	hives [háivz]《単複両扱い》／urticaria [ə̀ːrtəkə́əriə]
にきび	pimple [pímpl]／acne [ǽkni]
いぼ	wart [wɔ́ːrt]
ほくろ	mole [móul]
帯状疱疹 (たいじょうほうしん)	shingles [ʃíŋglz]《単数扱い》
ヘルペス，疱疹	herpes [hə́ːrpiːz]
水虫	athlete's foot
水膨れ	blister
蚊	mosquito [məskíːtou]

マダニ	tick
虫刺され（のあと）	insect bite／bug bite ＊I got bit by mosquitoes. (蚊に刺された)，Don't scratch your mosquito bites.（蚊に刺された所をかいてはいけませんよ）。insect [bug] repellent spray（虫よけスプレー），anti-itch cream（かゆみ止めクリーム）
かゆみがある	have an itch ＊itch [ítʃ]（かゆみ，むずがゆさ）。「背中がかゆい。」は，I have an itch on my back.／I feel itchy on my back.／My back itches.。
（火による）やけど	burn [bə́ːrn] ＊suffer a burn on ...（〜にやけどを負う）
（熱湯や湯気による）やけど	scald [skɔ́ːld]
ただれ	erosion [iróuʒən]
抜け毛（病気などが原因の）	hair loss

★外科・整形外科

手術	operation／surgery ＊an operation to remove the tumor（腫瘍の摘出手術）
手術を受ける	have an operation ＊a major [a difficult／a simple] operation（大[難しい／簡単な] 手術）
手術室	operating [operation] room《略：OR》／(operating) theatre (英)
移植手術	transplant surgery
麻酔剤	anesthetic

10 病気と健康

173

筋肉痛	sore muscles ／ pain in muscle
腰痛	backache
肩凝りがする	feel stiff in the [*one's*] shoulders [neck]
寝違える	get a crick in the [*one's*] neck ／ sleep wrong
関節リウマチ	rheumatoid arthritis
椎間板ヘルニア	herniated disk ／ slipped disk
ぎっくり腰	strained back
ぎっくり腰になる	throw [put] one's back out ／ strain *one's* back ＊I've put my back out again.（またぎっくり腰をやってしまった）
骨粗鬆症	osteoporosis [àstioupəróusəs]
肩を脱臼する	dislocate *one's* shoulder
骨折	fracture [frǽktʃər] ／ broken bone
松葉づえ	crutch [krʌ́tʃ] ＊walk on crutches（松葉杖をついて歩く）
負傷，けが	injury [índʒəri]
重傷	severe injury ＊severe [sivíər]（〔痛みなどが〕激しい，〔病気・けがなどが〕重い）
軽症	minor injury ＊minor [máinər]（〔病気・けがなどが〕生命の危険のない，割と軽い）
傷，けが	wound [wúːnd]
擦り傷	scrape [skréip]

かすり傷，引っかき傷	scratch [skrǽtʃ] ＊動詞は「体（の一部）をかく」。
擦りむき傷；擦りむく	graze [gréiz]
（短い）切り傷	cut [kʌ́t]
（長い）切り傷	slash [slǽʃ]
（棘などの）刺し傷	puncture [pʌ́ŋktʃər]
（針の）刺し傷	prick [prík]
（ナイフなどの）刺し傷	stab [stǽb]
あざ，打ち身，打撲傷	bruise [brúːz] ＊get a bruise on the knee（膝小僧にあざができる）
足を負傷［けが］する［している］	*be* wounded in the foot
出血	bleeding ／ loss of blood ＊The bleeding won't stop.（出血が止まりません）。bleed《動詞》／ get bleeding（血が出る）, diarrhea along with bleeding（出血を伴う下痢）, excessive bleeding（出血多量）。
かさぶた	scab [skǽb] ＊pick off a scab（かさぶたを〔剥ぎ〕取る）, pick at a scab（かさぶたを引っかく）
膿（うみ）	pus [pʌ́s] ＊draw out pus（膿を出す）。The wound on my leg is festering.（脚の傷が化膿しています）
傷跡，やけどの跡；心の傷	scar [skáːr]

★消化器科

腎臓病	kidney trouble ／ kidney disease ＊I have kidney trouble. （私は腎臓が悪い［腎臓病］です）
腎臓結石	kidney stone
血尿	bloody urine
排尿痛	painful urination
前立腺肥大症	enlargement of the prostate gland ／ prostatic hypertrophy
消化不良を起こす	have [get] indigestion ＊indigestion [ìndidʒéstʃən]（消化不良〔症〕），have a poor [a good] digestion（胃腸が弱い［強い］）
げっぷ（をする）	burp [báːrp] ＊feel a burp coming（げっぷが出そうになる）
口内炎ができている	have a canker sore ／ have a mouth ulcer
虫垂炎	appendicitis [əpèndəsáitis]
肝炎	hepatitis [hèpətáitəs]
血便	bloody stool
血便が出る	have blood in the stool
痔	piles ／ hemorrhoids

★脳神経外科

頭痛	headache
片頭痛	migraine [máigrein	míː-]
意識消失	unconsciousness
一時的な意識喪失	blackouts ／ fainting ／ syncope [síŋkəpi]
記憶障害	memory impairment

記憶喪失	loss of memory ／ amnesia
脳卒中	stroke
脳梗塞	cerebral infarction
脳出血	cerebral hemorrhage
認知症	dementia [diménʃə] ／ cognitive impairment
（脳卒中やてんかんなどの）発作，突然の発症	seizure [síːʒər]
（手足などの）麻痺（まひ）	paralysis [pərǽləsis]
自閉症	autism [ɔ́ːtìzm]

★神経内科・神経科

（筋肉の）痙攣（けいれん），ひきつけ	cramp [krǽmp] ／ spasm [spǽzm]
痙攣（けいれん），ひきつけ	convulsions [kənvʌ́lʃənz] ＊go into convulsions（ひきつけを起こす）
ピクピク痙攣（する）	twitch [twítʃ] ＊My right eye is twitching（右目がピクピク痙攣します）
しびれ	numbness [nʌ́mnəs] ＊My hand is numb.（手がしびれます）
てんかん	epilepsy [épəlèpsi]
うつ病	depression ＊suffer from depression（うつ病を患う）
抗うつ薬	anti-depressant
拒食症である	have anorexia [æ̀nəréksiə]
過食症	bulimia [bjuːlímiə]

10

病気と健康

不眠症	insomnia [insómniə] * I've been troubled with insomnia lately. (最近, 不眠症で悩んでいます)
統合失調症	schizophrenia [skìtsəfríːnjə]
妄想	delusion [dilúːʒən]
幻覚	hallucination [həlùːsənéiʃən] * experience hallucination (幻覚に襲われる)
アルコール依存症	alcohol dependence / alcoholism
パーキンソン病	Parkinson's disease
脳性まひ	cerebral palsy
多発性硬化症	multiple sclerosis
神経障害	nervous disorder
高所恐怖症	acrophobia
閉所恐怖症	claustrophobia
精神安定剤	tranquilizer

★小児科

ジフテリア	diphtheria [difθíəriə]
ダウン症	Down's syndrome
麻疹 (はしか)	measles [míːzlz] / rubeola [ruːbíːələ, -bióu-]
風疹	German measles / rubella [ruːbélɑ]
水ぼうそう	chicken pox
おたふくかぜ	mumps [mʌmps]
ポリオ	polio [póuliòu]
食物アレルギー	food allergy [ǽlərdʒi]
アトピー性皮膚炎	atopic dermatitis [eczema]

手足口病	hand-foot-and-mouth disease

★歯科

虫歯	tooth decay / bad tooth * prevent tooth decay (虫歯を防ぐ)
虫歯の穴	cavity [kǽvəti] * have one's cavity filled (虫歯を詰めてもらう)
入れ歯	false tooth [fɔ́ːls túːθ]
(歯の) 詰め物	filling [fíliŋ] * My filling fell out. (詰め物が取れた)
歯茎	gums [gʌmz]
歯槽膿漏	alveolar pyorrhea [ælvíːələr pàiəríːə]
歯垢を取る	remove dental plaque
歯石	scale / dental calculus / tartar * remove scale (歯石を取り除く)
歯列矯正器	braces 〈米〉 / brace 〈英〉
親知らず	wisdom tooth * One's wisdom teeth have come in. (親知らずが生えてきた)

★産婦人科

月経	period / menstruation
月経がある	undergo menstruation
月経がこない	one's period is late
月経異常	menstrual disorder
経口避妊薬	pill 〈口語〉 / oral contraceptive / (birth-control) pill

コンドーム	condom [kándəm, kʌ́n- | kɔ́n-, -dɔm]／rubber〈米・くだけて〉
不妊治療を受ける	have fertility treatment
妊娠する	get [become] pregnant
流産する	have a miscarriage
つわりがひどい	have bad morning sickness
女性ホルモン	female hormone
月経閉止期, 更年期	menopause [ménəpɔ̀ːz | mén(u)-] * male menopause（男性の更年期）
更年期障害	menopausal syndrome

★感染症内科・熱帯感染症

感染症	infection [infékʃən]
ばい菌	germ [dʒə́ːrm] * 通例, 複数形。
バクテリア, 細菌	bacteria [bæktíəriə] * bacteria coliform（大腸菌）, salmonella bacteria（サルモネラ菌）, bad bacteria（悪玉菌）, beneficial bacteria（善玉菌）
ウイルス	virus [váiərəs] * coronavirus（コロナウイルス）
殺菌, 滅菌, 消毒	sterilization * sterilize（～を殺菌 [消毒] する）
部屋の換気をする	ventilate a room
感染	infection [infékʃən] * prevent the spread of infections（感染の拡大を防止する）

接触感染	contact infection
飛沫感染	droplet infection [transmission]
濃厚接触	close contact * spread through close contact with an infected person（感染者との濃厚接触によって拡散される）
保菌者	carrier
抗体	antibody
ワクチン	vaccine [væksíːn] * a flu vaccine（インフルエンザワクチン）
治験	clinical trials
バイオ医薬品	biotechnology-based medicine
破傷風	lockjaw／tetanus
結核	tuberculosis [tju(ː)bə̀ːrkjəlóusəs]
狂犬病	rabies [réibiːz]
腸チフス	typhoid fever
性病	venereal disease [vəníəriəl dizíːz]
梅毒	syphilis [sífəlis]
淋病	gonorrhea [gànəríːə]
炭疽病	anthrax [ǽnθræks]
天然痘	smallpox [smɔ́ːlpɑ̀ks]
マラリア	malaria [məléəriə]
コレラ	cholera [kálərə]
赤痢	dysentery [dísəntèri]
A 型肝炎, B 型肝炎	Hepatitis A, Hepatitis B * Hepatitis（肝炎）の発音は [hèpətáitəs]。
食中毒にかかる [かかっている]	get [have] food poisoning

3. 治療薬・家庭常備薬など

★治療薬・家庭常備薬など

処方箋	prescription [priskrípʃən]
（医師の指示を必要とする）処方薬	prescription medicine [drug]
医師の処方箋なしで買える薬	over-the-counter medicine [drug] ／ nonprescription medicine [drug]
薬，内服薬	medicine [médəsn | médsn] ／ (an) oral medicine ＊medicine は通例，無冠詞で用いるが，修飾語を伴うと a がつくことが多い。take (a) cold medicine（風邪薬を飲む）
薬，薬剤	drug [drʌ́g] ＊medicine の方が一般的。「麻薬，（ドーピングなどに用いる）薬物」の意味もある。
漢方薬	Chinese medicine ／ herbal medicine
（薬の）副作用	side effect [sáid ifèkt]《しばしば複数形》
軟膏	ointment [ɔ́intmənt] ＊skincare ointment（肌荒れを防ぐ軟膏）
ハンドクリーム	hand cream
亜鉛華軟膏	zinc ointment [zíŋk ɔ́intmənt]
花粉症治療薬	hay fever remedy

解熱剤	antifebrile [æ̀ntifíːbrəl]
冷却ジェルシート	cooling gel sheet
アスピリン錠〔鎮痛解熱剤〕	aspirin [ǽspərin] ＊take two aspirins（アスピリンを2錠飲む）
抗生物質，抗生剤	antibiotic ＊take [be on] antibiotics（抗生物質を服用する［している］）
抗ヒスタミン剤	anti-histamine
副腎皮質ステロイド	adrenocorticosteroid [ədrìːnoukɔ̀ːrtikoustíərɔid]
殺菌剤，消毒剤	disinfectant
座薬	suppository [səpázətɔ̀ːri | -zitəri]
（主に飲み薬の）服用量（の1回分），（薬の）1服	dose ＊a dose of aspirin（1回（服用）分のアスピリン）
錠剤，丸薬	pill
錠剤，タブレット	tablet
（薬の）カプセル	capsule
粉末剤	powdered medicine
のど飴，トローチ，咳止めドロップ	lozenge [lázindʒ]
トローチ	troche [tróuki | tróuʃ]
湿布	compress ＊apply a cold compress to ...（～に冷湿布をする）
氷のう	ice bag [pack]

消毒薬	antiseptic ＊put some antiseptic on the cut（傷口を消毒する）	咳止めドロップ	cough drops
		制酸剤（胃酸過多などを中和する）	antacid
ガーゼ	gauze [gɔ́ːz]	消化剤	digestive medicine
（手術用の）ガーゼ	pack	胃腸薬	gastrointestinal medicine ／ a medicine for the stomach and intestines
脱脂綿	absorbent cotton〈米〉／ cotton wool〈英〉		
包帯（をする［巻く］）	bandage [bǽndidʒ]	下剤，便秘薬	laxative [lǽksətiv]
サージカルテープ	surgical tape	整腸薬	intestinal drug ／ intestinal remedy
ピンセット	tweezers		
絆創膏（ばんそうこう）	sticking plaster ／ Band-Aid〈米商標〉／ plaster〈英〉 ＊apply a (sticking) plaster on a cut（傷口に絆創膏を貼る）	かゆみ止め	anti-itch drug [medicine] ／ antipruritic drug
		虫よけスプレー	bug spray [repellent] ／ insect repellent spray
		浣腸	enema [énəmə] ＊give ... an enema（～に浣腸〔を〕する）
マスク	face mask ＊wear [pull off] a face mask（マスクをする［はずす］）. surgical mask（外科手術用マスク）		
		酔い止め	motion sickness drug [medication]
		目薬	eye drops ＊put eye drops in [into] one's eyes（目薬をさす）
鎮静剤	sedative [sédətiv] ＊be under the influence of a sedative（鎮静剤が効いている）		
		点鼻薬	nose [nasal] drops
		眼帯	eye bandage, (eye) patch ＊put on ／ apply ／ wear [take off] an eye bandage（眼帯をする［とる］）
鎮痛剤	painkiller ／ analgesics [æ`nəldʒíːzik, -sik] ＊take a painkiller（鎮痛剤を飲む）		
		（医療用の）リップクリーム	lip balm〈米〉／ lipsalve〈英〉
睡眠薬	sleeping pill [tablet]	うがい薬	gargle ／ mouthwash
頭痛薬	headache medication ／ headache pill [tablet]	膝のサポーター	knee supporter
		ワセリン	Vaseline [vǽsəlìːn]〈商標〉
咳止め薬	cough medicine	育毛剤	hair restorer ／ hair-growth drug ／ hair growth tonic
咳止めシロップ	cough syrup		

10
病気と健康

4. 診療科・入院・医学分野

★内科系

内科	internal medicine department
総合内科	general medicine
消化器内科	gastroenterological medicine
循環器内科	cardiovascular internal medicine
呼吸器内科	respiratory medicine
血液内科	hematology
内分泌内科	endocrinology
腎臓内科	nephrology [nifrálədʒi]
免疫・アレルギー科	immunology／allergy
神経内科	neurology
感染症内科	infectious diseases
腫瘍科	oncology
精神科	psychiatry
小児科	pediatrics
臨床検査科	clinical laboratory

★外科系

一般外科	general surgery
救急治療室，救急処置室	emergency room (ER)
集中治療室	intensive care unit (ICU)
消化器外科	gastrointestinal surgery
心臓外科	cardiac [heart] surgery
呼吸器外科	thoracic surgery
脳神経外科	neurological surgery
血管外科	vascular surgery
整形外科	orthopedic surgery
リハビリテーション科	rehabilitation (unit)
形成外科	plastic surgery
肛門科	colorectal surgery
皮膚科	dermatology [dəːrmətálədʒi]
泌尿器科	urology [juərálədʒi]
産科	obstetrics
婦人科	gynecology
眼科	ophthalmology
検眼科	optometry
耳鼻咽喉科	otorhinolaryngology [òutouràinouləríŋgələdʒi]
放射線科	radiology
歯科	dentistry／dental surgery
口腔外科	oral surgery

（調剤）薬局，病院内の薬局	pharmacy [fáːrməsi]
透析センター	dialysis [daiǽləsis] center
医療相談室	medical social services
訪問看護室	visiting nurse services

栄養指導室	nutrition services
一般診療所	general practice ＊general practitioner（一般開業医,《略》GP）

★入院

入院	hospitalization／hospital admission ＊stay at the hospital（入院する）, be in a hospital（入院している）
ナースステーション	nurses' station ＊nurse station は和製語。
病室	patient's room
一般病棟	general ward
入院患者	inpatient [ínpèiʃənt]
外来患者	outpatient
主治医, 担当医	primary doctor
担当看護師	primary nurse
同室者	(hospital) roommate
面会時間	visiting hours
個人の持ち物, 私物	personal belongings [items]

日常生活動作	ADL《＝activity of daily living》
反応	response
意識レベル	level of consciousness／consciousness level
主訴 (しゅそ)	chief complaint [kəmpléint] ＊患者が最も強く訴える症状のこと。
(長期の) ベッドでの静養, 安静	bed rest ＊need complete bed rest（絶対安静を必要とする）

介助	assistance／help ＊get to a bathroom without assistance（介助なしでトイレに行く）, walk without assistance（介助なしで歩く）
車椅子	wheelchair
医療処置, 治療, 手術	procedure [prəsíːdʒər] ＊surgical procedure（外科的処置）
患者を入浴させる	give a patient a bath ＊lukewarm water（ぬるま湯）
(人の) 身づくろい	personal grooming ＊入浴や身だしなみを整えることを指す。
血流がよい[悪い]	have good [bad] blood flow
(病気などで) 寝たきりの	bedridden ＊in a bedridden state（寝たきりの状態で）, become bedridden（寝たきりになる）, be confined to bed（寝たきりである）
転倒してけがをする	be injured in a fall
患者の体位を変える	change patient's position ＊Would you like me to change your position?（体の向きを変えましょうか）
床擦れを起こす	develop a bedsore [pressure sore]
(医師の) 往診	home visit ＊home-visit nursing (care)（訪問看護）
家族の介護者	family caregiver
要介護者	a person requiring long-term care
認知症になる	become demented
補聴器	hearing aid

10
病
気
と
健
康

在宅酸素療法	home oxygen therapy
在宅患者	home-bound patient
メンタルヘルス	mental health
生活習慣病	lifestyle disease
医療保険	medical insurance
労働災害	industrial accident

★主な学問分野

医学（特に内科学など）	medicine [médəsn | médsn]
解剖学	anatomy [ənǽtəmi]
麻酔学	anesthesiology [æ̀nəsθìːziάlədʒi] ／ anaesthesiology〈英〉
聴覚学	audiology
細菌学	bacteriology
心臓病学	cardiology
足病学，足病治療	chiropody [kərápədi] ／ podiatry [poʊdáiətri]〈米〉
歯科学	dentistry
皮膚病学	dermatology
診断学	diagnostics
発生学	embryology
内分泌学	endocrinology
疫学	epidemiology
病因学	etiology [ìːtiάlədʒi]
老年医学	geriatrics
血液学	hematology ／ haematology〈英〉 [hìːmətálədʒi]

衛生学	hygiene [háidʒiːn] ＊ dental [mental] hygiene （歯科［精神］衛生学）
免疫学	immunology [ìmjənálədʒi | -nɔ́l-]
助産術	midwifery
菌学	mycology [maikálədʒi]
神経学	neurology [njuərálədʒi]
疾病分類学	nosology [nousálədʒi]
看護学	nursing science
口腔外科学	oral surgery
歯列矯正学	orthodontics
整形外科学	orthopedics
病理学	pathology [pəθálədʒi]
薬学	pharmaceutics
物理療医学	physical medicine
生理学	physiology [fiziálədʒi]
精神医学	psychiatry [saikáiətri]
心理学	psychology [saikálədʒi]
放射線学	radiology [rèidiálədʒi]
外科学	surgery [sə́ːrdʒəri]
毒物学	toxicology [tàksikálədʒi]

5. 健康促進など

★健康

健康（状態）	health [hélθ] ＊ improve one's health by swimming（水泳で健康を増進する）, recover [regain] one's health（健康を取り戻す）, be out of health（健康を害している）	体力	physical strength [fízikl stréŋkθ] ＊ develop [build up] one's physical strength（体力をつける［養う］）
フィットネス, 健康（であること）；体力	fitness ＊ develop fitness（健康を増進する）	スタミナ	stamina [stǽmənə]
		持久力	staying power ／ endurance [endʒúərəns] ＊ have staying power（持久力がある）
健康診断を受ける	have [get / receive] a physical [medical] checkup [examination / exam]		
心身ともに健康である	be physically and mentally healthy	生まれつき病弱である	be born weak ／ be sickly from birth
栄養摂取［補給］；栄養状態	nutrition [nju:tríʃən]	エアロビクス	aerobics [eəróubiks]
体脂肪率	body fat rate [percentage]	ワークアウト, トレーニング, 運動	workout ＊ get a good workout（適度な運動をする）
運動（をする）	exercise [éksərsàiz]	有酸素トレーニング［運動］	cardio workout [exercise]

ウェート・トレーニング	weight training	サプリメント	supplement
ジョギング	jogging	ダイエット食品	diet food
マッサージ	massage	減量処方	weight loss formula
うつ伏せになる	lie on *one's* stomach	ダイエットバー	diet bars
仰向けになる	lie on *one's* back	ダイエット（シェイク）ミックスと食品	diet (shake) mixes & meals
マッサージ師《男性》	masseur [mæsə́ːr]	流動食	liquid diets
マッサージ師《女性》	masseuse [mæsúːz | mæsə́ːrz]	低糖質食品	low carb diets
リラックス効果のあるマッサージ	relaxation massage	ダイエット飲料	diet drink
		栄養比	nutritive ratio
腹式呼吸	abdominal [belly] breathing	食事療法学	dietetics
		食物繊維	dietary fiber
		カロリー	calorie
ロハス：健康と環境，持続可能な社会生活を心がける生活スタイル	LOHAS：lifestyles of health and sustainability ＊LOHAS 発祥の地は，Boulder, Colorado（コロラド州ボールダー）	炭水化物	carbohydrates
		タンパク質	protein
		脂肪	fat
		ビタミン	vitamins [váitəmin | vítə-, váitə-]
健康的なライフスタイル	healthy lifestyle	ダイエットをしている	*be* on a diet
		減量	weight loss
		脂肪減少剤	fat loss supplement

★健康食品とサプリメント

食品医薬品局	FDA (Food and Drug Administration)
栄養［健康］補助食品	dietary supplement
栄養食品	nutritional food
栄養剤，栄養補助食品	nutritional supplement
有機商品	organic product
自然食品	natural food(s)

★健康グッズ

頭皮マッサージ器	scalp massager
マッサージ用具	massage tools
健康（に関する）本	wellness book
万歩計	pedometer [pidámətər]
カロリーカウンター付き万歩計	pedometer with calorie counter
体脂肪モニター	body fat monitor
心拍計	pulse (rate) meter

ヨガマット	yoga mat [jóugə mæt]
トレーニング用具	workout kit
運動器具	exercise equipment [éksərsaiz ikwìpmənt]
（トレーニング用の）ランニングマシン	treadmill
ウェイトトレーニングの道具で運動する	exercise with weights
ダンベル	dumbbell ＊ work out with a dumbbell（ダンベルでトレーニングをする）
エリプティカル・マシン	elliptical (exercise) machine
空気清浄機	air cleaner

★療法

理学療法	physiotherapy [fìziouθérəpi]
指圧療法	acupressure [ǽkjuprèʃər]
アロマテラピー	aromatherapy [əròuməθérəpi]
熱と寒冷療法	heat & cold therapy
鍼療法	acupuncture
光線療法	light therapy
磁気治療	magnetic therapy
音療法	sound therapy
水療法	water therapy
自然療法	naturopathy [nèitʃərápəθi] ＊自然食，日光，空気などによる療法。
瞑想療法	meditation therapy

代替医療	alternative healthcare ＊通常医療の代わりに用いられる医療。

10 病気と健康

Elliptical machines
ペダルを踏むと足が楕円形を描くように作られている運動器具

11.

スポーツを楽しむ

1. 個人スポーツ

★いろいろなスポーツ

スポーツ	sports [spɔ́ːrts]
（スポーツの）試合	game [géim] ／ match [mǽtʃ] ＊《米》では団体競技や -ball の付く競技には game を使う。《英》ではどちらにも match を用いることが多い。watch a football game（サッカーの試合を見る）
試合に勝つ[負ける]	win [lose] a game [match]
運動競技	athletics [æθlétiks]
アスリート，スポーツ選手	athlete [ǽθliːt] ／ sportsperson
チーム・プレーをする選手，団結を乱さない人	team player
反則，不正[犯罪] 行為	foul play [fàul pléi] ＊⇔ fair play（フェアプレー）
3点を取る	score three goals [runs/points] ＊goal はサッカーなど，run は野球など。
ジョギング	jogging [dʒágiŋ	dʒɔ́giŋ]
ジョギング（をする）	jog
ジョギングをする人	jogger
リレー競技	relay [ríːlei]〈名〉
リレーの選手	relay runner

800メートルリレー	800-meter relay (race)
《トラック競技の》インコース	inside track [lane]
フライングする	jump the gun ＊陸上競技や競泳などでmake a false start ともいう。
バトンを渡す	pass the baton ＊baton pass（バトンタッチ）。バトンタッチは和製語。
サイクリングに出かける	go bike riding ／ go for a bike ride ／《英》go for a cycle ride
ヘルメット	helmet
ロードバイク	road bike
マウンテンバイク	mountain bike
ボウリング	bowling [bóuliŋ] ＊go bowling（ボウリングをしに行く）
ボウリングをする	bowl ／ play bowls
ボウラー，ボウリングをする人	bowler [bóulər]
レーン	alley [ǽli] ／ lane [léin]
ボウリング場	bowling alley
ピン	pin ＊I got 7 pins down.（7本倒した）．I got a strike [spare].（ストライク[スペア]を取った）
ピンを倒す	hit the pins
ストライク	strike [stráik] ＊bowl [hit] a strike（ストライクを取る）

スペア	spare [spéər]
スプリット	split [splít]
ガター（レーン両側の溝）	gutter [gʌ́tər] ＊ throw a gutter ball（ガターを投げる）

ゴルフ	golf [gálf ｜ gɔ́ːlf]
ゴルフ場	golf course
ゴルフ練習場（打ちっぱなし）	golf driving range [réindʒ] ／ golf practice range
練習用パッティング・グリーン	practice putting green
ゴルファー	golfer
キャディー	caddie ／ caddy [kǽdi]
（ゴルフなどの）観客，ギャラリー	gallery [gǽləri]
（ボールを打つ）ゴルフクラブ／（団体としての）ゴルフクラブ	golf club
ゴルフボール	golf ball
ホール，カップ	hole [hóul] ＊ eighteen-hole golf course（18 ホールのゴルフコース）
ピン	pin ／ flagstick
グリーン《ゴルフ》	green ＊ land on the green in two shots（2 打でグリーンをとらえる），the 18th green（18 番グリーン）
バンカー	bunker [bʌ́ŋkər] ＊ be trapped in a bunker（バンカーにつかまる），blast a ball out of a bunker（バンカーからボールを出す），fairway bunker（サイド・バンカー）

ウォーター・ハザードに入る	get into the water hazard
ホールインワン	hole in one ＊ get a hole in one（ホールインワンをする）

ゴルフをしに行く	go for golf ／ go playing golf
ゴルフをする	play golf
グリーンを捉える	hit the green ＊ You hit the green! で「ナイス・オン！」。
ゴルフコンペに出場する	participate [take part] in a golf competition
ラウンドする	go round
～（スコア）でラウンドする	go round in ＊ go round in 80's（80 代でラウンドする）
80 を切る	break 80
シングルプレーヤー	low handicapper ／ single handicapper
ハンデ "0" のプレーヤー	scratch player
ゴルフのハンディキャップ	golf handicap
ショートホール（パースリー）	par-three hole
ミドルホール（パーフォー）	par-four hole
ロングホール（パーファイブ）	long hole ／ par-five hole
ボールをティーに載せる	tee up the ball
アゲインスト，向かい風	headwind
フォロー，追い風	tailwind ／ downwind

クラブを握る	grip *one's* club		ナイスショット!	Good [Great] shot!
クラブを短く持つ	hold *one's* club short ＊ = choke down on the grip		パットする	putt a ball
			芝を読む	read the green
軸を固定する	fix the axis		3番アイアンで打つ	hit the 3 iron
頭を動かさない	keep *one's* head in place		こちらに向かって傾斜し下がっている	slope towards us
(ボール) を打つ構えを取る	address ＊ address the ball (アドレスする)		向こう側へ向かって傾斜し下がっている	slope away from us
ワッグルする	waggle [wǽgl] ＊ショットを打つ直前に, クラブヘッドを左右に軽く動かす動作のこと。 make a couple of waggles (ワッグルを2回ほどする)		順目でパットする	putt with the grain
			逆目でパットする	putt against the grain
			スライス (させる)	slice ＊ bend to right (スライスする)
2〜3回, 素振りをする	take a few practice swings ＊ groove *one's* swing (スウィングを作る)		フック(させる)	hook [húk] ＊ bend to left (フックする)
スウィングする	swing ＊ swing a club (クラブを振る)		トップする	top a ball
フルスイングする	make a full swing		トップ気味に打つ	half-top a ball
ゴルフボールを打ち抜く	hit through a golf ball		引っ掛け球	smothered ball
ボールを打つ	hit [strike] a ball		テンプラを打つ (ボールを高く上げる)	sky a shot
ボールにバックスピンをかける	put backspin on the ball			
オーバードライブ (する)	outdrive ＊ティーショット時に他の競技者よりも遠くへボールを飛ばすこと。		高く打ち [けり, 投げ] あげる	loft ＊ loft a ball (ボールを高く打ち [けり, 投げ] 上げる)
強烈なドライバー・ショット	screamer ＊野球では「痛烈なライナー」のこと。		ダフる	duff [dʌ́f] ／ sclaff ＊ duffer ([ゴルフが] 下手な人, よくダフる人)
軌道	trajectory [trədʒéktəri] ＊ with a high [low] trajectory (高い [低い] 軌道で)		ディボット	divot [dívət] ＊プレー中に削り取られた芝生や土。
いいショットを打つ	make a good shot		シャンクする	shank ＊クラブの芯ではなくヒール側に当たること。

手首をこねる	roll *one's* wrists
スウェイする	sway ＊体が横方向にぶれること。
空振り（をする）	whiff [hwíf] ＊＝ make an air shot （空振りする）

300 ヤードの 飛距離	a carry of 300 yards
スリーオンする	get on in three ＊ get on the green in three strokes の略。
右［左］ドッ グレッグ	dogleg to the right [left] ＊コースで，犬の後ろ足 のようにくの字型に急カ ーブしている場所。
上り坂のライ	uphill lie ＊ライは「打ったボールの 止まった位置・状態」のこと。
下り坂のライ	downhill lie
（球が）埋ま っているライ	buried lie ／ plugged lie
きついライ	tight lie
グリーンをは ずす	miss the green
グリーンにの せる	get on the green
パーオンする	hit the green in regulation
（ボール が） 境界線の外に 出た［て］	out-of-bounds《副》 ＊《ゴルフ》オービーの ［で］《略》OB
ひとつ大きめの クラブを使う	overclub
ひとつ小さめの クラブを使う	underclub

より遠くへ，より 正確なショット	far and sure shot
寄せワンにつ ける	hit the ball for one putt ／ up and down ＊「寄せワン」はアプロ ーチでボールをピンに寄 せて，1パットで入れる こと。
ニアピン	closest to pin ＊ play a closest [nearest] -to-the pin contest（ニア・ ピン・コンテストをする）
（ボールが）ピ ンそばにある／ ベタピン	*be* dead to the pin
40 フィート（約 12 メートル）の パットを沈める	sink a 40 footer
エージシュー トする	shoot *one's* age ＊ 18 ホールを自分の年 齢と年齢以下の打数で終 えること。
年齢以下のス コアで回る	shoot under *one's* age
年齢以上のス コアで回る	shoot over *one's* age
月例競技	monthly medal competition
ゴルフ・ウィ ドウ	golf widow ＊ゴルフ未亡人＝ゴルフ に過度に熱中する男性の 奥さん。

ピンポン，卓球	ping-pong
卓球	table(-)tennis
（卓球の）ラケット	paddle [pǽdl]《米》／ bat [bǽt]《英》
ラケット（テニス，バドミントン，卓球などの）	racket [rǽkət]
ネット	net [nét] ＊net は他動詞で「（サッカーなどで）ボールをゴールの中に入れる」「（テニスなどで）ボールをネットにあてる」の意味がある。
テニス	tennis [ténəs] ＊play tennis（テニスをする），The ball's in your court.（あなた次第です／あなたが決める番です）
テニス選手	tennis player
シングルス	singles
ダブルス	doubles
前衛	net player／ volleyer [válijər]
後衛	baseline player／ baseliner
コートチェンジ（する）	change sides／ change over
スマッシュ（する）	smash
スマッシュを打つ	hit a smash
（テニスやバドミントンの）オーバーヘッド・スマッシュ	overhead (smash)
ラブ（ゲーム中のゼロ点）	love
デュース	deuce [djúːs]
ブレークポイント	break point
タイブレーク	tie break
ウィナー	winner ＊相手ラケットに触れらずにポイントが決まったショットのこと。サッカーでは「決勝ゴール」の意。
フォールト	fault [fɔ́ːlt]
サービスエース（で得点する）	ace ＊return ace（リターンエース）
ドロップショット	drop shot
ロブ（を打つ）	lob [láb] ＊高くゆるい打球。
ボレー	volley [váli]
トップスピン	top spin ＊球の上部を打って前回転を与えること。
ダウンザライン	down-the-line ＊コートの端から，サイドラインに沿ってストレートに打つこと。
（ボール）をスライス（させる）	slice [sláis] ＊打球が利き手の方向に曲がって弧を描くように飛んでいく現象のこと。
ポーチ（する）	poach [póutʃ] ＊ダブルスのときに，パートナーの打つべきボールを自分で打ってしまうこと。
スカイダイビング	skydiving [skáidàiviŋ]
スカイダイビング（を）する	skydive／ enjoy skydiving

パラシュート （で降下する）	parachute [pǽrəʃùːt]	
ビリヤード	billiards [bíljərdz] ＊play billiards（ビリヤードをする）	
ビリヤード台	billiard table	
突き棒	cue [kjúː]	
（白い玉の） 突き玉	cue ball	
チョーク	chalk [tʃɔ́ːk]	
ラック	rack [rǽk] ＊ビリヤードで玉をそろえる三角形の枠。	
どのポケットに どの球を入れる か前もって言う	call one's shot	

乗馬	horse riding ／ horseback riding ＊go horseback riding （乗馬に行く）
乗馬者	horseback rider
手綱（たづな）	reins [réinz] ＊tighten [pull (on)/loosen] the reins（手綱を締める［引く／ゆるめる]）
鞍（くら），サドル	saddle [sǽdl]
あぶみ	stirrup 〈通例～ s〉 [stə́ːrəp, stír-	stírəp] ＊乗馬時に足を乗せる金具。

アイススケート をする	ice-skate ／ skate
アイススケート	ice skating

スポーツを楽しむ

アイススケート ト靴	ice skates ＊a pair of skates（スケート靴1足）
スキーをする	ski
マラソン（競技）	marathon ＊run a marathon（マラソン競技に出場する）
体操競技	gymnastics [dʒimnǽstiks] ＊rhythmic gymnastics （新体操）
ボクシング	boxing [báksiŋ] ＊boxing match（ボクシングの試合），do boxing（ボクシングをする）
レスリング	wrestling [résliŋ] ＊play [have] a wrestling match（レスリングの試合をする）
フェンシング	fencing
テコンドー	taekwondo [táikwándóu]
柔道	judo [dʒúːdou] ＊practice [do] judo（柔道をする）
空手	karate [kərɑ́ːti] ＊do [practice] karate （空手をやる）
剣道	kendo
相撲	sumo (wrestling)
アーチェリー	archery
ダーツ	darts
重量挙げ	weight lifting
ボディビル	body-building

2. チームスポーツ

★野球

野球	baseball [béisbɔ̀ːl] *play baseball（野球をする）, baseball field（野球場）	ネクストバッターズサークル	on-deck (batter's) circle
（観客席のある）野球場	ballpark《米》／ stadium [stéidiəm] *発音注意！	ピッチャー	pitcher [pítʃər] *comebacker（ピッチャー返し〔の打球〕）
屋内スタジアム	indoor stadium	キャッチャー	catcher [kǽtʃər]
《野球の》ファウル・ライン, 《バスケットボールの》フリースローライン	foul line [fául làin] *発音注意！	打者	batter [bǽtər]
		内野手	infielder [ínfìːldər]
		一塁手	first baseman
		二塁手	second baseman
ピッチャーズ・マウンド	pitcher's mound	三塁手	third baseman
ベース	base／bag	ショート	shortstop
一塁	first base *reach [go/get to] first base（一塁に出る）, play first base（一塁を守る）, round first base（一塁ベースを回る）	外野手	outfielder
		センター	centerfielder
		ライト	right fielder *make a hit to right (field)（ライトにヒットを打つ）
二塁	second base *ground ball to second base（セカンドゴロ）, slide into second base（二塁にすべり込む）	レフト	left fielder *hit a double over the left fielder（レフトオーバーの二塁打を打つ）, hit a liner down the left-field (foul) line（レフト線へライナーを打つ）
三塁	third base *third-base runner（三塁走者）, shoot the ball to third base（サードへ送球する）	監督《野球》	(field) manager *《米》では「〔野球以外の〕監督」は coach [kóutʃ] を用いる。
		ピッチングコーチ	pitching coach
ホーム・ベース	home plate [base] *anchor the home plate（〔キャッチャーが〕ホームプレートをブロックする）, throw to the plate（バックホーム）	バッティングコーチ	batting coach
		審判	umpire [ʌ́mpaiər]
		球審，主審	home-plate umpire

観客（スポーツの試合の）	spectator [spékteitər]
ファン（チーム・有名人などの）	fan [fǽn]
地元チーム	home team
来訪チーム，ビジター	visiting team

バット	bat [bǽt] ＊choke down on a bat（バットを短く持つ）。「グリップエンド」は knob [nɑb]。take a dry swing（素振りをする），play pepper（トスバッティングをする），fungo（ノック（する）），checked swing（ハーフスイング）
ヘルメット	helmet [hélmət] ＊wear a batter's helmet（バッター用ヘルメットをかぶる）
ユニフォーム	uniform [júːnəfɔ̀ːrm] ＊spikes／spike shoes（スパイク）
キャッチャーマスク	catcher's mask
グローブ	glove [ɡlʌ́v] ＊発音注意！
（野球の）ミット；（オーブン用の）ミトン	mitt [mít] ＊catcher's mitt（キャッチャーミット），first baseman's mitt [glove]（ファーストミット），oven mitt [mitten]（鍋つかみ）

イニング，回	inning [íniŋ]
（回の）表	top [tɑ́(ː)p | tɔ́p] ＊in the top of the ninth inning（9回の表）
（回の）裏	bottom [bɑ́təm]
キャッチボールをする	play catch ＊catchball は×。

ピッチング・カウント	(pitch) count
《カウントの言い方》ツー・ツー	2 balls and 2 strikes ＊ボールの数が先に来て，ストライクの数が後。
ストライク	strike [stráik]
ボール	ball [bɔ́ːl]
《名》ファウル（ボール）；《他》ファウルにする；《自》ファウルを打つ	foul [fául] ＊foul out（ファウルフライを捕球されてアウトになる）。foul out to second（セカンドへのファウルフライに倒れる），hit a fly (ball)（フライを打つ），take a foul tip off one's shin（自打球をすねに当てる）
《名》フォアボール；《自》フォアボールで歩く［を選ぶ］；《他》フォアボールを出す	walk [wɔ́ːk] ＊×four balls ではない。
敬遠（の四球［フォアボール］）	intentional walk ＊be walked intentionally（敬遠される），walk a batter intentionally（敬遠のフォアボールを与える）
三振	strikeout [stráikàut] ＊get a strikeout（三振を奪う）
三振する	strike out [stràik áut] ＊strike out three batters in a row（三者三振に打ち取る），strike out looking（見逃しの三振に倒れる）
アウト《野球》	out《名》
ストレート，直球，速球	fastball [fǽstbɔ̀ːl] ＊challenge a batter with a fastball（バッターに直球で勝負する），low fastball（低めの速球），sinking fastball（沈む速球）

フォーシーム・ファーストボール：ストレート，直球	four-seam fastball
ツーシーム・ファーストボール	two-seam fastball ＊投手の利き腕方向に変化する速球。
カットボール	cut fastball
スプリットフィンガー・ファストボール	split-fingered fastball ／ split-finger
スライダー	slider
カーブ	curve (ball) ／ curveball ＊throw a curve (ball)（カーブを投げる），down-breaking curve（縦に落ちるカーブ）
シンカー	sinker
シュートボール	screwball
チェンジアップ	change(-up)
フォークボール	fork-ball
パームボール	palm ball
ナックルボール	knuckleball
インコース	inside
アウトコース	outside

先発	starting pitcher
中継ぎ投手	middle reliever ／ setup man [pitcher/reliever]
抑え投手	(closing) reliever ／ closer ＊×stopper は和製語。
《名》投球，球数；《他》(打者に向かってボールを)投げる；《自》ピッチャーを務める	pitch ＊pitch a ball（ボールを投げる）

コントロールがいい	have good control ／ have great command
コントロールに苦しむ	struggle with one's control
ノーコン	bad control
満塁になる	fill the bases
打者を歩かせて満塁策をとる	walk the batter intentionally to load the bases
デッドボール，死球	hit by pitch ＊×dead ball は和製語。be hit by a pitch（死球を受ける），be hit by a pitch and take first (base)（デッドボールで一塁に出る）
デッドボール[死球]をぶつける	hit a batter by a pitch ＊rhubarb [rúːbɑːrb]（乱闘；抗議）
ダブルプレー	double play
トリプルプレー	triple play
投手戦	pitcher's battle [duel]
完封（試合）	shutout [ʃʌ́tàut] ＊three-hit shutout（3安打完封）
ノーヒット・ノーラン，無安打無得点試合	no-hitter [nóuhítər] ＊accomplish a no-hitter（ノーヒット・ノーランを達成する）

ヒットを打つ	have [get/make] a hit ／ single ＊single to right（ライト方向にヒットを放つ），2-for-4（4打数2安打）
二塁打を打つ	hit a double ＊ground-rule double（エンタイトルツーベース）
三塁打を放つ	hit a triple

得点	run ＊drive in three runs（3打点を挙げる），**score a run**（ホームインする，得点を挙げる）
クリーンナップ，中軸打線	**the heart of the (batting) order ／ the 3-4-5 hitters** ＊「クリーンナップ」は和製語。「4番打者」を clean(-)up (hitter [batter]) という。
スイッチヒッター	switch hitter
ピンチヒッター	pinch hitter
ホームランを打つ	hit a homer [home run] ＊two-run homer（2点本塁打）
満塁ホームランを打つ	hit a bases-loaded home run ／ hit a grand slam
ランニング・ホームラン	inside-the-park home run ＊× running home run は和製語。get *oneself* an inside-the-park home run（ランニング・ホームランとなる）
ハイタッチ	high five ＊ハイタッチは和製語。high-five ともつづる。give *A* a high five（A〈人〉とハイタッチする）
盗塁	steal ／ stolen base ／ base-stealing ＊steal second base（二塁へ盗塁する），a hidden-ball trick（隠し球），tag out（タッチアウト）
ヘッドスライディング	headfirst slide ＊slide head first（ヘッドスライディングする）
走者をバントで送る	bunt a runner

バントをする	lay down [make] a bunt ＊sacrifice bunt [fly]（犠牲バント［フライ］），bases full（満塁）
セーフティーバントをする	bunt for a base hit
スクイズ	squeeze bunt [skwíːz bʌnt]
バントを失敗する	fail to bunt
エラー	error ／ misplay ＊shortstop's error [misplay]（ショートのエラー）
二刀流選手	two-way player
ナイター	night game
延長戦	extra innings ＊go [run] into extra innings（延長戦に入る），send a game into extra innings（延長戦に持ち込む）
メジャー・リーグ	major league
アメリカン・リーグ	the American League
ナショナル・リーグ	the National League
オープン戦	exhibition game
ワールドシリーズ	the World Series
新人選手（プロスポーツチームの）	rookie [rúki]
2年目のジンクス	sophomore jinx

★アメリカン・フットボール

アメリカンフットボール	football 《米》 ＊《英》ではサッカー（soccer）を指す。
フットボール競技場	football field
フルバック	fullback
ランニングバック	running back
ハーフバック	halfback
ワイドレシーバー	wide receiver
タイトエンド	tight end
ライトガード	right guard
レフトガード	left guard
センター	center
クォーターバック	quarterback (QB)
キックオフ，試合開始時間	kickoff ＊試合開始時のキック。
ロングパスを投げる	heave a long pass ＊「ロングパス」は bomb [bám] ともいう。
下手投げのパス	shovel pass
ディフェンダーの上でパスを捕る	haul a pass over defenders
ボールを外に投げる	throw the ball away
（味方のボールを守るために）敵のタックルを阻止する	run interference [rán ìntərfíərəns]
ボールの前進を阻止する	hold the line
ラン	run ＊ボールを持ったまま相手プレーヤーの間を走ること。
フォワードパスを使った攻撃	passing game
ボールを投げるフリをすること	pump fake
ファーストダウン	first down ＊1回の攻撃権に与えられる4つの攻撃の最初。
タッチダウン	touchdown
タッチダウンの後の追加点	extra point
ハドル [円陣] を組む	huddle [hʌ́dl]
フィールドゴール	field goal ＊プレースキックまたはドロップキックによる得点（3点）。
クロスバー	crossbar ＊ゴールの横棒の部分。
ゴールポストにあたって跳ね返る	bounce off the upright
（反則に対する）ペナルティ	penalty [pénəlti]
第一クオーター	first quarter
ハーフタイム	halftime
ハーフタイムショー	halftime show
チアリーダー	cheerleader ＊× cheergirl
スーパーボウル	the Super Bowl ＊NFL の優勝決定戦。全米最大のスポーツイベント。

大学フットボール	college football
ローズボウル	the Rose Bowl ＊全米カレッジフットボールの王座決定戦。

★バスケットボール

バスケットボール	basketball [bǽskətbɔ̀ːl | báːs-] ＊play basketball (バスケットボールをする), wheelchair basketball (車椅子バスケットボール)
全米バスケットボール協会	NBA ＊＝National Basketball Association
(ゴールの) ネット，バスケット；1ゴール，得点	basket ＊miss a basket (ゴールをはずす), shoot [make] a basket (得点を入れる)
(バスケットボールの) リング [ゴール]	hoop [húːp] ＊hoops (バスケットボール), shoot hoops (バスケットボールをする)
バックボード 〔リングが付いている板〕	backboard
コート	court [kɔ́ːrt]
スリーポイントシュート	three-pointer ／ three-point shot ／ three 《口》 ＊成功すれば3点が与えられるシュート。make [shoot] a three (スリーポイントシュートを入れる [打つ])
レイアップ (シュート)	lay(-)up ＊ゴール下からのジャンプシュート。
得点	score

ジャンプボール	jump ball
反則，ファウル	foul [fául]
反則 (ファウル以外で非接触の反則)	violation
反則で退場する；《野球》ファウルフライを捕球されてアウトになる	foul out
第4クォーター	the fourth quarter
プレーオフに進出する	make [get into] the playoffs
スラムダンク	slam dunk ＊slam-dunk (ダンクシュートをする)
トリッピング	tripping ＊足で相手選手をひっかけて妨害する反則のこと。
ドリブル(する)	dribble
(ボールを) パス (する)	pass ＊fake a pass (パスするふりをする)
アシスト (する)	assist ＊得点を助けるプレー。
(得点を狙う) シュート	shot [ʃát | ʃɔ́t] ＊middle (range) shot ／ mid-range shot (ミドルシュート), shot on [off] target (ゴールの枠に飛んだ [枠を外れた] シュート)
トラベリング	walking ／ traveling
ダブルドリブル	double dribble

11 スポーツを楽しむ

★サッカー

サッカー	soccer [sákər]
サッカー選手	soccer player
ゴール	goal [góul] ＊score the winning goal（決勝点をあげる）, win by three goals to one（3対1で勝つ）
ゴールを決める，得点する	score [get/make] a goal
ペナルティーキック	penalty kick ＊be awarded a penalty kick（ペナルティーキックを与えられる）, lose in penalty kicks（PK戦で負ける）, save a penalty kick（PKを止める）
PK戦	penalty-kick shoot-out
直接フリーキック	direct free kick
間接フリーキック	indirect free kick
ハットトリック	hat trick ＊1人が1試合で3点入れること。
ワールドカップ	the World Cup ＊the Japanese World Cup squad（ワールドカップの日本代表チーム）
フォワード	forward
ハーフバック	halfback
フルバック	fullback
ゴールキーパー	goalkeeper

★アイスホッケー

アイスホッケー	ice hockey [áis hàki]
ナショナル・ホッケー・リーグ	NHL ＊= National Hockey League
ホッケー選手	hockey player
ゴールキーパー《アイスホッケー》	goaltender ／ netkeeper ／ goalminder
（アイス）スケートをする；（アイス）スケート靴	skate [skéit]
（アイス）スケート場；（スケート，アイスホッケーの）リンク	rink [ríŋk]
アイスホッケー用スティック	hockey stick
パック	puck [pʌk]
氷	ice
スタンリー杯	Stanley Cup ＊NHLでプレーオフトーナメントに優勝したチームに与えられる賞。

3. 水上・水中スポーツ, フィッシング

★水泳

水泳	swimming
泳ぎ手, 泳者	swimmer ＊long-distance [sprint] swimmer（長距離 [短距離] の水泳選手）
プール	(swimming) pool
クロール	crawl [krɔ́ːl]
平泳ぎ	breaststroke [bréststròuk]
背泳	backstroke
横泳ぎ	sidestroke
バタフライ	butterfly
自由形	freestyle
リレー	relay [ríːlei]
リレー競泳	medley relay [médli rìːlei]
高飛び込み	high dive
シンクロ（ナイズドスイミング）	synchronized swimming
アーティスティックスイミング	artistic swimming ＊シンクロの新しい競技名。

飛込台	diving board ＊jump off a diving board（飛込台から飛び込む）
（水深が）浅い場所, 浅瀬	shallow end
（水深が）深い場所	deep end

（海辺やプールの）監視員, 救助員, ライフセーバー	lifeguard
男性用水着	men's swimsuit ／ men's swimwear
女性用水着	women's swimsuit ／ women's swimwear
競技用水着	racing swimsuit ／ competition swimsuit
ビキニ	bikini ＊ツーピースの女性用水着。bikini briefs（《米》男性用水着 [下着], 《英》女性用下着）
日焼けローション	suntan lotion ／ tanning lotion
日焼け止めローション	sunblock (lotion) ／ sunscreen (lotion) ＊apply [put on ／ wear] sunscreen（日焼け止めを塗る）
日焼け防止指数	SPF ＊=sun protection factor

★水上スポーツ

スキューバダイビング	scuba diving [skúːbə dàiviŋ]
スキューバダイバー	scuba diver
潜水仲間	dive buddy
ウェットスーツ	wet suit
エア・タンク	air tank

調整弁	regulator [régjǝlèitǝr]
残圧計	(residual) pressure gauge [rizídʒuǝl préʃǝr gèidʒ]
（ダイビング）マスク	diving mask ＊ダイビング用水中メガネ。
潜水腕時計	dive watch
シュノーケル	snorkel [snɔ́ːrkl]
水深計	depth gauge [dépθ gèidʒ]
ダイブコンピュータ	dive computer
オクトパス（予備の空気源器材）	octopus
ウエートベルト	weight belt
フィン	fins
レック・ダイブ	wreck dive ＊海中に沈んだ船（人工的に沈めた船も含む）や飛行機を対象としたダイビングのこと。
ナイト・ダイブ	night dive ＊日没後の海に潜ること。
潜水指導員協会公認ダイバー	PADI certified diver ＊PADI ＝ Professional Association of Diving Instructors
フリーダイビング	freediving ＊呼吸するための器材を使わないダイビング。
耳抜きする	equalize one's ears
潜水病	the bends ／ diver's disease ／ caisson disease

ボート潜水エントリー	boat dive entry
岸からの潜水エントリー	shore dive entry

★サーフィン

サーフィン	surfing [sɔ́ːrfiŋ]
サーフィンをする；（海岸などへ）寄せる波	surf ＊go surfing（サーフィンに行く）
サーファー	surfer [sɔ́ːrfǝr]
サーフボード	surfboard ／ board
フル・ウェットスーツ	full wetsuit
陸に向かって吹く風	onshore breeze [wind]
沖へ向かって吹く風	offshore breeze [wind]
カモメ	seagull [síːgʌ̀l]
潮	tide [táid]
満潮（時）	high tide [hái táid]
干潮（時）	low tide
潮衝（ちょうしょう），激流	riptide [ríptàid] ＊潮流同士の衝突で起こる。
ビーチブレイク	beach break ＊海底が砂の場所でサーフィンすること。
リーフブレイク	reef break ＊海底が岩場の場所でサーフィンすること。
ポイントブレイク	point break ＊波が一定の場所で規則的にブレイクするポイントサーフィンすること。

ラインアップ	lineup ＊セットの波が何本もやってきて，海面が筋のようになっているさま。
パドリング	paddling ＊サーフボードに腹ばいになって水泳のクロールのように水を漕ぐこと。
ウィンドサーフィン	windsurfing
ウィンドサーファ	windsurfer
帆 (ほ)	sail [séil]
ボード《ウィンドサーフィン》	board

★セーリング

セーリング，帆走 (はんそう)	sailing
ヨット	yacht ／ sailboat《米》／ sailing boat《英》
マスト，帆柱	mast [mǽst | mάːst]
メインセール，主帆	mainsail [méinsèil]
ジブ，三角帆	jib ／ staysail
ブーム，帆桁 (ほげた)	boom
船体	hull [hʌ́l]
竜骨，キール	keel [kíːl] ＊船底中央を縦に船首から船尾にかけて通すように配置される強度部材。
舵 (かじ)	rudder [rʌ́dər]
舵棒	tiller
かじを取る	steer [stíər]
船尾側	aft side

左舷側	port side
右舷側	starboard side ／ bow side

★水上スキー・カヌーなど

水上スキー	water-skiing
水上スキーヤー	water-skier
水上スキーをする	water-ski
引き綱	towrope [tóuròup]
モーターボート	motorboat
（船などが通った後の）波の跡	wake
水上バイク	jet ski bike

ウェイクボード	wakeboard
ウェイクボードをする	wakeboarding

カヌー（をこぐ）	canoe [kənúː]
カヌー下り [競技]	canoeing
（カヌーの）パドル，櫂 (かい)	paddle ＊grip a paddle（パドルを握る）
（ボートの）オール	oar [ɔ́ːr] ＊pull on [with] the oars（オールをこぐ）
手漕ぎ舟	rowboat
漕ぎ手	rower
（白く泡立つ）急流，浅瀬	white water ＊white-water canoeing（〔白く泡立つ〕急流のカヌー下り）
急流	rapids

★フィッシング・フライフィッシング

釣り	fishing ＊offshore fishing（沖釣り）, sea fishing（海釣り）, river fishing（川釣り）
魚	fish ＊catch three fish（魚を3匹釣る）, Fish on!（〔魚が〕かかった！）
淡水魚	freshwater fish
川魚（かわうお）	river fish
海水魚	saltwater fish
海魚（かいぎょ）	sea fish
釣り人	angler [æŋglər] ＊angler は「（趣味, スポーツとして）魚を釣る人」。「（釣りを職業とする）漁師」は fisherman。
釣りざお	(fishing) rod ／ fishing pole
リール（釣りざおの）	(fishing) reel ＊Reel it!（〔リールを〕巻いて！）
釣り糸	fishing line
はりす	leaders
釣り針	hook ／ fishhook
（釣り針で）～（魚）を釣る	hook
たも（網）	landing net
（釣り針につける）餌	bait [béit]
ルアー, 擬似餌	lure [ljúər]
フライフィッシング	fly fishing ＊「フライフィッシングする人」は fly angler という。
マス釣り	trout fishing

漁獲許可証	fishing license
漁獲量制限	catch limit
キャッチ・アンド・リリース	catch and release
カゲロウ型毛針	mayfly
毛針を結ぶ	tie flies
結び	knot [nát] ＊barrel knot（《釣り》筒形結び）

川	river
渓流	mountain streams
（魚などの）産卵	spawning [spɔ́ːniŋ]
茶色のマス	brown trout
ニジマス	rainbow trout
大西洋サケ	Atlantic salmon
黒バス／ブラックバス	black bass
オオクチバス	largemouth bass
コクチバス	smallmouth bass
カワカマス	pike
ナマズ	catfish
キャスティング（釣り糸を投じること）	casting
バックハンドによるキャスティング	backhand cast
回転キャスティング	roll cast
海釣り用の長靴	wading boots
（魚釣り用の）防水ゴム長靴［ズボン］	waders [wéidərz]

12.

自然・動物・植物を愛する

★天気・天候の表現

（ある地域・期間における）天気，天候	weather [wéðər] ＊ "What's the weather like tomorrow? (明日の天気はどう？) — The TV says it's bad weather. (テレビでは天気が悪いんだって)"。通例 the weather だが，good weather のように形容詞がつく場合は無冠詞となる。How's the weather today? (今日のお天気はどうですか). — It's raining. (〔いま〕雨が降っています)
気候（年間を通じての）	climate [kláimət]
いい天気	good weather
悪天候	bad weather
荒天，暴風雨の天候	stormy weather
穏やかな天気	calm weather
雨のち晴れ	rainy, (and) later sunny
曇りのち晴れ	cloudy, (and) later sunny
晴れのち曇り	sunny, (and) later cloudy ＊ fair to [later] cloudy (晴のち曇り) という言い回しもある。It'll be fair to rainy today, so take your umbrella. (今日は晴れのち雨だから傘を持っていってね)
晴れ時々雨	sunny, (and) sometimes rainy
曇り時々晴れ	cloudy, (and) occasionally sunny ／ cloudy, (and) sometimes sunny ／ cloudy, with occasional sun
所により雨	rainy in some areas
所によりにわか雨	showery in some areas
晴天，快晴	clear [fair] weather
晴れている，天気がいい《形》	sunny〈米〉／ fine〈主に英〉
晴れる	clear up
雲	cloud [kláud] ＊ a rain cloud (雨雲)
曇った，雲の多い《形》	cloudy ＊ It's cloudy today. (今日は曇りです)，be cloudy all day long (一日中曇りである)
曇る	become [get] cloudy
曇った／どんよりした	overcast ＊ an overcast sky (どんより曇った空)
雲で覆われた	cloud-covered
雨（が降る）	rain ＊ It began [started] to rain. (雨が降り出した)
小雨が降る	rain lightly ／ drizzle ＊ It's raining lightly. ／ It's drizzling. (〔いま〕小雨が降っています)。It's sprinkling. (雨がパラパラ降っています)

雨が降りそう。	It looks like rain. / It's likely to rain. / It's going to rain.
雨がだんだん強くなってきた。	It's raining harder.
雨はやみそうにない。	The rain shows no sign of stopping. / The rain shows no sign of letting up.
雨がやんだ。	The rain has stopped. / The rain has let up. / It has stopped raining.
（季節・時期などが）雨の多い, 雨の, 雨降りの《形》	rainy ＊It's rainy today. （今日は雨〔模様〕です）
ゲリラ豪雨	a sudden heavy downpour
雷（が鳴る）	thunder ＊It is thundering. （雷が鳴っている）, thunder and lightning （雷鳴と稲妻）
稲妻	lightning
雷が落ちる	be hit [struck] by lightning ＊The building was hit [struck] by lightning. （雷が落ちる）
雪（が降る）	snow ＊powder snow ／ powder （粉雪）, snow in large flakes （ぼたん雪）, eternal [perpetual, everlasting] snow （万年雪）, new-fallen snow ／ fresh snow （新雪）
雪の降る, 雪の多い；雪に覆われた, 雪深い《形》	snowy ＊a snowy road （雪道）

12 自然・動物・植物を愛する

（雪・ほこりなどが）積もる	lie ／ pile up ／ settle ＊The snow lay about five centimeters deep on the ground. / The snow piled [heaped] up about five centimeters high. （雪が5センチほど積もった）, Snow settled on the roofs. （雪が屋根に積もった）
（雪・霜・氷が）解ける	thaw [θɔ́ː] ／ melt ＊The snow thawed [melted] completely. （雪はすっかり解けた）
雹（ひょう）（が降る）	hail [héil]
霜	frost
氷の張った, 氷で覆われた, 氷の多い	icy [áisi] ＊slip on an icy road （凍結した道ですべる）。「氷が張る」は ice up/over. The windows of my car iced over. （車の窓ガラスが氷結した）
霧	fog [fɔ́(ː)g] ＊a dense [thick] fog （濃い霧）
霧の立ち込めた《形》	foggy ＊a foggy morning （霧の立ち込めた朝）
スモッグ	smog [smág] ＊smoke と fog の二語が組合わさってできた言葉。
もや／かすみ（がかかる）	haze [héiz]
虹	rainbow ＊A rainbow appeared [hung in the sky]. （虹が出た［空にかかっていた］）

天気図	weather map	気象学	meteorology
高気圧	high (atmospheric) pressure／an anticyclone	気象学者	meteorologist
		気象予報士	weather forecaster
高気圧の地域	high-pressure area	お天気キャスター	weather presenter
低気圧	low (atmospheric) pressure／depression／cyclone	ウェザーリポート，天気予報	weather report／weather forecast
低気圧の地域	low-pressure area		

前線	front	気圧計，晴雨計	barometer
寒冷前線	cold front	風	wind
温暖前線	warm front	風の強い《形》	windy ＊a windy day（風の強い日）
停滞前線	stationary front		
梅雨前線	seasonal rain front	ジェット気流	jet stream
		微風	breeze ＊a cool breeze（涼風）
暴風雨	storm／rainstorm	陸に向かって吹く風	onshore breeze
台風	typhoon		
ハリケーン	hurricane ＊西インド諸島に発生する熱帯性低気圧。	沖に向かって吹く風	offshore breeze
		突風	gust
サイクローン	cyclone ＊インド洋の熱帯低気圧。	風向計	weather vane
竜巻	tornado《米国中西部の竜巻》／twister《米口語》	ものすごく暑い／焼けつくように暑い	be hot as hell／be scorching hot ＊as hell「《形容詞の後ろに用いて，くだけて，ぞんざいに》とても，ものすごく」。
		外はうだるように暑い。	It's boiling outside.
大雨注意報	heavy rain advisory		
乾燥注意報	dry air advisory	降ればどしゃ降り／二度あることは三度ある	when it rains, it pours [pɔ́ːrz]. ＊不運が続くことのたとえ。
大雨洪水警報	heavy rain and flood warning		
暴風警報	strong wind warning		
津波警報	tsunami warning		
波浪警報	high wave warning		

歩道で卵を焼けるほど暑いね。	(It's) so hot you can fry an egg on the sidewalk.

★気温・季節

摂氏 28 度	28 degrees Celsius [sélsiəs] ／ 28 degrees Centigrade [séntəgrèid | sénti-] ＊The temperature is [stands at] 28℃. （気温は摂氏 28 度だ）
華氏 82.4 度（摂氏 28 度）	82.4 degrees Fahrenheit [fǽrənhàit, fάːr-]
氷点下，零下	below freezing (point) ／ below zero ＊a temperature below freezing (point) （氷点下の気温），The temperature dropped to 10 degrees below freezing (point) [below zero]. （気温は氷点下 10 度に下がった）
零下 5 度	five (degrees) below zero
マイナス 5 度	minus five (degrees)
最高気温	the maximum [highest] temperature
最低気温	the minimum [lowest] temperature
暑い天気	hot weather
寒い天気	cold weather

蒸し暑い	muggy
涼しい	cool
季節	season ＊the hay fever season （花粉症の季節），in the sowing season ／ the season for sowing （種まきの時期に）
季節（ごと）の	seasonal ＊seasonal item （季節商品），non-seasonal weather （季節外れの天気［天候］）
春／春期	spring ／ springtime
梅雨	the rainy season ＊the start of the rainy season （梅雨入り），the end of the rainy season （梅雨明け）
渇水期	the dry season
夏／夏期	summer ／ summertime
秋	fall [fɔ́ːl] ／ autumn [ɔ́ːtəm] ＊米語では，autumn よりも fall を日常的にはよく使う。
秋期	autumn (season) ／ fall (season)
収穫期	harvest(time) ／ harvest season
小春日和	Indian summer
冬／冬期	winter (season)
冬期	wintertime
クリスマス・シーズン	the Christmas season
昼夜平分時	equinox ＊1 年の中で昼夜の時間が同じ時。

12 自然・動物・植物を愛する

夏至	the summer solstice
冬至	the winter solstice
旬である	*be* in season
季節はずれである	*be* out of season
狩猟期 (しゅりょうき)	the hunting season
（動物の）発情期，交尾期	the mating season

★地震などの自然災害

災害，災難	disaster [dizǽstər | -ά:s-]
災害	calamity
国全体に影響が及ぶ災害	national disaster
自然災害，天災	a natural disaster
人災	human disaster / a man-made [human-made] disaster
被災地	disaster-stricken area
被災者	disaster victim
災害に見舞われる	suffer a disaster

自宅から避難する	evacuate *one's* home
断水する	cut off (the) water (supply)
停電	blackout / power failure / power outage 〈米〉, power cut 〈英〉

救援する	relieve ＊relieve earthquake victims（地震の被災者を救援する）
人命を救助する	save human life
援助する	aid ＊aid for the flood victims（洪水被災者への援助）
災害保険	disaster insurance
災害救助	disaster relief
災害救助訓練	disaster relief drill
災害対策	disaster prevention measures

震災	earthquake (disaster)
地震がある	have an earthquake
震災地	an area damaged [destroyed] by an earthquake
地震	earthquake ＊earthquake swarms（群発地震）
余震	aftershock
マグニチュード	magnitude
地震予知	an earthquake prediction / a prediction of earthquakes
猛吹雪	blizzard [blízzərd]
雪崩 (なだれ)	avalanche [ǽvəlæ̀nʃ] / snowslide ＊avalanche warning（なだれ注意報）
地滑り	landslide
津波	tsunami
洪水	flood

氾濫	flooding
火山の噴火	a volcano eruption
火事，火災	fire
山火事	forest fire
干ばつ	drought

★環境保護・エネルギーなど

生態系	ecological system / ecology / ecosystem
環境問題	environmental problem
環境保護	environmental protection
環境汚染	the pollution of the environment / environmental pollution
環境を破壊する	damage [harm] the environment
自然環境を保護する	protect the natural environment
エコツーリズム	eco-tourism ＊環境保護と観光業・地域振興の融合をめざす観光の考え方。
環境保護活動家	ecoactivist
生態系破壊，環境破壊	ecocide
環境（保護）を意識した	eco-conscious
熱烈な環境保護論者	ecofreak
（製品の）環境安全ラベル	eco-label

生態学者，環境保護論者	ecologist
地球温暖化	global warming
地球温暖化ガス，温室効果ガス	greenhouse gas
二酸化炭素排出量	CO₂ [carbon dioxide] emission ＊ reduction of carbon dioxide emissions（二酸化炭素排出量の削減）
フロンガス	CFC ＊＝ chlorofluorocarbon
オゾンホール	the ozone hole
紫外線	ultraviolet
熱帯雨林	tropical rain forest
森林伐採	deforestation
酸性雨	acid rain
ヒートアイランド現象	urban heat-island phenomenon
砂嵐，砂塵嵐	dust storm
（砂漠の）砂嵐	sandstorm
砂漠化する	desertify ＊ desertification（砂漠化）
黄砂	yellow sand
エルニーニョ（現象）	El Niño
赤潮	red tide

異常気象	abnormal [unusual] weather
猛暑	extreme heat
京都協定	Kyoto Agreement ＊ United Nations Framework Convention on Climate Change（気候変動に関する国際連合枠組条約）

12 自然・動物・植物を愛する

リサイクルする	recycle ＊recycle empty bottles （空き瓶をリサイクルする）
リサイクル	recycling
ゴミ	garbage〈米〉／ trash〈英〉
産業廃棄物	industrial waste
ポリ袋	plastic bag
使い捨てプラスチックごみ	disposable plastic waste
環境にやさしい	eco-friendly ／ green ／ environment-friendly ／ environmentally friendly ＊an eco-friendly [a green, an environment-friendly] product（環境にやさしい製品）
再生紙	recycled paper
再生可能な	renewable
再生可能なエネルギー	renewable energy
再生可能な資源	renewable sources
省エネを促進する	promote energy savings
省エネ効果	energy-saving effect
省エネを怠る	cut back on energy conservation
省エネルギー技術	energy conservation technology
省エネ対策	measures to conserve energy
エネルギーを貯蔵［節約］する	conserve energy

エコに関心を持つようになる	become eco-conscious
エコカー	eco-car
排気ガス規制車	emission-free automobile
ハイブリッド車	hybrid car [vehicle]
エコマーク	eco-label
エコバッグ	eco-friendly shopping bag
電力不足	power shortage
エネルギー不足	energy shortage
太陽エネルギー	solar energy
原子力発電	nuclear [atomic] power generation
原子力発電所	nuclear power plant
太陽光発電システム	solar electricity system
ソーラーパネル	solar panel
ソーラー電気	solar electricity
太陽光発電	solar energy generation
水力発電所	hydroelectric power plant
ダム	dam
火力発電所	thermal power plant
風力発電	wind power generation
地熱発電	geothermal power generation
天然資源	natural resources
海底資源	submarine resources

水資源	water resources
鉱物資源	mineral resources
化石燃料	fossil fuel
石油	oil / petroleum
石炭	coal
メタンハイドレート	methane hydrate
レアメタル, 希少金属	rare metal
レアアース, 希土類元素	rare earth element

★公害

公害	pollution
排気ガス	exhaust gas
廃棄物	waste ＊radioactive waste（放射性廃棄物）
光化学スモッグ	photochemical smog
大気汚染	air pollution
水質汚染	water pollution
放射能汚染	radioactive contamination [pollution]
公害病	pollution-caused illness
公害病患者	victim of a pollution-caused illness
公害問題	pollution problem (issue)
公害対策	anti-pollution measures

公害対策基本法	(Japan's) Environmental Pollution Prevention Act

★宇宙・天体など

宇宙	the universe
宇宙空間	(outer) space
天の川銀河	the Milky Way
（銀河系外）銀河	the Galaxy
星座	constellation
星	star
惑星	planet
恒星	fixed star
太陽	the sun ＊sunspot（黒点）
太陽系	the solar system
水星	Mercury
金星	Venus
地球	the Earth
月	the moon
火星	Mars
木星	Jupiter
土星	Saturn
土星の環	Saturn's rings
天王星	Uranus
海王星	Neptune

三日月	crescent (moon)
満月	full moon
半月	half moon

12 自然・動物・植物を愛する

北極星	the polestar
流れ星，流星	shooting star
流星雨，流星群	meteor swarm
彗星，ほうき星	comet ＊Halley's comet [Comet] (ハレー彗星)
隕石	meteorite
日食	solar eclipse ／ eclipse of the sun
月食	lunar eclipse
ビッグバン	the big bang
ブラックホール	black hole
暗黒物質，ダークマター	dark matter ＊宇宙を形作っている光・電波・X線でも観測されない物質。
天体	heavenly bodies
プラネタリウム	planetarium
宇宙船	spaceship ／ spacecraft
ロケット	rocket [rá(:)kət | rók-]
宇宙ステーション	space station
人工衛星	(artificial) satellite
小惑星探査機	asteroid explorer
宇宙飛行士	astronaut ／ spaceperson

★主な元素名

水素	hydrogen [háidrədʒən]
ヘリウム	helium [hí:liəm]
リチウム	lithium [líθiəm]
炭素	carbon [ká:rbn]
窒素	nitrogen [náitrədʒən]
酸素	oxygen [á(:)ksidʒən | ɔ́ks-]

フッ素	fluorine [flúərì:n]
ナトリウム	sodium [sóudiəm]
マグネシウム	magnesium [mægní:ziəm]
アルミニウム	aluminum [əlú:minəm]
ケイ素	silicon [sílikn, -kàn]
リン	phosphorus [fá(:)sfərəs]
イオウ	sulfur 〈米〉／ sulphur 〈英〉
塩素	chlorine [klɔ́:ri:n]
カリウム	potassium [pətǽsiəm]
カルシウム	calcium [kǽlsiəm]
チタン	titanium [taitéiniəm, ti-]
鉄，鉄分	iron [áiə(r)n]
コバルト	cobalt [kóubɔ:lt]
ニッケル	nickel [níkl]
銅	copper [ká(:)pər | kɔ́pə]
亜鉛	zinc [zíŋg]
スズ	tin [tín]
ヨウ素	iodine [áiədàin]
ウラン	uranium [juəréiniəm]
プルトニウム	plutonium [plu:tóuniəm]

★科学技術

科学技術	technology
最先端技術	state-of-the-art technology
ハイテク，先端技術	high tech(nology)
バイオテクノロジー	biotechnology
エコテクノロジー	eco-technology ／ ecological technology
ナノテクノロジー	nanotechnology

光ファイバー	optical fiber
形状記憶合金	shape-memory alloy
形状記憶樹脂	shape-memory polymer
抗菌処理	antibacterial treatment
半導体	semiconductor [sèmikəndÁktər]
発光ダイオード	light-emitting diode
IC タグ	integrated circuit tag
開発	development
発明	invention [invénʃən]
実証研究	empirical study ／ experimental study
特許	patent [pǽtnt] ＊apply for [file] a patent（特許を申請する）, obtain [get] a patent（特許を取る）

研究する	study ／ research
（学問，自然科学上の）法則	law ／ principle
理論	theory
仮説	hypothesis
調べる，調査する	examine
実験（する）	experiment
観察［観測］する	observe
記録する	record
人工知能	artificial intelligence (AI) [à:rtifiʃl intélidʒəns]
ロボット	robot [róubɑt, -bət] ＊発音注意。a humanoid robot（人型のロボット）

★遺伝子工学など

遺伝する	inherit [inhérət]
遺伝子	gene [dʒí:n]
遺伝子工学	genetic engineering
ヒトゲノム	human genome
遺伝子情報	genetic code
遺伝子地図	genetic map
遺伝子操作	gene manipulation
遺伝子治療	gene therapy
遺伝子組み換え	genetic modification
遺伝子組み換え食品	genetically modified [engineered] food(s)
クローン技術	cloning technology [techniques]
ES 細胞，胚性幹細胞	embryonic stem cell
iPS 細胞，人工多能性幹細胞	induced pluripotent stem cells
再生医療	regenerative medicine

（ウイルスの）突然変異した株	mutated strain
細胞	cell ＊a cancer cell（がん細胞）, cell division（細胞分裂）
絶滅する	become extinct

12 自然・動物・植物を愛する

2. 地理

★地図のいろいろ

地図	map
大縮尺図	large-scale map
小縮尺図	small-scale map
実測図	measured map
地質図	geological map
イラスト地図	illustrated map
平面図	planimetric map
等高線地図	contour map
地勢図	topographical map
起伏地図, 立体地図	relief map
森林地図	forestry map
壁掛け地図	wall map
歴史地図	historical map
星図	star map [chart]
市内地図	city map
分布地図	distribution map

測地系, 地理的な座標系	geographical coordinate system
全地球測位システム	GPS ＊ = Global Positioning System
地理学	geography
地形学	geomorphology
方位 (角)	azimuth [ǽziməθ]
目印, (土地の) 境界標	landmark
陸地区画	quadrangle ＊米国地質調査部の標準地図の一区画。

★地理の重要語句

地図製作者	cartographer
地図作成 (法)	cartography
(地図の) 投影図, 図法	projection [prəʤékʃən]
メルカトル図法	Mercator projection
モルワイデ投影図法	Mollweide projection [mɔ́:lvaidə prəʤèkʃən]
サンソン図法	sinusoidal projection [sáinjəsɔ̀idl]
正射投影法図	orthographic projection
平面図法	planar projection
(地図・図表などの) 凡例	legend ／ (map) key
コンパス, 羅針盤	compass [kʌ́mpəs]
羅針図, 方位図	compass rose
縮尺	scale
緯度	latitude [lǽtətjùːd]
経度	longitude [làndʒətjùːd]
子午線	meridian [mərídiən]
中心子午線	central meridian
グリニッジ子午線	the prime meridian ＊Greenwich (Mean) Time (グリニッジ標準時: GMT)
(国際) 日付変更線	the (International) Date Line
～度線	~ parallel (of latitude)

回帰線	tropic *《しばしば T ～》
北回帰線	the Tropic of Cancer
南回帰線	the Tropic of Capricorn
赤道	equator [ikwéitər] *〈the ～ / the E ～〉

北	north * in the north of Japan（日本の北の方に）
南	south * south of Kagoshima （鹿児島の南）
東	east
西	west
北東	northeast
北西	northwest
南東	southeast
南西	southwest
北北東	north-northeast
北北西	north-northwest
東北東	east-northeast
西北西	west-northwest
東南東	east-southeast
西南西	west-southwest
南南東	south-southeast
南南西	south-southwest
北の	northern * in the northern part of Japan（日本の北部）
南の	southern
東の	eastern
西の	western

北極	the North Pole
南極	the South Pole
北極圏	the Arctic Circle
南極圏	the Antarctic Circle
北半球	the Northern Hemisphere
南半球	the Southern Hemisphere
東半球	the Eastern Hemisphere
西半球	the Western Hemisphere
磁北極	the north magnetic pole
磁南極	the south magnetic pole

大陸	continent [ká(:)ntənənt]
海	《通例 the ～》 sea
海洋	ocean [óuʃən] *発音注意。《米》では しばしば sea の代用語。
(平均) 海面	sea level * a drop [rise] in sea level（海面の低下 [上昇]）
水平線, 地平線	the horizon
波	wave [wéiv]
岸, 海岸	shore
ビーチ, 砂浜	beach
潮（の干満）	tide [táid] * the ebbing [falling] tide（引き潮）, the flood tide（満ち潮）, It is high [low] tide.（満潮 [干潮] だ）

海流	current [kə́:rənt | kə́r-] ＊a sea [an ocean] current〈海流〉, a strong current of the river〈川の急流〉
環礁	atoll [ǽtɔ(:)l]
岩礁，暗礁	reef [rí:f] ＊a coral reef〈サンゴ礁〉
海峡	channel [tʃǽnl] ／ strait [stréit] ＊-nn- の発音は [n]。the English Channel〈イギリス海峡〉, the Bering Strait〈ベーリング海峡〉。
湾，入り江	gulf [gʌ́lf] ／ bay [béi] ／ cove [kóuv] ＊bay は cove より大きく gulf より小さい。
地峡	isthmus [ísməs] ＊二つの主な陸地を結ぶ細くて狭い陸地のこと。
諸島／列島	archipelago
島	island ＊the northernmost point of the island〈島の最北端〉
島／小島	isle [áil]〈発音注意〉
半島	peninsula [pənínsələ | -sjulə]
（海上わずかに頭を出した）小島	key ／ tiny island
山	mountain
山脈	mountains ／ a mountain range [chain]

（山，飛行機などの）高度，海抜，標高《海面からの高さ》	altitude ＊an *altitude* of 3,776 meters〈標高 3,776 メートル〉
海抜，海面上の	above sea level ＊10 meters above sea level〈海抜 10 メートル〉。below sea level〈海面下〉。
火山	volcano [vɑ(:)lkéinou | vɔl-]
活火山	an active volcano
休火山	a dormant volcano
間欠泉	geyser [gáizər]
岩丘，ビュート	butte [bjú:t] ＊米国西部で見られる側面が切り立って上部が平らな巨大な岩。
メーサ	mesa ＊主に米国西部の頂上が平らで周囲が絶壁の地形。
崖，絶壁	cliff [klíf]
森林，森，山林	forest ＊forest fire〈森林火災〉
小さな森，木立ち	grove [gróuv]
ジャングル	jungle
岩	rock [rá(:)k | rɔ́k]
石	stone [stóun]
地面	ground
（植物生育のための）土	soil
（地層の一部としての）土	earth
（靴底についた）土	dirt

泥	mud
砂	sand [sǽnd]
砂漠	desert [dézərt] 《発音注意》 ＊ the Arizona desert （アリゾナの砂漠）
泉	fountain [fáuntn | -tin]
オアシス	oasis [ouéisis] 《発音注意》
谷	valley [vǽli]
峡谷	canyon [kǽnjən]
丘	hill
丘陵	hills ＊ rolling hills（なだらか に起伏している丘陵地）
（川などの） 水源（地）	the source
（植物の群生す る）湿地（帯）	《通例，〜s》wetland
（樹木が育つ）湿 地（帯），沼地	swamp [swámp]
沼地，（海と陸 の間の）湿地帯	marsh [máːrʃ] ＊草の生える沼地を指す。
（川・湖に通じる） 小さな沼, 潟（かた）	lagoon [ləgúːn]
高原, 台地	plateau [plætóu] ＊ plateau には「（学習・ スポーツ・生産などの）停 滞期」の意味もある。 reach a plateau（停滞 期に入る，伸び悩む）
平野	plain [pléin] ＊ the plain below（眼 下に広がる平野）
大草原, 草原 地帯	prairie [prέəri]
牧草地	pasture [pǽstʃər | páːs-, -tj(u)ə]

滝	waterfall [wɔ́ːtərfɔ̀ːr, 《米》wá-]
湖	lake
洞窟	cave [kéiv] ＊ cave painting（洞窟 壁画）
池	pond [pá(ː)nd | pɔ́nd]
貯水池	reservoir [rézərvwàːr, -vwɔ̀ːr]
川	river
支流	branch ／ tributary [tríbjətèri | -təri]
本流	the main stream [current]
河口	the mouth of a river
（潮の干満のあ る大河の）河口	estuary [éstʃuèri | -tjuri]
デルタ	delta
運河	canal [kənǽl]
氷河	glacier [gléiʃər | glǽsiə] ＊ a giant glacier（巨大 な氷河）

ツンドラ	tundra [tʌ́ndrə]
フィヨルド	fjord ／ fiord [fjɔ́ːrd, fiɔ́ːrd | fíːɔːd]
棚氷, 氷棚	ice shelf

3. 動物

★動物

動物園	zoo
水族館	aquarium [əkwéəriəm]

ライオン	lion
➤（ライオン・馬などの）たてがみ	mane [méin]
➤（ライオン，クマ，キツネなどの）子	cub [kʌb]
トラ	tiger
➤（ネコ・イヌ・クマなどかぎ爪のある動物の）足	paw [pɔ́ː]
ヒョウ	leopard [lépərd] ＊A leopard cannot change its spots. （そう簡単に性格［性質］は変わらない）。spotは「斑点」。
黒ヒョウ	(black) panther
ゾウ（象）	elephant
➤（象・イノシシなどの）牙	tusk [tʌ́sk]
➤（象・イノシシなどの）鼻	trunk [trʌ́ŋk]
サイ	rhinoceros [rainásətəs]
カバ	hippopotamus [hìpəpátəməs] ／ hippo [hípou]
クマ	bear [béər]
シロクマ	polar bear
バッファロー	buffalo

シマウマ	zebra [zíːbrə	zé-, zíː-]
➤しま（模様）	stripes
ラクダ	camel
➤こぶ	hump [hʌ́mp]
キリン	giraffe [dʒəráef	dʒərúːf]
シカ	deer
➤（シカの）角	antler [ǽntlər]
ラマ	llama [láːmə] ＊スペル注意。

トナカイ	reindeer [réindìər]
カリブー	caribou [kǽrəbùː] ＊（北米産の大型の）トナカイ
オオカミ	wolf [wúlf]
コアラ	koala bear
ナマケモノ	sloth [slɔ́ːθ	slóuθ]
カンガルー	kangaroo [kæ̀ŋgərúː]
➤（カンガルーなど有袋類の）腹袋（はらぶくろ）	pouch [páutʃ]
アリクイ	anteater [ǽntìːtər]
バク（獏）	tapir [téipər]

（一般に小形で尾のある）サル	monkey [mʌ́ŋki]
（尾のない大形の）サル	ape [éip]
ニホンザル	Japanese macaque
ゴリラ	gorilla [gərílə]
ヒヒ	baboon

チンパンジー	chimpanzee [tʃimpænzíː]
オランウータン	orangutan [ɔːrǽŋətæ̀n]

キツネ	fox
アライグマ	raccoon
タヌキ	raccoon dog [ræːkúːn	rək- dɔ̀(ː)g]
イノシシ	(wild) boar
アルマジロ	armadillo [ɑ̀ːrmədílou]
ヤマアラシ	porcupine [pɔ́ːrkjəpàin]
ハリネズミ	hedgehog [hédʒhɔ̀(ː)g]
モグラ	mole [móul]
イタチ	weasel [wíːzl]
ヤマネコ	wildcat
コウモリ	bat

ネズミ，ドブネズミ，クマネズミ	rat [rǽt]
マウス，ハツカネズミ	mouse [máus]
リス	squirrel [skwə́ːrl, skwʌ́rl	skwírl]
シマリス	chipmunk [tʃípmʌ̀ŋk]

(牛・ヤギ・羊・サイなどの) 角	horn [hɔ́ːrn]
(肉食動物の) 牙 (きば)，犬歯，(蛇の) 毒牙 (どくが)	fang [fǽŋ]
(犬・猫・馬などの) 鼻づら，鼻口部	muzzle [mʌ́zl]

(馬・犬・魚などの) 尾，しっぽ	tail [téil]
(キツネ・リスなどのふさふさした) 尾，しっぽ	brush [brʌ́ʃ]

★ペット

ペット	pet
犬	dog ＊ bowwow [bàuwáu] (ワンワン《大型犬の鳴き声》)，woof [wúf,wúːf] (ワン《中型犬の鳴き声》，ウー《犬のうなり声》)，小型犬は "arf" [ɑ́ːrf] (キャン)。
子犬	puppy [pʌ́pi]
猫	cat ＊ mew [mjúː] (ニャー《猫の鳴き声》)，meow meow [miáu miáu] (ニャオ，ニャー《猫の鳴き声》)
子猫	kitten [kítn] ／ kitty
(猫の) ほおひげ	whiskers [(h)wískərz]
オウム	parrot [pǽrət]
インコ	parakeet [pǽrəkìːt]
アレチネズミ	gerbil [dʒə́ːrbl]
ハムスター	hamster
モルモット	guinea pig [gíni pìg]
ウサギ	rabbit
子ウサギ	bunny
金魚	goldfish [góuldfìʃ]
金魚鉢	fish bowl
熱帯魚	tropical fish

12 自然・動物・植物を愛する

★家畜・家禽など

家畜	domestic animal ／ livestock
（家畜の）牛 ／畜牛	cattle [kǽtl]
➤雌牛	cow [káu]
➤去勢雄牛	ox [áks]
➤去勢していない雄牛	bull [búl] *moo [múː]（モー《牛の鳴き声》）
水牛	water buffalo
ウマ	horse *neigh [néi]（ヒヒーン《馬のいななき》）
ロバ	donkey [dáŋki	dóŋ-]
ラバ	mule [mjúːl]
ヒツジ	sheep *baa [bǽː	báː]（メー《羊やヤギの鳴き声》）
➤雄羊	ram [rǽm]
➤雌羊	ewe [júː]
➤子羊	lamb [lǽm]
ヤギ	goat
ブタ	pig *oink [ɔ́iŋk]（ブーブー《ブタの鳴き声》）
（ブタなどの突き出た）鼻	snout [snáut]
子ブタ	piggy ／ piglet
ガチョウ	goose [gúːs] *鳴き声は gabble-gabble。
アヒル	duck *鳴き声は quack-quack。
ニワトリ	chicken *cock-a-doodle-doo [kákədùːdldúː]（コケコッコー《ニワトリの鳴き声》）

★主な爬虫類，両生類など

爬虫類	reptile [réptl	-tail]
ヘビ	snake
コブラ	cobra [kóubrə]
ガラガラヘビ	rattlesnake
カメレオン	chameleon [kəmíːliən]
トカゲ	lizard
イモリ	newt [njúːt]
ヤモリ	gecko [gékou]
カエル	frog
ヒキガエル	toad [tóud]
ウシガエル	bullfrog
アマガエル	tree frog
オタマジャクシ	tadpole [tǽdpòul]
オオサンショウウオ	giant salamander
（魚介類・カエルなどの）卵	spawn [spɔ́ːn] ／ roe [róu]

★主な鳥類

鳥	bird
（鳥，コウモリ，昆虫などの）翼，羽	wing *spread [flap] one's wings（翼を広げる［羽ばたきをする］）
（1本の）羽，羽毛	feather [féðər] 《発音注意》
くちばし	bill ／ beak *bill は「細長く平たいくちばし」，beak は「タカ・ワシなどの鋭く曲がったくちばし」。

（鳥，動物などの）爪，かぎ爪	claw [klɔ́ː]
（ペンギンの翼など）ひれ足	flipper
とさか	cockscomb ／ crest
鳥の巣	bird's nest
（鳥・虫などの）卵	egg

トキ	Japanese crested ibis
キジ	pheasant [féznt]
タカ	hawk [hɔ́ːk]
ワシ	eagle
オオワシ	Steller's sea eagle
ハゲワシ，ハゲタカ	vulture [vʌ́ltʃər]

フラミンゴ	flamingo
ペリカン	pelican [pélikn]
白鳥	swan
コウノトリ	stork [stɔ́ːrk]
ツル	crane [kréin]
タンチョウヅル	red-crowned crane
ペンギン	penguin [péŋgwin]
ダチョウ	ostrich [ástritʃ	ɔ́s-]
クジャク	peacock
アホウドリ	albatross [ǽlbətrɑs]
フクロウ	owl [ául] 《発音注意》
キツツキ	woodpecker

カッコウ	cuckoo [kúːkuː	kúkuː]
ヒバリ	(sky)lark
カワセミ	kingfisher
コマドリ	robin
アオカケス	blue jay
ハチドリ	hummingbird
ツバメ	swallow
カラス	crow [króu] 《発音注意》
鳩	pigeon [pídʒən, -dʒin]
カモメ	gull [gʌ́l]
スズメ	sparrow [spǽrou]

★昆虫・害虫・家のまわりの生き物たち

昆虫，虫	insect ／ bug 《米》
幼虫	larva [láːrvə] ＊複数形は larvae [láːrviː]。
（カブトムシなどの）幼虫	grub [grʌ́b]
（チョウ・ガなどの）幼虫，イモムシ	caterpillar [kǽtərpìlər]
サナギ	pupa [pjúːpə]
（チョウなどの）サナギ	chrysalis [krísəlis]
成虫	imago [iméigou]

テントウムシ	ladybug 《米》 ／ ladybird 《英》
コオロギ	cricket
トンボ	dragonfly
セミ	cicada [sikéidə	-káːdə] ／ locust 《米》

12 自然・動物・植物を愛する

ホタル	firefly ／ lightning bug 〈米〉
カブトムシ	beetle
クワガタ	stag beetle
カミキリムシ	long-horned beetle
カゲロウ	mayfly ／ dayfly
カマキリ	mantis
コガネムシ	gold beetle ／ goldbug
チョウ（蝶）	butterfly
モンシロチョウ	cabbage butterfly
アゲハチョウ	swallowtail (butterfly)
イナゴ	grasshopper
カメムシ	stinkbug
ゴキブリ	cockroach
ノミ	flea
ハエ	fly
蚊	mosquito [məskíːtou]
蛾	moth [mɔ́(ː)θ]
カイコ	silkworm
シャクトリムシ	looper ／ inchworm 〈米〉
毛虫	(hairy) caterpillar
シロアリ	termite ／ white ant
アリ	ant ＊worker ant（働きアリ），soldier ant（兵隊アリ），queen ant（女王アリ）
ハチ（蜂）	bee ＊queen bee（女王バチ），worker (bee)（働きバチ）
ミツバチ	bee ／ honeybee

スズメバチ	hornet ／ wasp
ハチの巣	honeycomb
ハチの巣箱	beehive
クモ	spider
クモの巣	spider's web ／ cobweb
クモの糸	spider's thread
ムカデ	centipede [séntəpìːd]
カタツムリ	snail [snéil]
ナメクジ	slug [slʌ́g]
ミミズ	earthworm ＊ちなみに，「ミミズ腫れ」は welt ／ weal。

★海や川・湖で生活する生物

クジラ	whale [hwéil]
シロナガスクジラ	blue whale
マッコウクジラ	sperm whale
ザトウクジラ	humpback whale
シャチ	killer whale
イルカ	dolphin [dɑ́(ː)lfin ｜ dɔ́l-]
ジュゴン	dugong [dúːgɑ(ː)ŋ]
アザラシ（類）	seal [síːl] ＊アザラシ，オットセイなどの総称。
オットセイ	(fur) seal
アシカ，トド	sea lion ＊アシカ，トド類の総称。
セイウチ	walrus [wɔ́ːlrəs]
サメ	shark ＊ちなみに「鮫肌」は，dry and rough skin。

ジンベエザメ	whale shark
ノコギリザメ	saw shark
ウミガメ	sea turtle
カワウソ	otter [á(:)tər | ɔ́tər]
ラッコ	sea otter
カモノハシ	duckbill / platypus
ビーバー	beaver
魚	fish ＊ farm-raised fish / hatchery(-raised) fish (養殖魚), natural fish (天 然魚)
ひれ	fin ＊ tail fin（尾びれ）, anal fin（尻びれ）, abdominal fin（腹びれ）, pectoral fin（胸びれ）
鱗（うろこ）	scale
浮袋	air bladder
白子（魚類の 精巣）	soft roe / milt
（魚類などの） えら	gill
スズキ	sea bass
マス	trout [tráut]
ニジマス	rainbow trout
ハゼ	goby
カサゴ	scorpion fish
メバル	dark-banded rockfish
アイナメ	(fat) greenling

クマノミ	Clark's anemonefish
トビウオ	flying fish ＊ flying fish roe（とびっこ）
フグ	blowfish
マンボウ	sunfish
エイ	ray [réi]
マンタ	manta ray
アカエイ	red stingray
アナゴ	conger (eel)
ハモ	conger pike / pike eel
アユ	sweetfish
イワナ	char
ヤマメ	brook char [trout]
ウナギ	eel
メダカ	(Japanese) killifish
ドジョウ	loach
カジカ	bullhead
サケ	salmon [sǽmən] ＊ smoked salmon（ス モークサーモン）, salmon roe（イクラ）
マグロ	tuna ＊ slices of raw tuna (fish)（マグロの刺身）, moderately-fatty tuna （中トロ）
ハマチ	young yellowtail
ブリ	yellowtail
タイ	sea bream / red- snapper
マダイ	red sea bream

イシダイ	striped beak-perch / parrot fish
キンメダイ	alfonsino / bright-red fish with golden goggle eyes
アマダイ	tilefish [táilfiʃ]
カレイ	flatfish
ヒラメ	(left-eyed) flounder [fláundər]
舌平目	sole [sóul]
カツオ	bonito [bəníːtou] * sliced bonito lightly grilled with its inner flesh still raw（カツオのたたき）
カンパチ	amberjack
のどぐろ, アカムツ	rosy seabass / blackthroat seaperch
サバ	mackerel [mǽkərl] *「しめさば」は, raw mackerel sprinkled with salt and pickled in vinegar。
アジ	horse mackerel
サンマ	(Pacific) saury
イワシ	sardine [sɑːrdíːn]
コハダ	gizzard shad
タチウオ	scabbard fish
シラス	whitebait [(h)wáitbèit] * boiled and dried whitebait（しらす干し）
シラウオ	icefish
コチ	flathead
マカジキ	striped marlin
イサキ	grunt [grʌ́nt]

ニシン	herring * herring roe（数の子）
カワハギ	filefish / leatherjacket
キス	sillago
クエ	longtooth grouper
サヨリ	halfbeak
（甲のない）イカ	squid * ヤリイカ, スルメイカなど。bigfin reef squid（あおりいか）
コウイカ	cuttlefish
ホタルイカ	firefly squid
タコ	octopus
（タコなどの）触手	tentacle

ホタテ, 貝柱	scallop
アワビ（鮑）	abalone
ツブ貝	whelk
とり貝	Japanese cockle
ミル貝	trough shell
赤貝	arch shell
青柳（あおやぎ）	the meat of surf clams
サザエ	turban [top] shell

ロブスター	lobster [lá(ː)bstər｜lɔ́b-]
伊勢エビ	(spiny) lobster
（小）エビ	shrimp
アマエビ	sweet shrimp
車エビ	prawn [prɔ́ːn] * fried prawns（エビフライ）

ボタンエビ	spot prawn
カニ	crab [krǽb]
タラバガニ	king crab
シャコ	squilla [skwílə]

★観賞魚など

古代魚	archaic fish
ハイギョ	lungfish
コンゴハイギョ	Protopterus dolloi
アミメウナギ	reedfish
アロワナ	arowana
ピラルクー	pirarucu [pirɑ́:rəkù:]

ピラニア	piranha [pirɑ́:njə]
ナマズ	catfish
デンキウナギ	Electrophorus electricus
コイ	carp
闘魚	fighting fish

レッドビーシュリンプ	red bee shrimp
グッピー	guppy [gʌ́pi]
ブルーダイヤモンド・ラミレジィ	diamond blue ramirezi
コリドラス	Corydoras
テトラ	tetra
アカヒレ	white cloud
プリステラ	pristella maxillaris
プラティー	platyfish
エンゼルフィッシュ	angelfish

シクリッド	cichlid [síkləd]
ディスカス	discus

タツノオトシゴ	sea horse
チョウチョウウオ	butterflyfish
キンチャクダイ	blue striped angelfish
ベラ	wrasse [rǽs]
ツノダシ	Moorish idol
ダニオ	danio [déiniòu]
ブラックモーリー	black molly
クーリーローチ	kuhli loach
ソードテール（ツルギメダカ）	swordtail
ベタ	betta [bétə]

★藻類，水の中の小さな生き物など

藻	algae [ǽldʒiː]
（海藻）トチャカ	Irish moss
海草	seaweed
シダ（類）	ferns
昆布	kelp

プランクトン	plankton
アオミドロ	pond scum
ミドリムシ	euglena [juglínə]
アメフラシ	sea hare [héər]
ウミウシ	sea slug
イガイ	mussel [mʌ́sl]
二枚貝	clam [klǽm]

12 自然・動物・植物を愛する

オオシャコガイ	giant clam		オオクチホシエソ	stoplight loosejaw
エボシガイ	barnacle		オオタルマワシ	phronimasedentaria
			オニボウズギス	black swallower
ヒトデ	starfish		コウモリダコ	vampire squid
オニヒトデ	crown of thorns starfish		ザラビクニン	careproctus trachysoma
イソギンチャク	sea anemone		ゾウギンザメ	elephant shark
フジツボ	acorn shell		ウリクラゲ	order beroidea
ケヤリムシ	feather worm		オキフリソデウオ	desmodema lorum
			クダクラゲ	siphonophore
ヤドカリ	hermit crab		クリオネ	clione ／ sea angel
キンチャクガニ	boxer crab		クロカムリクラゲ	periphylla periphylla
カメノテ	capitulum mitella		ジュウモンジダコ	dumbo octopus
			リュウグウノツカイ	oarfish/ribbonfish
ウニ	(sea) urchin [ə́ːrtʃən]		ウミグモ	sea spider
バフンウニ	green sea urchin		ウミウリ	crinoid
ムラサキウニ	purple sea urchin		ウルトラブンブク	linopneustes
			オタマボヤ	larvacea
ウツボ	moray eel		ガラパゴスハオリムシ	riftia pachyptila
ウミヘビ	sea serpent			
クラゲ	jelly fish			

★深海生物

ダイオウグソクムシ	giant isopod
ダイオウイカ	giant squid
オニアンコウ	linophrynidae
オオグチボヤ	predatory tunicate
メガマウス	megamouth shark
ラブカ	frilled shark
シーラカンス	coelacanth [síːləkæ̀nθ]

4. 植物

★植物

植物，草木	plant ＊grow a plant（植物を育てる），alpine plants（高山植物）tropical plants（熱帯植物），wild plants（野生植物），garden plants（栽培植物）
庭園	garden ＊a landscape garden（山水式庭園）
植物園	botanical garden
園芸	gardening
庭に植物を植える，ガーデニングをする	plant a garden

花	flower
花言葉	flower language

つぼみ	bud
芽	seedling
おしべ	stamen [stéimən | -men]
めしべ	pistil [pístl]
花粉	pollen [pá(:)lən | pɔ́l-]
花粉媒介者	pollinator
受粉	pollination
子房（しぼう）	ovary [óuvəri]
花びら，花弁	petal [pétl]
葉	leaves
胚珠（はいしゅ）	ovule [ávju:l, óu-]
（花の）がく	calyx [kéiliks, kǽ-]
枝	branch

幹（木の）	(tree-)trunk
茎	stalk ／ stem
根	root
実，果実	fruit ＊bear a lot of fruit（たくさんの実がなる）
木の実，堅果	nut
イチゴなどの小果実	berry

月下美人	a Queen of the Night
アロエ	aloe [ǽlou]
ツツジ	azalea [əzéiliə]
かすみ草	baby's breath
ベゴニア	begonia [bigóunjə]
キンポウゲ	buttercup
サボテン	cactus [kǽktəs]
カムミール	c(h)amomile [kǽməmàil]
カーネーション	carnation [kɑːrnéiʃən]
ガマ	cattail《米》／bulrush《英》
サクラの花	cherry blossom
キキョウ	Chinese bellflower
キク	chrysanthemum [krəsǽnθəməm]
ヒナゲシ	corn [field] poppy
クローバー	clover [klóuvər]
サルスベリ	crape myrtle

ヒナギク	daisy [déizi]
タンポポ	dandelion [dǽndəlàiən]
ダリア	dahlia [dǽljə, dά:l- | déiliə]
ハナミズキ	dogwood
ワスレナグサ	forget-me-not [fərgétminàt]
エノコログサ	foxtail
フリージア	freesia
ホウセンカ	garden balsam [bɔ́:lsəm]
ゼラニウム	geranium [dʒəréiniəm]
ヒョウタン	gourd [gɔ́:rd, gúərd]
ハイビスカス	hibiscus
ヒヤシンス	hyacinth [háiəsinθ]
アジサイ	hydrangea [haidréindʒə, -dʒiə]
アヤメ	iris [áiəris]
ツタ	ivy [áivi]
カキツバタ	rabbit-ear iris
スイカズラ	Japanese honeysuckle
フジ	Japanese wisteria
ジャスミン	jasmine [dʒǽzmin, dʒǽs-]
ラベンダー	lavender
ライラック	lilac
ユリ	lily
ハス（の実）	lotus
モクレン	magnolia [mægnóuliə]
マリーゴールド	marigold [mǽrəgòuld]
ミモザ	mimosa [mimóusə | -zə]
アサガオ	morning glory

スイセン	narcissus [nɑ:rsísəs]
ラッパスイセン	daffodil [dǽfədil]
（アヘンを採る）（アヘン）ケシ	opium poppy
ラン	orchid [ɔ́:rkəd]
パンジー	pansy
ペチュニア	petunia [pətjú:njə | -niə]
ナデシコ	(fringed) pink
ポインセチア	poinsettia [pɔinsétiə]
アシ	reed [rí:d]
バラ	rose [róuz]
ベニバナ	safflower [sǽflàuər]
キンギョソウ	snapdragon
ヒマワリ	sunflower
ショウブ	sweet flag
スイートピー	sweet pea
オオアワガエリ	timothy (grass)
チューリップ	tulip [tʃú:ləp]
スミレ（の花）	violet [váiələt]
ニオイアラセイトウ	wallflower
スイレン	water lily
ヒャクニチソウ	zinnia [zíniə]

★植物の主な病気と病原菌

うどん粉病／（衣類・革などの）白かび	mildew [míldju:]
灰色かび病	gray mold
立ち枯れ病	damping-off

根こぶ病	clubroot
さび（病）	rust [rʌst]
菌類が引き起こす病気，菌類	fungi [fʌ́ndʒai | fʌ́ŋgi:] ＊単数形は fungus。
カビ／糸状菌	mold [móuld] ＊bread mold（パンカビ）
枯草菌 (こそうきん)	Bacillus subtilis
酵母（菌）	yeast ＊酵母菌で土壌改良し，堆肥やボカシ肥料の発酵をスムーズに進める働きがある。

★牧草，芝草，穀草など

草，牧草，芝草	grass ＊集合的に用いる。種類を表す場合は可算名詞。
ギョウギシバ／（芝生・牧草用）バミューダグラス	Bermuda grass
イチゴツナギ	bluegrass ＊牧草・芝生用の草。
雑草	weeds
胡麻	sesame [sésəmi]
竹	bamboo [bæmbú:]
《集合的に》穀物，穀類，穀草	grain [gréin]
モロコシ	sorghum [sɔ́:rgəm] ＊トウモロコシに似た温帯・熱帯の穀類。
フェンネル，ウイキョウ	fennel [fénl]
チョウセンニンジン	ginseng [dʒínseŋ]
ペパーミント	peppermint
スペアミント	spearmint

★樹木

樹木	trees
アンズ	apricot [ǽprikɑ̀t, éi-]
西洋トネリコ	ash [ǽʃ]
ハコヤナギ	aspen (tree)
ブナノキ	beech (tree)
樺 (かば)	birch (tree)
トチノキ	buckeye [bʌ́kài]
ツバキ	camellia [kəmí:liə, -mél-]
クスノキ	camphor (tree) [kǽmfər trì:]
サクラ	cherry (tree)
栗（の木）	chestnut [tʃésnʌ̀t] (tree)《発音注意》
カリン	Chinese quince
ニレ	elm (tree)
ユーカリ	eucalyptus (tree)
イチジク	fig (tree)
モミ	fir (tree)
キンモクセイ	fragrant orange-colored olive
クチナシ	gardenia [gɑrdí:njə]
イチョウ	ginkgo [gíŋkou] (tree) ＊gingko nut（ぎんなん）
鉄樹	ironwood
ウメ	Japanese apricot (tree)
杉	Japanese cedar
ヒノキ	Japanese cypress
ビワ	Japanese loquat
ネズ, 杜松 (としょう)	juniper
金柑 (きんかん)	kumquat [kʌ́mkwɑt]

12 自然・動物・植物を愛する

月桂樹	laurel [lɔ́(ː)rl] (tree)
マホガニー	mahogany
カエデ，モミジ	maple [méipl] (tree) ＊カエデもモミジも同じ maple tree。
桑（の木）	mulberry (tree)
オーク，カシ，ナラ	oak (tree)
オリーブ（の木）	olive (tree)
ヤシ	palm [páːm] (tree)
キリ	paulownia [pɔːlóunia]
ボタン（牡丹）	peony [píːəni] (tree)
柿（の木）	persimmon (tree)
松（の木）	pine (tree)
ザクロ	pomegranate [páməgrǽnət] (tree)
アメリカスギ，セコイア	redwood ＊＝sequoia

ビャクダン	sandalwood
サザンカ	sasanqua [səsáːŋkwə]
クヌギ	sawtooth oak
セコイア	sequoia
グミ	silverberry
アメリカスズカケノキ	sycamore
チャノキ（茶の木）	tea plant
チーク（の木）	teak [tíːk]
クルミ	walnut (tree)
シラカバ	white birch
ヤナギ	willow (tree)
イチイ	yew (tree)
ゆず	*yuzu* citron
ケヤキ	zelkova [zélkəvə] (tree)

Cherry blossoms

13.

余暇を楽しむ

1. 映画

★基本単語

映画	movie [múːvi] 《主に米》／ film 《主に英》／ cinema 《主に英》
《一般的に》映画（を見）に行く	go to (the) movies／ go to (see) a movie
（特定の）映画を見に行く	go to the movie／《米口語で》go see the movie
（映画館で）映画を見る	see a movie
（テレビや DVD などで）映画を見る	watch a movie

洋画《映画》	foreign movie
邦画	Japanese movie
映画スター	movie star／film star
映画ファン	movie fan
よく映画に行く人，映画ファン	moviegoer 《米》／ filmgoer 《英》

映画館	movie theater 《米》／ movie house《米》／ cinema 《英》／ flick 《英》 ＊ the flicks で「《英》映画館（での上映）」。go to the flicks（映画を見に行く）。flick は「《主に米》《通例，単数形で》映画」の意。horror flick で「ホラー映画」。

複合スクリーン映画館，シネコン	multiplex 《米》／ cinema complex 《英》(cineplex [sínəplèks])
ドライブイン・シアター	drive-in theater
封切り映画館	first-run theater
チケットカウンター	ticket counter／ box office
前売券	advance ticket
当日券	same-day ticket／ today's ticket
（映画の）スクリーン，《時に the ～ で》映画[テレビ]（界），画面	screen ＊ movie [cinema] screen（映画のスクリーン）。動詞は，「（映画・テレビ番組を）上映［放映］する，（小説・劇などを）映画化する」。

主要上映作品	feature film ＊短編映画やドキュメンタリー映画に対して使う。
（映画・演劇などの）開演時間，ショータイム，見せ場	showtime [ʃóutàim]
休憩時間	interval [íntərvl]
二本立て	double feature
三本立て	triple feature

新着映画	newly released movie [film]
前編	the first part

後編	the second [latter] part
続編	sequel [síːkwəl] ／ continuation ＊ sequel to ˝Star Wars˝ （スターウォーズの続編）, continuation of ˝Mission: Impossible˝ （ミッション・インポッシブルの続編）
リメイク版	remake [riméik]
近日公開予定の映画	upcoming movie
予告編	(movie's) trailer
（映画の一般公開前の）試写会	preview ＊演劇なら「試演会」,《米》で映画・テレビ番組の「予告編」の意もある。
（観客の反応を調査するための）覆面試写会	sneak preview
概要／あらすじ	synopsis [sinápsis] ／ outline
ネタばれ,（映画・本などの内容をばらして）台なしにする記事, 台なしにする人［物］	spoiler
大ヒット映画	blockbuster film
傑作映画	cinematic masterpieces
（新刊本・映画・演劇などの）批評, 論評, 書評, レビュー	review [rivjúː]
映画評論家	movie critic
興行収入	box-office revenue [révənjùː]

★映画の感想

映画どうだった？	How was the movie? ／ How did you like the movie?
──素晴らしかった！	It was amazing [great, fantastic]!
──悪くなかった。	Not so bad.
──続編を楽しみにしています。	I'm looking forward to its sequels.
──絶対見るべきです！	You must see! ／ It's a must see!
──まあまあでした。	It was OK.
──つまらない映画だった。	It was a boring movie.
──駄作でした。	That was trash.
──失敗作だね。	It's a flop. ＊ flop は「（映画・ショービジネスなどの）失敗（作）」。

★キャストなど

（映画などの）配役（を決める）, 役を割り当てる	cast ＊ cast (the parts of) a play （劇の配役を決める）, The play is well cast. （その芝居は配役がよい）
配役（を割り当てること）	casting
（劇・小説・映画などの）悪役, 敵役	villain [vílən] ＊ play the villain （悪役を演じる）
ヒーロー, 英雄	hero [híːərou ｜ híərou] ＊男女兼用で用いる。特に女性を指す場合は, heroine.

13 余暇を楽しむ

235

（映画・劇・小説などの男性の）主人公	hero
（映画・劇・小説などの女性の）主人公	heroine [hérouən]《発音注意》

役	role [róul]
演技	acting
映画俳優	movie [film, screen] actor ＊「女優」も含めて actor ということが多い。最近では女優自身も actress より actor と呼ばれることを好む傾向がある。
（劇・映画・テレビの）俳優, 役者, 男優《男女問わず用いる》	actor ＊ character [leading] actor（性格［主演］俳優）
女優	actress ＊ -ess 語尾の付いた語で女性を表すのは性差別的であると考える人が増えている。
主人公, 主役	protagonist [proutǽgənist	pro(u)-]
主演, 主役	the leading role ／ the lead ＊ play the leading [main] part [role] ／ act the leading character ／ star（主役を務める［演じる］）
敵役	antagonist [æntǽgənist]
助演, 脇役《役》	the supporting role
脇役《人》	supporting actor [player] ＊「バイプレイヤー」は和製語。

共演者	co-star [kóustà:r] ＊「～と共演する」は co-star with....。
特別出演	cameo [kǽmiòu]
エキストラ	extra [ékstrə] ＊ play as an extra（エキストラをやる）

声優	voice actor [actress]
映画俳優組合	Screen Actors Guild《SAG》
俳優経歴	actor biography
映画作品目録	filmography

★観客年齢制限《表示》

観客年齢制限《表示》	movie [film] rating
一般向け映画	G = General Audiences ＊年齢制限がなく誰が見てもよい映画。
保護者の指導を望む	PG = parental guidance suggested ＊子どもは親と一緒に見るべき映画。
13歳以下の子供達には父兄等の同伴が望ましい映画	PG-13 = parents strongly cautioned ＊ 13歳以下は見るべきではなく, 親にとって要注意の映画。
保護者の同伴を要す	R = restricted ＊ 17歳以下は親と一緒に見るべき映画。
17歳未満入場禁止	NC-17 = no one 17 and under admitted ＊ 18歳未満は見てはいけない映画。

★ジャンル

ジャンル	genre [ʒɑ́:nrə] ＊ What genre of movies do you like?（どんなジャンルの映画が好き？）
アクション	action
ドラマ	drama
恋愛もの	romance
コメディー	comedy
冒険もの	adventure
ファンタジー	fantasy
アニメーション，アニメ	animation／cartoon
犯罪もの	crime
刑事もの	detective
家族もの	family
スリラー	thriller
ホラー	horror
サスペンス	suspense
戦争もの	war
SF	science fiction ＊省略する場合は，sci-fi [sáifái]。
ドキュメンタリー	documentary
サイレント映画	silent movie
短編映画	short movie
フィクション	fiction
ノンフィクション	nonfiction

★映画製作

映画会社	movie company／film company
配給会社	distributor／distributing agency
（映画の）配給	distribution
映画制作	film production／moviemaking
映画制作者，映画監督	film(-)maker
制作総指揮者	executive producer
制作者，プロデューサー	producer
共同制作者	co-producer

映画撮影所	film studio
野外撮影，ロケ，ロケ地	location
ロケ中で	on location
16mm のカメラ	16mm camera
撮影	shooting [ʃúːtiŋ]
映画を撮影する	shoot a film
カチンコ	clapperboard

特殊効果 (略: SFX)	special effects ＊特殊撮影 (特撮)。爆破シーンなど。effects の発音に FX [efeks] が似ているため FX。F/X ともつづる。
視覚効果 (略: VFX)	visual effects ＊例えば，背景の合成や，ワイヤーアクションで撮影後，ワイヤーを削除すること。
音響効果	sound effects
コンピュータ・グラフィックス (略: CG)	computer graphics
台本，脚本	script / screenplay / scenario
脚本家	screenwriter / script writer
(脚本の) 柱	scene heading
(劇・小説の) 筋 (の運び)，ト書き	action
役名	character's name
台詞，セリフ	《通例，複数形で》lines ＊learn one's lines (セリフを覚える)
セリフ	dialogue ＊(劇・映画・小説などの) 対話，会話 (の部分)，(一般に) 会話。

字幕	subtitles ＊English subtitles (英語字幕)
吹き替え	dubbing
吹き替え版	dubbed version ＊「日本語吹き替え版」は a Japanese-dubbed version。
(アナウンサーなどの) とちり，NG	blooper [blú:pər]

ストーリーボード，絵コンテ	storyboard
フレーム，コマ	frame [fréim]

監督	director
助監督	assistant director
カメラマン	cameraman
仕掛撮影主任	key rigging grip
(映画・テレビなどの) 照明係	gaffer [gǽfər]
美術監督	art director
セットデザイナー	set designer
音響ミキサー	sound mixer
音響デザイナー	sound designer
視覚効果プロデューサー	visual effects producer
デジタル効果合成担当	digital effects compositor
合成画アーティスト	compositing artist
デジタルアーティスト	digital artist
振付師	choreographer
スタント	stunt

★映画祭

映画祭	movie [film] festival
カンヌ映画祭	the Cannes Film Festival
ベネチア映画祭	the Venice Film Festival
ベルリン映画祭	the Berlin Film Festival

有名人	celebrity
レッドカーペット	red carpet ＊ the red carpet は「歓待，丁重な歓迎」の意。 roll out the red carpet for guests（客を丁重にもてなす）

★アカデミー賞

アカデミー賞	the Annual Academy Awards
オスカー（米国アカデミー賞の略称）	Oscar
最優秀作品賞	Best Picture
最優秀監督賞	Best Director
最優秀主演男優賞	Best Actor
最優秀主演女優賞	Best Actress
最優秀助演男優賞	Best Supporting Actor
最優秀助演女優賞	Best Supporting Actress
最優秀脚本賞	Best Writing, Screenplay Witten Directly for the Screen
最優秀脚色賞	Best Writing, Screenplay Based on Material from Another Medium
最優秀撮影賞	Best Cinematography
最優秀美術監督・装置監督賞	Best Art Direction-Set Direction
最優秀編集賞	Best Film Editing

最優秀メイクアップ賞	Best Makeup
最優秀視覚効果賞	Best Effects/Visual
最優秀音響効果賞	Best Effects/Sound
最優秀作曲賞（ミュージカル・コメディ）	Best Music, Original Musical or Comedy Score
最優秀作曲賞（ドラマ）	Best Music, Original Dramatic Score
最優秀歌曲賞	Best Song
最優秀長編アニメ映画賞	Best Animated Featured Film
最優秀短編（アニメ賞）	Best Short, Film, Animated Film
最優秀短編賞（実写）	Best Short Film, Live Action
最優秀ドキュメンタリー映画賞（長編）	Best Documentary, Features
最優秀外国語作品賞	Best Foreign Language Film
名誉賞	Honorary Award
アービン・G・サルバーグ賞	Irving G. Thalberg Memorial Award
功労賞	Academy Award of Merit

★基本単語

芝居；（役割・役柄を）演じる	play ＊perform [put on] a play（芝居をやる，劇を上演する），play a bad guy（悪役を演じる）
演劇ファン	theatergoer
劇場	theater／theatre〈英〉
劇場街	theater district
国立劇場	National Theater
演劇界	the theater (world)／theatrical circle
劇団	theatrical [dramatic] company
劇団員	a member of a theatrical company
ブロードウェイ	Broadway theater
オフブロードウェイ	Off-Broadway theater ＊ニューヨーク市マンハッタンにある小さい劇場で上演されるプロの演劇を指す。
アングラ演劇	underground theater
地方の劇場	regional theater
出演者の紹介, 名士録	Who's Who
ロングラン, 長期公演	long run
悲劇	tragedy
コメディ	comedy ＊stand-up comedy（〔独りで行う〕漫談, お笑い）
チケット売り場	ticket office／box office

前売券	advance ticket
当日券	day-of-performance ticket
演劇のビラ [ポスター], （演劇の）プログラム《米》	playbill
初日, 初演	premiere [primíər, pre-]
初演の夜	opening night
開場時間	opening time
開演時間	start time
（映画・番組・CD・劇などの）総上映 [演奏・放送・上演] 時間	running time
（演劇やコンサートの）昼の部, マチネー	matinee [mæˈtənéi	mǽtinèi]
（演劇やコンサートの）夜の部, ソワレ	soiree [swɑːréi	swáːrei]
チケットを予約する	reserve [book] a ticket
小冊子, パンフレット	brochure [brouʃúər	bróuʃə]／pamphlet
座席表	seating chart
キャパ, 客席数	seating capacity
（舞台前方の）特別席, 一等席	orchestra (seat)／stalls〈英〉
（劇場の）1階席前部席, 《主に米》1階席	parquet／stalls〈英〉

（劇場・映画館の）2階席	balcony
（劇場の）2階正面席	first balcony《米》／ dress circle《主に英》 ＊正装を必要とする特等席。
中2階席,《米》（劇場の）2階桟敷（の前列）	mezzanine [mézənìːn | métsə-]
緞帳（どんちょう）	drop curtain
ステージ, 舞台	stage ＊ the stage で「（舞台での）俳優業」「（映画・小説などに対して）演劇, 舞台」。go on the stage（舞台に上がる,〔舞台〕俳優になる）。動詞は,「（劇などを）上演する,（コンサート, スポーツ大会など を）開催する」。
上手（かみて）	stage left ＊英語では舞台から見ていう。
下手（しもて）	stage right
舞台のそで	the wings of the stage
舞台装置, 舞台背景	(stage) set ／ scenery
舞台の奥［後方］で［へ］	upstage
舞台の前方で［へ］	downstage
回り舞台	revolving stage
奈落	trap cellar
場内放送装置, PA	PA [public-address system]
（劇場やホールの）観客席	auditorium [ɔ̀ːditɔ́ːriəm]
観客, 聴衆	audience [ɔ́ːdiəns]
楽屋	dressing room ／ back stage
ドーラン	greasepaint ＊ put on greasepaint（ドーランを塗る）
美術（セット）デザイン	set design
服飾デザイン	costume design
照明デザイン	lighting design
音響デザイン	sound design
小道具	property ＊しばしば -ties。props。
大道具	large props ／ stage set

13 余暇を楽しむ

★キャスト・スタッフ，舞台用語など

キャスト，配役	cast ＊映画・劇の出演者全員。 **a member of the cast** （キャストの一員）
舞台係，裏方	stagehand ／ stage crew
音響係	sound crew
照明係	lighting technician
小道具方	《男女共用》property coordinator [handler]
大道具方	sceneshifter
（劇場・競技場などの）座席案内係	usher [ʌ́ʃər]
プロデューサー	producer
舞台演出家	stage director
舞台監督	stage manager
舞台俳優	stage actor
プロンプター，セリフ付け役	prompter ＊演劇で舞台の陰で俳優にセリフ（のきっかけ）を教える係。
劇作家	playwright
戯曲	play
即興劇	improvisation
劇中劇	play within a play ＊劇の中に挿入された劇。
リハーサル，下稽古	rehearsal
場当たり	technical rehearsal ＊照明・音響・大道具・小道具などのきっかけの確認，俳優の立ち位置，道具を含む出ハケなどを，本番と同じような状況で確認する稽古。

全通し稽古	run through
全通し	full
（衣装を着けての）最終舞台稽古，ゲネプロ	dress rehearsal
演出，ト書き	stage directions
台詞	lines ＊ **learn** one's **lines**（せりふを覚える），**fluff [mess up]** one's **lines**（せりふをとちる），**stumble at** one's **lines**（セリフを噛む）。fluffは「（せりふ・演奏・試合などでの）とちり」。**make a fluff**（とちる）
滑舌，（明瞭な）発音；（思考・感情の明瞭な）表現	articulation ＊ **He is good [bad] at articulation.**（彼は滑舌がいい［悪い］）
行間を読む	read between the lines
本読みをする	read the script with other actors
大根役者	ham [hǽm]
着ぐるみ	mascot costume
メソッド演技	method acting ＊アメリカで有名な演技技法のひとつで，リー・ストラスバーグらによって 1940 年代に確立された。
演技，公演，上演，演奏	performance ＊ **give a performance**（演技［公演，演奏］する）
上演する，（役などを）演じる，（楽器などを）演奏する	perform

（ステージや人前で）あがる，緊張する，硬くなる	get stage fright ＊ He always gets stage fright before performing.（彼は演じる前になるといつも緊張します）

（劇・オペラなどの）（第〜）幕	act
第一幕	act I
場，場面	scene [síːn] ＊ act（幕）の中の小区分。
第二幕第八場	Act II, Scene viii ＊ [ǽkt túː, síːn éit] と読む。
暗転	blackout
ギャラ	performance fee ／ appearance fee
頑張って！《演者に対して》	Break a leg! ＊演者に対して公演前に言う励ましの決まり文句。
ブラーヴォ！／ブラーヴァ！／ブラーヴェ！／ブラーヴィ！	Bravo! ／ Brava! ／ Brave! ／ Bravi! ＊イタリア語で演奏［演技］者を称賛するかけ声。Bravo! は "男性ひとりに向けて"，Brava! は "女性ひとりに向けて"，Brave! は複数女性に向けて，Bravi! は "複数の男性や複数の男女混合に向けて"。海外の演奏［演技］者に向けては使い方にお気をつけて。
カーテンコール	curtain calls ＊ take many curtain calls（何度もカーテンコールを受ける）
アンコール	encore [ɑ́ŋkɔːr	ɔ́ŋkɔː]
打ち上げ	afterparty ＊パーティー・会合・コンサートなどのあとの二次会，アフターパーティー。

オペラ	opera [ɑ́pərə	ɔ́p-]
オペラハウス	opera house
オペレッタ	light opera
オペラグラス	opera glasses
喜歌劇	comic opera
京劇	classical Chinese opera
（オペラの）プリマドンナ，歌姫	diva [díːvə] ／ prima donna

バレエ	ballet [bæléi]
バレエ・ダンサー	ballet dancer
バレリーナ《伊》	ballerina [bæ̀ləríːnə]
プリマ[主役の]バレリーナ	prima ballerina
モダン・バレエ	modern ballet
チュチュ（バレリーナの衣裳）	tutu [túːtu]
（バレリーナの）トーシューズ	pointe shoes

白鳥の湖	Swan Lake
くるみ割り人形	The Nutcracker
ジゼル	Giselle [dʒizél]
ロミオとジュリエット	Romeo and Juliet
眠れる森の美女	The Sleeping Beauty

★ジャンル

音楽, 曲	music ＊ listen to music while working（仕事をしながら音楽を聴く）。dance to (the) music（音楽に合わせて踊る）。the を付けると特定の音楽を指す。What kind of music do you like?（どんな音楽が好き？）
ロック	rock music ／ rock and roll（略：rock'n'roll）
アール・アンド・ビー	R&B ／ rhythm and blues
ソウル	soul
ポップス	pop music ／ pop
ラップ	rap
ヒップホップ	hip-hop
クラッシック	classical music
ジャズ	jazz
フュージョン	fusion
シャンソン	chanson [ʃɑːnsɔ́ːn]
カンツォーネ	canzone [kænzóuni]
カントリー	country music ／ country western
ハワイアン	Hawaiian

演歌	*enka* ballad
昭和時代の歌 謡曲	Japanese popular songs of the Showa era
民謡	folk music

ラテン音楽	Latin music
サンバ	samba
マンボ	mambo [mɑ́ːmbou]
タンゴ	tango [tǽŋgou]
サルサ	salsa [sɑ́ːlsə]
レゲエ	reggae [régei]
ジプシーの音楽	gypsy music
フラメンコ	flamenco

管弦楽	orchestral music
器楽	instrumental music
バレエ音楽	ballet music
室内楽	chamber music
交響曲	symphony [símfəni]
協奏曲	concerto [kəntʃéərtou]
コラール	choral [kərǽl	kɔrɑ́ːl]
オペラ	opera
声楽	vocal music
琴曲 (きんきょく)	koto music
古楽	early music
雅楽	ancient Japanese court music

★主な演奏家など

音楽家, ミュージシャン	musician [mju(ː)zíʃən]
作曲家	composer [kəmpóuzər]
作詞家	lyricist [lírəsist]

編曲家	(music) arranger ／ orchestrator
ギタリスト	guitarist
ベース奏者	bassist [béisist]
キーボード奏者	keyboard player ／ keyboardist
ドラム奏者	drummer
ボーカル	vocalist
歌手	singer
指揮者	conductor
バイオリニスト	violinist
ピアニスト	pianist
トランペット奏者	trumpeter
オペラ歌手	opera singer

★楽器など

楽器	musical instrument ＊play a musical instrument（楽器を演奏する）
アンプラグド	unplugged ＊アンプを用いないで生楽器だけで演奏することをいう。
弦楽器	stringed instrument
木管楽器	woodwind instrument
金管楽器	brass instrument
打楽器	percussion instrument
吹奏楽器，管楽器	wind instrument
鍵盤楽器	keyboard instrument

（オーケストラの）弦楽器群	the strings
（オーケストラの）木管楽器群	the woodwinds
（オーケストラの）金管楽器群	the brass
（オーケストラの）打楽器群	the percussion
（オーケストラの）管楽器	the winds

ヴァイオリン	violin
ヴィオラ	viola
チェロ	cello
ヴィオラ・ダ・ガンバ	viola da gamba
バス，ベース	bass
コントラバス	contrabass ／ double bass
フルート	flute
オーボエ	oboe
クラリネット	clarinet
ファゴット	bassoon
サクソフォーン	saxophone
ホルン	French horn
トランペット	trumpet
トロンボーン	trombone
チューバ	tuba [tjúːbə]
ユーフォニウム	euphonium
ハープ	harp
ティンパニ	timpani
マリンバ	marimba [mərímbə]
ビブラホン	vibraphone [váibrəfòun]

木琴	xylophone [záiləfòun, zí-]
ピアノ	piano [piǽnou]
キーボード	keyboard
シンセサイザー	synthesizer
オルガン	organ [ɔ́ːrgən]
リードオルガン	reed organ
パイプオルガン	pipe organ
ハープシコード	harpsichord
アコーディオン	accordion
バンドネオン（アコーディオンの一種）	bandoneon
コンセルティーナ	concertina ＊鍵盤がなく半音階的に配列したボタンのある六角形のアコーディオン。
ギター	guitar [gitáːr] ＊「ストローク」は strumming [strʌ́miŋ]。「アルペジオ」は arpeggio [ɑːrpédʒiòu, -dʒou]。
エレキギター	electric guitar
ギターシンセサイザー	guitar synthesizer
エフェクター	effects
チョーキング	bend ／ bending
リムショット	rim shot
アドリブ	improvisation
シールド	cable
エレキベース	electric(al) bass
バンジョー	banjo
リュート	lute
マンドリン	mandolin

琴	koto [kóutou]
三味線	samisen ／ shamisen ／ a three-stringed Japanese instrument
ウクレレ	ukulele [jùːkəléili]
バグパイプ	bagpipes
ハーモニカ	harmonica ＊ play the harmonica （ハーモニカを吹く）
オカリナ	ocarina
パン・フルート	pan flute
リコーダー，縦笛	recorder
ミュージカル・ソー（楽器として使うノコギリ）	musical saw
パーカッション	percussion
ドラム，太鼓	drum
バチ，ドラムスティック	drum stick
打楽器用小槌	mallet [mǽlət]
和太鼓	Japanese drum
スチールドラム	steel drum ＊ドラム缶から作られた打楽器。
タブラ	tabla ＊インド音楽で用いられる大小の２個の手打ち組太鼓。
（タンバリンのような形をした）フレームドラム，片面太鼓	frame drum ＊ tambourine [tæ̀mbəríːn]（タンバリン）

ボンゴ	bongo
コンガ	conga
ドラムマシン	drum machine
(手で振り鳴らす) ハンドベル	handbell
シンバル	cymbals

★西洋音楽の時代区分

中世	Medieval
ルネッサンス	Renaissance
バロック	Baroque
古典派	Classical era
ロマン派	Romantic era
ポストロマン派	Post-Romantic era
近代	modern
コンテンポラリ	contemporary

★音楽の三要素と楽譜など

音楽の三要素	the three elements of music
リズム	rhythm [ríðm]
メロディー	melody [mélədi]
ハーモニー	harmony [háːrməni]

作曲	composition
作曲する, 曲を書く	write [compose] music
五線紙	music paper / music sheet
一つの楽曲, 一曲	a piece of music ＊ compose a piece of music (作曲する)
ト音記号	G clef / treble clef

ヘ音記号	F clef / bass clef
ハ音記号	C clef
音符	(musical) note ＊「全音符」は whole note〈米〉/ semibreve〈英〉,「二分音符」は half note〈米〉/ minim〈英〉,「四分音符」は quarter note〈米〉/ crotchet〈英〉,「八分音符」は eighth note〈米〉/ quaver〈英〉,「十六分音符」は sixteenth note〈米〉/ semiquaver〈英〉
(音が) 半音高い, 嬰音の	sharp
(音が) 半音低い, 変音の	flat
休符	rest
拍子, リズム, ビート, 強拍音	beat ＊ a four beat rhythm（4拍子のリズム）
8ビート	eighth note beats / eighth note groove
ウラ, ウラ拍	offbeat
シンコペーション	syncopation ＊弱拍 (ウラ) と強拍 (オモテ) のリズムがタイで結ばれてアクセントの位置が移動したリズム。
音程	interval ＊ a third interval (3度の音程), be in key [tune] (音程が合っている)
歌詞	lyrics ＊ set [put] these lyrics [words] to music (この歌詞に曲をつける)
調律器／調律師	tuner

うまく (正確に) 歌う	carry a tune

13 余暇を楽しむ

音痴である	*be* tone-deaf ／ have no ear for music
音域	range〈通例, 単数形で〉 ＊ This song has notes of a wide range.（この歌は音域が広い）
移調	transposition ＊「この曲をニ長調に移調して演奏する」は play the tune transposed to D major。

メトロノーム	metronome [métrənòum]
モデラート, ほどよい速度で	moderato [màdərá:tou]
アンダンテ, 歩く速さで	andante [ɑːndáːntei]
アレグロ, 軽快に速く	allegro [əlégròu]
長調	major [méidʒər]
短調	minor [máinər]
フォルテ, 強く	forte [fɔ́ːrtei]
メゾフォルテ, やや強く	mezzo forte [mètsou fɔ́ːrtei]
ピアノ, 弱く	piano
メゾピアノ	mezzo piano
楽譜, スコア	score
譜面台	music stand
(綴〔と〕じられていない) 数枚の楽譜	sheet music
楽譜を読む	read music

伴奏	accompaniment [əkʌ́mpənimənt] ＊ sing with a guitar accompaniment（ギターの伴奏で歌う）。動詞「伴奏（を）する」は accompany。

ライブ	live concert
ライブハウス	club with live music
ハウリング	feedback
音楽に合わせて踊る	dance to (the) music
おはこ, 十八番	favorite ／ one's forte [fɔ́ːrt] ＊ forte は「得意（分野），強み」。
追っかけ	groupie

DTM《和製語》	computer music
サンプラー	sampler
録音	recording

ディスコグラフィー	discography ＊音楽家・作曲家の全作品目録。
(著作権物の) 海賊 [違法録音, 違法複製] 版(の)	bootleg ＊ bootleg CD（海賊版CD）
環境音楽	ambient music
音楽療法	music therapy
オルゴール	music box《米》／ musical box《英》

ジャンボリー	jamboree ＊主に野外で大勢で催される盛大な催し物やパーティー。

4. 絵画・彫刻, 工芸

★絵画・彫刻

(絵画・彫刻などの) 美術, 芸術	art
美術	fine arts 《常に複数形で》
美術品《集合的に》	fine art
芸術家	artist
画家	painter
彫刻家	sculptor [skʌ́lptər]
展覧会	exhibition

絵画	painting * a painting by Henri Rousseau (アンリ・ルソーの絵)
洋画《絵画》	Western [European] painting
油絵	oil painting／oils
水彩画	watercolor painting 《米》／watercolour painting 《英》 * a watercolor painting of a landscape (風景を描いた水彩画)
アクリル画	acrylic painting
フレスコ画	fresco painting
テンペラ絵の具 [画法]	tempera
肖像画	portrait (painting)
人物画	portrait／figure painting
風景画	landscape／scenery

自画像	self-portrait * paint [draw] a self-portrait (自画像を描く)
静物画	still-life painting
抽象画	abstract painting
細密画 (さいみつが)	miniature painting
宗教画	religious painting
織物絵	fabric painting
壁画	wall painting／mural painting

イラスト	illustration
フェイス・ペイント	face painting

(線で描いた) 絵, デッサン, 線画	drawing * make a rough drawing (下絵を描く)
パステル (画)	pastel
チョーク (画)	chalk
木炭 (画)	charcoal
コンテ (画)	conté crayon
ペン画	pen and ink
鉛筆画	pencil

版画	block print
エッチング (による版画 [作品])	etching
リトグラフ	lithography
木版画	woodcuts／woodprint

13 余暇を楽しむ

彫刻（する）《像を作る》	sculpture [skʌ́lptʃər]
彫刻（する）《彫って作る》	carving《名》，carve《動》
（像などを）彫刻する	sculpt ／ sculpture
（表面などに）彫刻する	engrave
（何でも）彫刻する	curve
彫刻のように均整のとれた	sculpturesque
のみ；のみで彫る	chisel
立像	statue

レリーフ	relief [rilíːf]
ブロンズ像	bronze
木彫	wood carving

（画材道具）

アクリル絵の具	acrylics
油絵の具	oil colors ／ oil paints ／ oils
水彩絵の具	watercolors
パステル	pastel ＊絵画で使うクレヨンの一種。
ステンシル	stencil ＊板金・紙・皮革などに図柄や文字を切り抜いた刷込み型。
接着剤	adhesive ／ glue ＊ adhesive for plastic(s)（プラスチック用接着剤），wood [hide] glue（木工［皮革］用接着剤）

エアブラシ	airbrush [éərbrʌ̀ʃ] ＊圧縮空気によって絵の具，塗料などを吹きつける工具。
エアブラシ用絵の具	airbrush colors
コンプレッサー	compressor ＊空気を圧縮する工具。

スモック	smock [smá(ː)k ǀ smɔ́k]
（絵）筆	(paint) brush [brʌ́ʃ]
筆洗いバケツ	brush basin
筆入れ	brush case
パレット	palette
パレットナイフ	palette knife
キャンバス	canvas
カゼイン塗料	casein [kéisiːn] paint
色鉛筆	colored pencil
クレヨン	crayon
画用紙	drawing paper
製図器具	drafting instruments
製図用机	drawing (drafting) table
カッティング・マット	cutting mat
スケッチ用品	sketching supplies
画帳	drawing pad
ポスター・カラー	poster color
顔料	pigment
顔料すり棒	pigment muller
インク	ink
蜜蝋（みつろう）	beeswax

粘土	clay
マーカー	marker
色見本マニュアル	color reference manual

（用語）

作品	work ＊ Van Gogh's earlier works（ゴッホの初期の作品）
心象風景《心理的情景》	mindscape
遠近法	perspective
遠近法のための格子線	perspective grid
コレクション	collection
構成	composition
色の理論	color theory
陰影	shadow
三次元	three dimension
三次元見通し	three dimensional vista
深さ	depth
水平な線	horizontal line
縦線	vertical line
割合	proportions
線を描く	draw a line
（定規などの器具を用いない）手書きの［で］,自在画法の［で］	freehand
マージン	margin

★工芸

工芸	craft
工芸品	craftwork
手工芸	handicraft
手工芸品	handcrafts
伝統工芸	traditional crafts
美術工芸品	arts and crafts
工芸家	craftspeople
装飾芸術（品）	decorative art ＊インテリアや家具などの調度類を飾るための美術。

織物	fabric
編む	knit
編み物	knitting
編み棒	knitting needle [pin]
刺繍	embroidery
（織機で）（～を）織る	weave ＊ weave fabric from [out of] wool（羊毛から布地を織る）
織機 (おりき)	loom

陶芸	ceramics《単数扱い》／ ceramic art
陶芸家	ceramist ／ ceramic artist ／ potter
陶芸品	《集合的に》 ceramics ＊個々に言うときは，a piece of ceramic art.
陶器	pottery ＊磁器を除く焼き物の総称。
陶磁器	ceramic ware

13 余暇を楽しむ

磁器	porcelain ／ china(ware)
ろくろ	potter's wheel * turn a potter's [pottery] wheel（ろくろを回す）
窯 (かま)	kiln [kíln] * fire pottery in a kiln（陶器をかまの中で焼く）
(陶器などに)うわ薬（をかける），表面の艶	glaze [gléiz] * glaze pottery in a kiln（窯で陶器にうわぐすりをかける）
壷	pot
皿	plate
花瓶	vase [véis, véiz | vάːz]

漆器	lacquerware ／ japan
漆工	japanner
木工品	woodwork
木工（技術）	woodworking〈主に米〉／ woodwork〈主に英〉
染色，染め物	dyeing
金属細工（品）	metalwork
竹細工	bamboo work
石細工	stonework

★伝統文化など

茶道	tea ceremony
茶会	tea party
茶釜	tea kettle
茶碗	teacup
茶せん	tea whisk
盆	tray
ひしゃく	dipper

茶菓子	tea cake
華道	flower arrangement
書道，習字	calligraphy [kəlígrəfi]
日本舞踊	Japanese dance
歌舞伎	kabuki
猿楽	monkey dance
能	Noh [nóu]
狂言	kyogen
文楽，人形浄瑠璃	bunraku puppet theater

書	calligraphy
古典	classical book
古文書	old literature

国宝	national treasure * be designed as a national treasure（国宝に指定される）
文化遺産	cultural assets
文化財	cultural property
重要文化財	important cultural asset
無形文化財	intangible cultural asset

世界文化遺産	world cultural heritage
世界自然遺産	world natural heritage
古代の遺物	antiquities

5. 娯楽・ギャンブル

★娯楽

娯楽，気晴し，楽しませるもの	entertainment ＊ the entertainment industry（娯楽産業）
気晴し，娯楽	pastime
気晴し，娯楽，レクリエーション	recreation [rèkriéiʃən]
娯楽施設	amusement facilities
遊園地	amusement park
遊具	playground equipment
移動遊園地	carnival
お化け屋敷	hunted house
ろう人形館	wax museum ＊ wax figure（ろう人形），mechanical doll（からくり人形）
パチンコ店	pachinko parlor
雀荘	mahjong parlor
ボウリング場	bowling alley
ゲームセンター	game arcade
賭博	gambling
カジノ	casino
ルーレット	roulette
宝くじ	lottery
競馬	horse racing
競輪	bike race
競艇	motor boat race

★演芸・エンターテインメント

ボードビル，寄席演芸	vaudeville [vɔ́:dəvil]〈米〉／ variety show〈英〉
コメディアン，お笑い芸人	comedian [kəmí:diən]
女性コメディアン	comedienne [kəmi:dién]
ものまね（人の声・動作などの）	mimicry [mímikri]
（話し方・しぐさを）まねる，〜のものまねをする	mimic ／ imitate ＊ be good at mimicking the teachers（先生たちの物まねが得意だ）
ものまね（芸人などの）	impression ／ imitation ＊ do an impression of a movie star（映画俳優のものまねをする）
腹話術	ventriloquism [ventríləkwìzm]
娯楽番組	entertainment program
著名人	celebrity ／ famous person
テレビタレント	TV personality ／ TV celebrity ／ TV performer
（芸能人の）芸名	stage name
（映画俳優の）芸名	screen name
曲芸師	acrobat [ǽkrəbæt]
手品師	magician [mədʒíʃən]
司会者	emcee [émsí:]

13

余暇を楽しむ

スター	star
アイドル	idol
アイドル歌手	pop idol / singing idol
スターの座	stardom ＊ rise [shoot] to stardom（スターの座に駆け上がる）
DJ	disc jockey
ファッションモデル	fashion model

★競馬

馬	horse
騎手	jockey
競馬場	racetrack《米》／ racecourse《英》
重勝式（の賭け）	daily double
チャーチル・ダウンズ（ケンタッキー州にある有名な競馬場）	Churchill Downs ＊【馬券】tip（予想）, exacta（馬単）, trifecta（3連単）, trio（3連複）, win（単勝）, place ／ show（複勝）, quinella（馬連）, dividend ／ payoff（配当金）
ケンタッキー・ダービー	Kentucky Derby
（馬・競技者などを）出場名簿から消す	scratch ＊名詞は,「出場中止［辞退］の競走馬［選手］」。
本領を発揮する，本調子になる	hit one's stride
ダークホース，穴馬	dark horse
激戦する，接戦を演じる	get a run for one's money

楽勝する	win hands down
最後までわからない	go right down to the wire
接戦である	be neck and neck
ホームストレッチで〔ゴール前の直線コースに入って〕	in [on] the homestretch
僅差で勝つ	win by a nose

★トランプ

トランプ（の札）	(playing) card
トランプ（遊び）	(playing) cards
トランプをする	play cards ／ have a game of cards
カードを切る	deal the cards ／ shuffle the cards
カードを伏せて配る	deal out the cards face down
カードをめくる	flip the cards over
カードの山から1枚引く	take a card from the deck
カードの山から2枚引く	draw two cards from the deck
カードを1枚捨てる	discard one card
カードを数枚捨てる	get rid of the cards
山札	deck ＊ place the deck of cards（カードの山札を置く）
バカラ	baccarat
ブラックジャック	Blackjack
ブリッジ	Bridge

ポーカー	Poker
ババ抜き	Old Maid
大富豪	President ／ Career Poker
神経衰弱	Concentration ／ Memory
七並べ	Domino ／ Sevens
ソリティア	Solitaire
ハートの組札	hearts ＊ the two of hearts（ハートの2）
ホールデム（ポーカーの一種）	Hold'em (Poker)
カナスタ（同位札7枚の組合わせ）	Canasta
クリベッジ	Cribbage
ピノクル	Pinochle
ジュースワイルド（ポーカーの一種）	Deuces Wild
ピラミッド	Pyramids
ゴーフィッシュ（札合わせ）	Go Fish ／ Fish

はったり	bluff [blʌ́f] ＊ play a game of bluff（はったりをかける）
切り札（を出す）	trump [trʌ́mp] ＊ play a trump（切り札を出す），trump someone's ace（〜のエースに切り札を出す）
（トランプのカードを）配る番：カードを配る	deal ＊ It's your deal.（きみが配る番［親］だよ）

カジノ	casino [kəsí:nou]
ハウス・ルール	house rules
スロット	slots
ロット，宝くじ	lotto [lá(:)tou｜lɔ́t-] ＊ bingo に似た数合わせゲーム。
サイコロ	dice [dáis]
（サイコロ博打の）クラップス	craps [krǽps]
スペード札を過半数獲得すること	spades
1のぞろ目	snake eyes ＊ 2つのサイコロの目がともに1。
ギャンブラー	gambler
（特にギャンブルゲーム専門の）いかさま師	shark ＊ card shark（トランプのいかさま師）
病みつきのギャンブラー，ギャンブル狂	compulsive gambler
ノミ屋	bookmaker ／ bookie
悪徳高利貸	loan shark
ディーラー	dealer
チップを換金する	cash in one's chips

13 余暇を楽しむ

6. 写真, その他の主な趣味・余暇

★写真

写真	photograph ／ picture ／ photo ＊ photo は省略形で，くだけた文脈で使われる。 take a picture with a digital camera（デジカメで写真を撮る）
写真を撮る	take a picture [photo] ＊ take a photo with ... in the background（〜をバックに写真を撮る）
写真撮影	photography ＊ No Photography（《掲示》写真撮影禁止），My biggest interest is photography.（私の最大の趣味は写真です）
カメラマン, 写真家	photographer
カメラ	camera
デジタルカメラ	digital camera
デジタル・コンパクト・カメラ	digital compact camera
一眼レフカメラ	single-lens reflex camera《略：SLR camera》
インスタントカメラ	instant camera
ポラロイドカメラ	Polaroid camera
35ミリフィルム	35 millimeter film
画像	image
（カメラなどの）絞り，（レンズの）口径	aperture [ǽpərtʃuər]

〜にズームインする，〜を拡大する	zoom in on ... ＊ zoom in on her face（彼女の顔にズームインする）
〜をズームアウトする，〜を縮小する	zoom out ...
〜にカメラのピントを合わせる	focus a camera on ... ＊ focus a camera on his face（彼の顔にカメラのピントを合わせる）
ピントが合っている	be in focus
ピントがボケている	be out of focus ／ be blurred ／ be not clear ＊ This photograph is out of focus.（この写真はピントが合っていません）
ソフトフォーカス	soft focus ＊故意に輪郭をぼやけさせる。
明度を上げる	brighten
（カメラの）フラッシュライトをオンにする	put a flash on
逆光で《形》	backlit [bǽklìt] ＊ This picture is backlit.（この写真は逆光になっています）
（写真の）露出（時間）	exposure [ikspóuʒər]
手動による露出	manual exposure
自動露出	automatic exposure

シャッター速度	shutter-speed
シャッターを押す	push [press] the button
連写する	take continuous photos
シャッターチャンス	Kodak moment ／ photo opportunity
シャッターチャンスを狙う	watch for a best [great] shot
シャッターチャンスを逃す	miss a best [great] shot

スナップ写真	snapshot
集合写真	group photo ＊ use the timer to take a group photo（セルフタイマーで集合写真を撮る）
三脚を立てる	set one's tripod [tráipɑd]
（人が）写真映りがよい	photogenic 《形》
自撮り	selfie ＊ take a selfie（自撮りする）
自撮り棒	selfie-stick
写真撮影スポット	photo spot

カラー写真	color photo [picture]
黒白写真	black and white photo
証明写真	ID photo
風景写真	landscape picture
結婚写真	wedding photo

プリントする	print
引き伸ばす	enlarge ／ blow up
写真［動画］を SNS に投稿する	post a photo [video] on SNS
旅のフォト日記をつける	keep a photo diary of one's travel

写真を編集する	edit a photo
トリミングする	trim
画像を加工する	process [edit] an image
（写真などから不要な部分を）切り取る	crop
合成写真	composite photograph
印画紙	photographic (printing) paper

★写真を撮る

私の写真を撮ってもらえますか。	Could you take my photo?
（私たちの）写真を撮っていただけますか。	Could you take a picture for us?
ここをタップするだけです。（スマートフォンのカメラで）	Just tap here.
少し右にずれていただけますか。	Could you move to the right?
はい，チーズ！	Say cheese!
まばたきしたので，もう 1 枚！	You blinked. Once more, please!

13 余暇を楽しむ

もっと詰めてください。	Squeeze in!
うまく撮れていればいいけど。	I hope it'll come out well.

★その他の主な趣味・余暇

ところで Bob, 余暇をどのように過ごすのが好きですか。	So, Bob. How do you like to spend your leisure time?
自由な時間にやりたいことは何ですか。	What do you like to do in your free time?
自由時間にはどんなことを楽しんでいますか。	What do you enjoy doing in your free time?
どのくらいギターを弾いているのですか。	How long have you been playing the guitar?
読書	reading books ＊ I'm into reading comic books now. (今マンガにハマっています)
音楽鑑賞	listening to music ＊ I really like listening to music. (私の趣味は音楽を聴くことです)
映画鑑賞	watching movies ＊ I enjoy watching movies in my free time. (空いた時間には、映画鑑賞を楽しんでいます)
筋トレ	strength training
料理	cooking
海外旅行	overseas trip
散歩	walking

テレビゲーム	video game ＊ I'm currently into playing a video game. (最近、ゲームにハマっています)
オンラインゲーム	online game
買い物	shopping ＊ I really like going shopping. (私はショッピングに行くのが好きです)
絵を描くこと	painting pictures
ガーデニング	gardening ＊ What made you start gardening？(ガーデニングを始めたきっかけは何ですか)
釣り	fishing ＊ How often do you go fishing？(どのくらい〔の頻度で〕釣りに行くのですか)
コイン収集	coin collecting
切手収集	stamp collecting
昆虫採集	insect collecting ＊ magnifying glass（拡大鏡、虫眼鏡）, tweezers（ピンセット）
バードウォッチング	bird watching
天体観測	astronomic observation ＊ astronomy（天文学）, astronomical telescope（望遠鏡）
動画編集	editing videos
ハイキング	hiking ＊ One of my favorite leisure activities is hiking. (私の好きな趣味のひとつはハイキングをすることです)
キャンプ	camping

14.

学ぶ

1. 教育

★重要単語

教育	education [èdʒəkéiʃən | èdju-]
教育的な	educational
教育する	educate [édʒəkèit | édju-] ＊ be educated to be a lawyer（法律家になるように教育を受ける）
普通教育	ordinary education
義務教育	compulsory education
教育改革	educational reform

カリキュラム，教育過程	curriculum [kəríkjələm]
シラバス，授業計画	syllabus [síləbəs]
遠距離教育，通信教育	distance learning ／ correspondence education
学区	school district
学習指導要項	teaching guidelines
教材	teaching material
教科書	textbook ／ text
参考書	reference book
生涯教育	lifelong education
生涯学習	lifelong learning
独学，独習	self-study

★教育の費用

授業料	tuition〈米〉／ tuition fees〈英〉
授業料免除	tuition waiver
入学金	entrance fee
奨学金	scholarship [skálərʃip] ＊ receive scholarship（奨学金を受ける），scholarship student（奨学生）
学費	school expenses

★教育問題

学級崩壊	classroom disruption ／ classroom collapse
校内暴力	school violence ／ violence at school ＊ suffer from school violence（校内暴力を受ける）
（窓ガラスなどの）器物破棄行為	vandalism [vǽndəlìzm]
いじめ	bullying [búliŋ]
いじめる	bully [búli] ＊ He was bullied at school.（彼は学校でいじめにあった）
不登校	truancy [trúːənsi]
不登校生	truant [trúːənt]
中退者	dropout [drápàut]
仲間からの圧力	peer pressure ＊集団の中で同じ行動をとらせようとする精神的圧力。

2. 教育機関と教育関係者

★教育機関

学校	school
保育所	preschool ／ nursery school
保育園児	preschool child
幼稚園	kindergarten [kíndərgàːrtn]
幼稚園児	kindergarten child
公立学校	public school
私立学校	private school
小学校	elementary school ／ grade school 〈米〉／ primary school 〈英〉
小学生	elementary schoolchild ／ primary schoolchild 〈英〉
中学校	junior high school 〈米〉〈満 12 ～満 14 歳〉／ middle school
中学生	junior high school student ／ middle school student
高校	(senior) high school 〈米〉〈満 14 ～ 18 歳〉
高校生	high school student
専門学校	vocational school

専門学校生	vocational school student
職業訓練校	job-training school
塾，予備校	test coaching school ／ coaching school
予備校生	coaching school student
プレップスクール	preparatory school ＊米国で大学準備教育のための私立の学校。
全寮制学校	boarding school
大学	college ／ university ＊ college は複数の学部・研究科は存在しない。大学院課程を設けていない小さな大学。university は複数の学部・研究科から成る。大学院課程を設けている大きな大学。
大学生	college [university] student
共学	coeducation ／ mixed education
共学の学校	coeducational school ＊省略して coed, coed school と呼ぶ場合もある。
別学	single-sex education
男子校	boys' school ／ all-boys school

14
学ぶ

女子校	girls' school ／ all-girls school
学年度	academic year
（大学前までの学校の）学年	grade ＊ What grade are you in?（何年生？）《小・中・高校生に対して》
学部生	undergraduate student
学年	year ＊ the first [second, third, fourth] year student（1年生，2年生，3年生，4年生）。What year are you in?（何年生ですか）
《米》大学1年生，高校1年生	freshman
《米》大学2年生	sophomore
《米》大学3年生，高校2年生	junior
《米》大学4年生，高校3年生	senior
卒業見込みの大学生	prospective college graduate
短期大学，短大	junior college
短大生	junior college student
リベラルアーツカレッジ	liberal arts college ＊アメリカの四年生大学の中で、特に寮生で小規模な私立大学。
国立大学	national university
州立大学	state university ／ state-run university

学部，教授陣	faculty [fǽkəlti] ＊ the faculty of economics（経済学部）
学科	department [dipáːrtmənt]
課程，科目	course [kɔ́ːrs]
専攻（科目），専攻学生	major [méidʒər] ＊ What's your major?（専攻は何ですか）— I'm an English Literature major.（英文学を専攻しています）
大学院	graduate school
大学院生	graduate student ／ graduate
大学院医学専攻課程	school of medicine
修士課程	master's course ／ master's program
博士課程	doctor's course ／ doctor's program
ビジネススクール	business school
ロースクール，法科大学院	law school
メディカルスクール	medical school

★アメリカの名門大学

アイビーリーグ	IVY League ＊アメリカの名門大学8校からなるグループの総称。ハーバード／イエール／コロンビア／プリンストン／ダートマス／ブラウン／コーネル／ペンシルベニア大学，全て私立大学。

パブリックアイビー	Public IVY ＊アメリカの州立大学の名門校。特に明確な区分けはないが，州立で伝統ある大学を指す。
セブンシスターズ	Seven Sisters ＊アメリカの名門女子大7校の総称。ラドクリフカレッジやバーナードカレッジ等。

★教育関係者

教育実習生	trainee teacher
将来の先生，教師候補	would-be teacher
チューター，家庭教師	tutor
進路指導教員	guidance counselor
講師	lecturer
非常勤講師	part-time lecturer

専任講師	full-time lecturer
専任教員，専任講師	instructor
准教授	associate professor
教授	professor
客員教授	visiting professor
名誉教授	professor emeritus
学部長	dean [díːn]
副学長	vice president
学長	president
理事長	chairman of the board of trustees

教頭，副校長	vice principal

14
学ぶ

Exterior of the university library of Columbia University

3. 入試・学校生活

★入試

入試係	admission office
入学申請	application
入学試験	entrance exam ／ entrance examination ＊take an entrance examination（入学試験を受ける），pass the entrance exam（入学試験に合格する）
大学入学学力テスト（略：SAT）	Scholastic Assessment Test
入学許可	admission
合格者	successful examinee [applicant, candidate]
不合格者	unsuccessful examinee [applicant, candidate]
入学手続き	registration
入学手続きをする	register [rédʒistər]
授業料を収める	pay tuition fees
入学式	entrance ceremony
履修登録	course registration

★授業参加

授業に出席する	attend a class
授業をさぼる	cut a class
ズル休みをする	play hooky [húki]
遅刻する	be late [《主に米》be tardy]《for, to》 ＊「遅刻」《名》は lateness，《主に米》tardiness。
欠席	absence
（正当な理由のない）常習的な欠席	absenteeism
授業参加	participation in class
（〔試験以外に〕履修期間に出される）課題	course work ＊成績に加味される。
レポート，論文	paper [péipər] ＊write a paper（レポートを書く），turn in [hand in, submit] a paper（レポートを提出する）
学期末レポート	term paper
（口頭）発表，プレゼン（テーション）	presentation
ディスカッション，話し合い，討議	discussion
ディベート，討論会	debate [dibéit] ＊論題をめぐって賛成派，反対派に分かれて行なう討論会。
ペアワーク	pair work ＊2人1組になって，授業内で与えられた課題などをこなす。
グループワーク	group work
宿題をする	do homework
（学生に対する）課題	assignment [əsáinmənt]
（～に関する学習のための）研究課題，自主研究	project〈名〉[prádʒekt] ＊do a project on pollution（汚染についての研究課題に取り組む）

★科目・授業・講義

必修科目	compulsory [required] subject
選択科目	elective subject
基礎必修科目, 先修科目	prerequisite *高度な内容の科目を履修する前に, 履修が完了していなければならない基礎的な内容の科目。
単位取得外科目	non-credit course
ゼミナール, ゼミ	seminar [sémənɑ̀ːr]
教育実習	teaching practicum
補習クラス	remedial course
夏期講習	summer school / summer session
学校暦	academic calendar
課外クラブ活動	extracurricular club activities
校外学習, 遠足	field trip * go on a field trip (校外学習に行く)
野外活動日	field day

★試験

試験	examination / exam *入学や成績評価のための重要な試験を指す。
試験がある	have an examination
試験を実施する	give [administer] an examination
試験を採点する	mark an examination
受験申込者	applicant [ǽplikənt]
受験者	examinee [igzæməníː, egz-]
試験官	examiner
試験監督官 (を する)	proctor 〈米〉／ invigilator 〈英〉
入学試験	entrance examination
中間試験	midterm 〈米〉／ midterm exam
学期末試験	final [final exam]
追試	makeup exam
テスト, 試験	test
抜き打ちテスト	pop test
達成テスト	achievement test *学習到達度を測るための学力テスト。
能力テスト	proficiency test
客観テスト	objective test
主観テスト	subjective test
穴埋め	fill in the blanks
並べ替え	rearrangement
正誤問題	error correction
クローズ・テスト, 空欄穴埋めテスト	cloze test
多肢選択形式	multiple-choice
語句選択	word choice
内容真偽	true or false [fɔ́ːls]
面接試験	interview test
面接官	interviewer
面接試験受験者	interviewee

14

学ぶ

就職の面接（試験）	job interview
筆記試験	written test
口述試験	oral test
小テスト	quiz

★成績

成績（をつける）	grade
得点	point
合格点	passing point
落第する，落第させる	fail
単位	credit
成績優秀者名簿	honor roll ＊ Lisa got on the honor roll.（リサは成績優秀者名簿に載った）
成績証明書	transcript
停学	suspension
除籍	expulsion

★論文・卒業

学術論文	article
卒業論文	graduation thesis

修士論文	master thesis
博士論文	dissertation
修士号	master's degree ＊ get a master's degree（修士号を取る）
博士号	doctor's degree／Doctor of Philosophy (PhD degree)
卒業	graduation
卒業式，学位記授与式	commencement ＊ gown（ガウン），cap（キャップ）
卒業証書	diploma
卒業証明書	certificate
卒業記念アルバム	yearbook

同窓会《組織》	alumni association [əlʌ́mnai əsòusiéiʃən]
同窓会パーティー	alumni party
同窓会（の会合）	class reunion

4. 学習

★学習

知能，知性	intelligence
知能指数（略：IQ）	intelligence quotient [kwóuʃənt]
感情指数（略：EQ）	emotional intelligence quotient ＊IQ の不足部分を補いながら，人間関係内で起こりうるさまざまな問題を解決する能力など，自分の心や感情をコントロールする能力値を示す指数。
学力	academic ability
情報	information
知識	knowledge [nálidʒ]
学習	learning
学習障害（略：LD）	learning disabilities
発達障害	development disabilities
限局性学習症	specific learning disorder ＊全般的な知的発達に遅れがなく，聞く・話す・読む・書く・計算する又は推論する能力のうち，特定のものの習得と使用に著しい困難を示す状態。
注意欠如・多動症（略：ADHD）	attention-deficit hyperactivity disorder
読み書き能力	literacy [lítərəsi]
文盲	illiteracy [ilítərəsi]
能力	competence [kámpətəns] ＊何かを達成するために必要な資質。

有能な	competent
無能な	incompetent
コミュニケーション能力	communicative competence
技能	skill ＊skilled（熟練した），skillful（上手な），unskillful（下手な）
言語技能	language skills
創造性	creativity ＊creative（創造的な），create（～を創造する），creation（創造）
潜在能力	potential ＊maximize each student's potential（生徒ひとりひとりの潜在能力を最大限に引き出す）
才能	talent ＊talented（才能のある），gifted（才能に恵まれた）
達成感	a sense of achievement [fulfillment]
記憶	memory ＊memory lapse（記憶違い），memory loss（記憶喪失）
記銘（する）	imprint ＊情報が記憶に刻まれること。
保持	retention ＊retain（保持する）
想起（する），思い出す（こと）	recall

14
学
ぶ

267

短期記憶	short-term memory
長期記憶	long-term memory

★学問・研究領域

（人文科学）

哲学	philosophy
倫理学	ethics [éθiks]
宗教学	religion
民俗学	folklore
美学	aesthetics
文学	literature [lítərətʃər]
言語学	linguistics [liŋgwístik]
音声学	phonetics
心理言語学	psycholinguistics
英語学	English linguistics
歴史学	history
考古学	archaeology [àːrkiάlədʒi]
地理学	geography [dʒiάgrəfi]
文化人類学	anthropology [æ̀nθrəpάlədʒi]

（社会科学）

法学	law
政治学	political science
国際関係論	international relations
経済学	economics
ミクロ経済学	microeconomics
マクロ経済学	macroeconomics

計量経済学	econometrics
統計学	statistics
財政学	finance
経営学	business management ／ business administration
商学	commerce
会計学	accounting
社会学	sociology
社会福祉学	social welfare
心理学	psychology
社会心理学	social psychology
教育心理学	educational psychology
臨床心理学	clinical psychology
認知心理学	cognitive psychology
実験心理学	experimental psychology
教育学	pedagogy ／ education

（理工系ほか）

数学	mathematics * mathematician（数学者）, arithmetic（算術）, algebra（代数学）, geometry（幾何学）, arithmetical analysis（解析学）, differential calculus（微分学）, integral calculus（積分学）
化学	chemistry * chemical reaction（化学反応）, chemist（化学者）

天文学	astronomy [əstránəmi] ＊astronomer（天文学者），astronomical（天文学的な）
物理学	physics ＊physical（物理的な，身体的な），physical phenomenon（物理現象），physicist（物理学者），physician（医者），physique（体格）
機械工学	mechanical engineering
電子工学	electronic engineering
土木工学	civil engineering
ロボット工学	robotics

建築学	architecture ＊architect（建築士）
生物学	biology [baiálədʒi] ＊biologist（生物学者）
農学	agriculture [ǽgrikʌ̀ltʃər] ＊agriculturalist（農学者）
水産学	fisheries [fíʃəriz]
海洋学	oceanography [òuʃənágrəfi] ＊oceanologist（海洋学者）
海洋生物学	marine biology
火山学	volcanology
畜産学	animal science

医学	medicine [médəsn]／medical science

解剖学	anatomy [ənǽtəmi]
生理学	physiology [fìziálədʒi]
遺伝学	genetics [dʒənétiks]
病理学	pathology [pəθálədʒi]
免疫学	epidemiology [èpidì:miálədʒi]
衛生学	hygiene [háidʒi:n]
法医学	forensic medicine
歯学	dentistry [déntəstri]
看護学	nursing science
獣医学	veterinary medicine [vétərənèri médəsn]
薬学	pharmacy [fáːrməsi]

14 学ぶ

★英語学習

（学習法）

音読	reading aloud ＊英文に目を通しながら声を出して読むこと。英語の語感を身につけるのに有効な方法で，例文をひととおり読み終えたうえで，正確な発音やイントネーションを学ぶ。
リピーティング	repeating ＊正しい英文の発音が聞こえた後に，真似して声に出し発音練習する方法。
オーバーラッピング	overlapping ＊英文テキストを見た状態で音声を流し，その音声に被せて音読練習をすること。

シャドウイング	shadowing ＊英文が聞けた直後，またはほぼ同時に声を出し繰り返す方法。元来は同時通訳者の養成法であるが，リスニング力を高め，英文がチャンクとして記憶に定着し，正確な発音やイントネーションが身につく。
ウィスパーリング	whispering ＊英文が聞けた直後，またはほぼ同時にささやき繰り返す方法。シャドウイングの前段階として，自分の声が気になったり邪魔に感じる人や周囲に人がいて迷惑をかけられない時などに適している。
特定の情報の聞き取り	focused listening ＊特定の情報に焦点を合わせて聞き取る方法。例えば，「動詞」「形容詞」などの品詞，「数字」「大きさを表わす語句」などの意味，種類に応じて聞き取る焦点をまず決め，聞きながら該当する語句を書き出す。

（語彙）

語彙，語彙力	vocabulary [voukǽbjəlèri] ＊ build up one's vocabulary（ボキャブラリーを増やす）
受動語彙（力）	passive vocabulary
発信語彙（力）	active vocabulary

（英文の構造など）

主語	subject [sʌ́bdʒikt]
目的語	object [ábdʒikt] ＊ direct object（直接目的語），indirect object（間接目的語）
補語	complement [kámpləmənt]
修飾語句	modifier [mádəfàiər]
先行詞	antecedent [æ̀ntisíːdnt]
文字	letter
表意文字	ideogram／ideograph
表音文字	phonogram
接頭辞	affix
語根	root
接尾辞	suffix
語	word
同義語	synonym
反意語	antonym
同音異義語	homonym
派生語	derivative
発音	pronunciation
抑揚	intonation
音節	syllable
句	phrase [fréiz] ＊ noun phrase（名詞句），verbal phrase（動詞句），adjectival phrase（形容詞句），adverbial phrase（副詞句）
節	clause [klɔ́ːz]
文	sentence

平叙文	declarative sentence
疑問文	interrogative sentence
否定文	negative sentence
否定疑問文	negative interrogative sentence
命令文	imperative sentence
付加疑問文	tag question

単文	simple sentence
複文	complex sentence
重文	compound sentence
段落	paragraph
文章	passage

（品詞～動詞と関連語）

品詞	parts of speech
動詞	verb [vɔ́ːrb]
➤活用	conjugation
➤現在	present
➤過去	past
➤過去分詞	past participle
➤ BE 動詞	be-verb
➤一般動詞	general verb
➤助動詞	auxiliary verb
➤使役動詞	causative verb
➤自動詞	intransitive verb
➤他動詞	transitive verb
➤規則動詞	regular verb

➤不規則動詞	irregular verb
➤三人称単数現在の"s"	the third-singular present "s"

（品詞～名詞と関連語）

名詞	noun [náun]
➤可算名詞	count [countable] noun
➤不可算名詞	uncount [uncountable] noun
➤一般名詞	common noun
➤固有名詞	proper noun
➤抽象名詞	abstract noun
➤物質名詞	material noun
➤集合名詞	collective noun

（品詞～代名詞と関連語）

代名詞	pronoun [próunaun]
➤人称代名詞	personal pronoun
➤指示代名詞	demonstrative pronoun
➤所有代名詞	possessive pronoun
➤関係代名詞	relative pronoun

（品詞～形容詞と関連語）

形容詞	adjective [ædʒiktiv]
➤指示形容詞	demonstrative adjective ＊ some，any など。

14
学
ぶ

（品詞～副詞・接続詞ほか＆関連語）

副詞	adverb [ǽdvəːrb]
➤関係副詞	adverbial pronoun
接続詞	conjunction [kəndʒʌ́ŋkʃən]
不定詞	infinitive [infínətiv]
冠詞	article
➤定冠詞	definite article
➤不定冠詞	indefinite article
限定詞	determiner [ditə́ːrminər]
数詞	numeral
現在分詞	present participle
過去分詞	past participle
間投詞	interjection [ìntərdʒékʃən]

（文法項目）

文法	grammar
時制	tense ＊present（現在），past（過去），future（未来），sequences of time（時制の一致），present perfect（現在完了），past perfect（過去完了），future perfect（未来完了）
進行形	progressive [prəgrésiv] ＊past progressive（過去進行形），present progressive（現在進行形），present perfect progressive（現在完了進行形），future progressive（未来進行形）

不定詞	infinitive
動名詞	gerund [dʒérənd]
能動態	active voice
受動態	passive voice
話法	narration ＊direct narration（直接話法），indirect narration（間接話法）
同格	apposition [æ̀pəzíʃən]
結合性，つながり	cohesion [kouhíːʒən] ＊文法・意味に基づく文と文をつなげる関係。
省略	ellipsis [ilípsis]
倒置	inversion [invə́ːrʒən]
比較	comparison [kəmpǽrisn]
比較級	comparative form
最上級	superlative form
仮定法	subjunctive mood
分詞構文	participle construction

15.

仕事をする

1. 企業形態，企業内組織，経営，契約

★企業形態など

（法人）

会社，企業	company [kʌ́mpəni] ＊launch a new company （新会社を発足させる）
会社，企業，事務所	firm [fə́ːrm]
大企業，大会社	big company ／ giant (company)
法人，株式会社	corporation [kɔ̀ːrpəréiʃən] ＊特に子会社を持つ大企業を指す。
中小企業	small and medium-sized company
有限会社《略：Ltd.》	limited company
合資会社	limited partnership company
合名会社	general partnership company ／ unlimited partnership company
合同会社《略：LLC》	limited liability company
医療法人	healthcare [medical] corporation
社団法人	incorporated association
財団法人	incorporated foundation
宗教法人	religious corporation
学校法人	education [school] corporation

社会福祉法人	social welfare corporation
特定非営利活動法人（NPO法人）	incorporated non-profit organization
独立行政法人	incorporated administrative agency
会計事務所	accounting firm
法律事務所	law office [firm]
コンサルティング会社	consulting firm
オーナー会社	owner-managed firm
企業，会社	business ／ company
上場企業	listed company ＊Our company is now listed.（我が社は上場しました）
ベンチャー（企業）	venture business ＊新しい技術の開発，新しい市場の開拓（新製品や新サービスの提供）を志向した事業，または起業家が設立した規模は小さいが専門分野に強い企業。
企業，会社，大事業	enterprise [éntərpràiz]
コンツェルン，複合企業体	conglomerate [kənglάmərət]
多国籍企業	multinational company
人材派遣業	temporary staffing agency
派遣労働者	temporary worker

株，株式	stock ／ share ＊stock は会社が発行する株全体，share は stock を分割した売買の単位としての株，株式。
株式会社	stock company〈米〉／ joint-stock company〈英〉
株主	stockholder〈主に米〉／ shareholder〈主に英〉
株主総会	stockholders' meeting
株式上場	stock listing

（主な業種）

製造業者，メーカー	manufacturer ／ maker ＊computer manufacturer（コンピュータメーカー），auto maker（自動車メーカー）
卸売り業者，問屋	wholesaler [hóulsèilər]
小売業	retail business [trade] ＊retailer（小売業者），retail store [shop]（小売店）
建設業	the construction industry
建設・土木	construction and engineering
情報通信業	information and communications
運輸業，郵便業	transport and postal activities ＊home-delivery service ／ door-to-door delivery service（宅配業，宅配便）

金融業，保険業	finance and insurance ＊banking（銀行業）
不動産業・物品賃貸業	real estate and goods rental and leasing
宿泊業・飲食サービス業	accommodations, eating and drinking services
教育・学習支援業	education, learning support
医療・福祉	medical, health care and welfare
医薬品	pharmaceuticals
ヘルスケア機器・用品	health care equipment and supplies
バイオテクノロジー	biotechnology
航空宇宙・防衛	aerospace and defense
商社・流通業	trading companies and distributors
航空貨物・物流サービス	air freight and logistics
旅客航空輸送業	airlines
海運業	marine
陸運・鉄道	road and rail
メディア	media
インターネット・カタログ販売	internet and direct marketing retail
情報技術サービス	IT services
電気通信サービス	telecommunication services
食品	food products
家庭用品	household products

15 仕事をする

275

（系列）

系列会社	affiliate ／ affiliated company
持ち株会社，親会社	holding company
親会社	parent company
子会社	subsidiary company
同族会社	family business
本社	headquarters 〈単・複両扱い〉
本店	the head [main] office
支店	branch [brǽnʧ]
店舗，販売店	outlet [áutlèt]
工場直売店	factory outlet
チェーン店	chain ＊同一資本による直系のホテル，スーパー，レストラン，映画の興行網など。
チェーンストア	chain store ／ multiple store 〈主に英〉
代理店	agency

★企業内組織

（人事）

人事	personnel [pə̀:rsənél]
人事管理	personnel management
人材	human resources
業績，成果	performance [pərfɔ́:rməns]
能力	competence

才能	talent
技能	skill
適性能力	competence [kámpətns]
熟練の技，専門知識	expertise [èkspəːrtíːz]
業績評価	performance review ／ performance evaluation
多面的人事査定，360度評価	360-degree feedback
（経験豊富な）助言者，よき指導者	mentor
余剰人員	surplus personnel
企業家，起業家	entrepreneur [ɑ̀ːntrəprənə́ːr]
起業家精神	entrepreneurship
取締役会	board of directors ／ corporate board of directors
（～に）異動になる	be transferred to ...
（～に）左遷される	be relegated to ...
（～に）栄転する，昇進する	be promoted to ... ＊ He has been promoted to the head office. （彼は本店に栄転になりました）
（～に）降格される	be demoted to ...

（役職）

取締役	director [dəréktər]
会長	chairperson ／ chairman 《男性》／ chairwoman 《女性》
名誉会長	honorary chairman
社長	president
代表取締役	representative director
代表取締役社長	President and Representative Director
副社長	vice-president ＊米国では社長に次ぐ地位とは限らない。特定の部門を担当する部長級にあたる。
専務取締役, 専務	executive managing director ＊専務というポジションは一般的に米英にはない。
常務取締役, 常務	managing director ＊常務というポジションは一般的に米英にはない。
社外取締役	outside director
相談役（企業の）	senior adviser
顧問弁護士	legal adviser ／ legal counsel
管理職	managerial position
中間管理職	mid-level manager ／ middle-management
上級管理職	executive
部長	department manager ＊sales department manager（販売部長）

課長	section manager
課長代理	acting [deputy] section manager
課長補佐	assistant section manager
係長	sub-section manager ／ chief clerk
最高経営責任者《略：CEO》	Chief Executive Officer
最高執行責任者《略：COO》	Chief Operating Officer
最高財務責任者《略：CFO》	Chief Financial Officer
最高情報責任者《略：CIO》	Chief Information Officer
最高技術責任者《略：CTO》	Chief Technical Officer

★経営

（経営方針）

経営	management
経営理念	management principles ＊企業の存在意義・価値観や将来の理想像を言葉で表現したもの。経営をするうえで最も大切にしている考えや根本となる考え。
経営方針	business policy ／ management policy ＊企業活動の方向性を決める重要な方針で，事業を展開するために必要な行動や考え方を目標として具体的に示したもの。
経営戦略	management strategies

事業戦略	business strategies ＊formulate business strategies（事業戦略を立てる）
経営戦術	management tactics
事業戦術	business tactics ＊look over one's business tactics（事業戦術を見直す）
スウォット分析	SWOT analysis ＊経営戦略立案のための分析方法のひとつ。市場における自社の強み（Strength）と弱み（Weakness）という内部分析、市場環境における機会（Opportunity）と脅威（Threat）という外部分析の4つの要因を組み合わせて最適な意思決定を行うための分析手法。
（事業の）多角化，多角経営	diversification [dəvə̀ːrsəfikéiʃən]

（企業統治）

企業統治，コーポレート・ガバナンス	corporate governance ＊株主などによる企業経営への関与・統制。
コンプライアンス	compliance [kəmpláiənsi] ＊企業などにおける法令遵守。
企業の社会的責任	corporate social responsibility
社会的責任投資	socially responsible investment
定款（ていかん）	the articles of an association／the statutes of a company
倫理規定	code of ethics

営利主義，金儲け主義	commercialism [kəmə́ːrʃlìzm]

（ビジネスプラン）

ケース・スタディ	case study ＊個人・集団・状況の一定期間における変化などを調査・研究する。
経営計画（書），事業計画（書）	business plan
ビジネスモデル	business model
長期計画	long-term planning
中期計画	medium-term planning
短期計画	short-term planning
要員計画	workforce planning
人員管理計画	staff management plan
設備計画	facility plan
製造計画	manufacturing plan
実現可能調査	feasibility study
採算性，営利性，収益性	profitability ＊achieve profitability（収益性を高める）
採算性の高い	profitable ＊highly profitable business（非常に収益性の高い事業）
採算性の低い	unprofitable ＊unprofitable product（採算の取れない製品）

（マーケティング）

市場	market
マーケティング	marketing ＊市場調査，商品企画，宣伝広告といった企業活動を指す。do marketing（マーケティングを行う）

市場調査	marketing research
市場性	marketability
マーケット分析	market analysis
一次データ	primary data ＊調査者自身が原資料や直接観察などから集めた情報。他者が収集したものや文献などは「二次データ（secondary data）」。
マーケティング・ミックス	marketing mix ＊製品（Product），価格（Price），プロモーション（Promotion），流通チャネル・物流（Place）という４つのＰを効果的に組み合わせた，標的市場においてマーケティング目標を達成する手段。
（広告以外の）販売促進活動《略：SP》	sales promotion ＊消費者の購買意欲を刺激し，また販売店の業務を効率化することで商品の販売増進を図る企業の活動。ただ認知してもらうだけでなく，その先にある購入（契約）を目的としている。店頭プロモーション，イベントプロモーション，キャンペーンプロモーション，ダイレクトマーケティングなどがある。

★契約・入札・特許

（契約）

契約，契約書	contract [kántrækt]
契約内容	terms of a contract
契約者	contractor
契約を交わす	exchange contracts
契約を履行する	fulfill a contract
契約を更新する	renew a contract
更新	renewal
仮契約，一時契約	temporary contract

商談	business negotiation
下請け契約	subcontract
契約違反	breach of contract
契約に違反する	break a contract
契約を取り消す	cancel a contract
契約金，頭金	down payment

注文（する）	order
～に注文する	place an order with ...
ＡにＢを注文する	put an order to A for B
受注する	receive an order
注文品を完納する	complete an order
クーリングオフ	cooling-off

（入札）

入札	bidding
入札する	bid
入札手続き	bidding procedures
入札価格	bidding price／the price tendered

（特許）

特許	patent [pǽtnt]
特許を申請する	apply for a patent
特許を与える	give [grant] a patent
特許権利	patent rights
特許権利所有者	patentee

2. 生産・製造，価格・販売，財務など

★生産・製造

（生産）

生産	production
生産者	producer
生産量	production quantity
受注生産	make-to-order production
生産管理	production control
品質管理	quality control
原価管理	cost management
工程管理	process control
安全管理	safety control
安全第一	safety first
検査台	inspection table
生産能力	production capacity
過剰生産	overproduction
生産不足	underproduction
生産効率	production efficiency
組立工場	assembly plant
組み立てライン	assembly line
生産ライン	production line
歩留まり	yield rate ＊製造した商品のうちの良品割合。
シックスシグマ	Six Sigma ＊米モトローラ社が開発した品質管理の手法。
圧縮機械	compressor
圧力容器	pressure vessel
研磨機	grinding machine
延伸加工機	swaging machine

ベルトコンベアー	conveyer belt
製造工程能力	manufacturing process capability
価値分析	VA (=value analysis)
コスト・テーブル	cost table ＊原価計算のための表データ。
製造指示書	production order
ファクトリーオートメーション，工場自動化	factory automation
稼働率	capacity utilization

（製品）

製品	product
商品コンセプト	product concept
ブランド品	brand-name product
製品のラインアップ，品ぞろえ	line-up
製品群	product line
製品ライフサイクル	product life
製品構成	product mix

★価格・販売

（価格）

価格	price
手頃な価格	reasonable price
手が届く価格	affordable price
値上げする	raise prices
値下げする	lower prices

生産者価格	producer price
卸売価格	wholesale price
小売価格	retail price
希望小売価格	suggested retail price
オープン価格	open price
消費者価格, 消費者物価	consumer price
消費者物価指数《略：CPI》	consumer price index
総額表示	total price with tax
下取り価格	trade-in price
市場価格	market price

（価格設定）

価格設定	pricing
価格戦略	pricing strategy
コスト・プライシング	cost-based pricing *費用に基づき製品やサービスなどの価格を設定すること。
マーケット・プライシング	market pricing *市場価格を考慮して価格を決定すること。
バリューベース・プライシング	value-based pricing *個別の品物やサービスのみによる他社との価格比較を回避し, 全体の所要コストの観点から価格設定をすること。
価格競争	price competition
価格支配力	price leadership

（販売ルート）

販売経路	sales channel
店頭販売	over-the-counter sale

通信販売	mail-order sale
訪問販売	door-to-door sale
委託販売	consignment sale
フランチャイズ契約	franchise contract
カタログ・ショッピング	catalog shopping
在庫一掃セール, クリアランス・セール	clearance sale

（e コマース）

e コマース	e-commerce (electronic commerce)
インターネットショッピング	e-shopping
オンライン・ショッピング	online-shopping
仮想商店街	cybermall ／ virtual mall
ネットオークション	net auction
電子決済	electronic settlement
電子署名	electronic signature
電子マネー	electronic money
インターネット銀行	Internet bank
モバイル・バンキング	mobile banking
ネット販売	sales through the Internet
テレビショッピング	TV shopping

15 仕事をする

（在庫）

在庫，在庫表	inventory [ínvəntɔ̀ːri]
在庫管理	inventory management
倉庫	warehouse
在庫不足	inventory shortage
発注要請書	purchase requisition
在庫調査する	take inventory
在庫にタグ付けをする	tag the inventory
財産目録	inventory of property
在庫回転率	inventory turnover
在庫調整	inventory adjustment
在庫調整する	adjust the stock
販売時点情報管理《略：POS》	point of sale

（流通）

流通，物流	distribution
流通システム	distribution system
流通チャンネル，販売ルート	distribution channel
流通産業	distribution industry
マーチャンダイジング	merchandizing ＊小売店が販売価格や時期などを含め，どのような製品をどんな販売形態で提供すべきかを総合的に企画立案すること。

納品書	delivery note ／ bill of goods

（広報）

広報《略：PR》	public relations ／ advertisement
バナー広告	banner advertisement
広告代理店	advertising agency
パブリシティ，広報	publicity
商標	trademark
ブランド	brand [brǽnd]
セールスポイント	selling point
差別化戦略	differentiation strategy
製品の差別化	product differentiation
プル戦略	pull strategy
プッシュ戦略	push strategy

（顧客サービス）

顧客	customer
依頼人，得意客	client [kláiənt]
顧客ロイヤリティ	customer loyalty ＊顧客が企業やその商品に対して高い信頼を持ち，持続的に顧客であり続けること。
顧客維持	customer retention
顧客流出	customer defection
顧客満足度《略：CS》	customer satisfaction

カスタマイズ	customize
アフターサービス	after-sales service
コールセンター	all center
クレーム，苦情	complaint
商品回収（する），リコール（する）	recall
製品保証書	product warranty
保証	warrant [wɔ́(ː)rənt] ＊購入された商品を一定期間は無料で修理，手入れすることを約束するサービス。
消費者心理	consumer confidence
消費者団体	consumers' association

（支払い）

現金払い	cash payment
現金払いする	pay in cash
代金引換《略：COD》	cash on delivery
一括払い	lump-sum payment
分割払い	installment payment ＊pay in installments（分割で支払う）
滞納金，未払金	《常に複数形で》arrears
支払延滞分	overdue payment
買掛金	account payable
売掛金	account receivable
返金する	refund ／ give a refund

（競争）

企業業績	business performance
競争力	competitiveness ＊competitive price（他社と競争力ある価格）
市場占有率	market share ＊set [gain] a 60% market share（60 パーセントの市場占有率を得る）
独占	monopoly
寡占	oligopoly [àləgάəpəli]
カルテル	cartel [kɑːrtél]

（M&A）

合併・買収，吸収合併	M&A (merger and acquisition)
株式公開買付け《略：TOB》	takeover bid
敵対的買収	hostile takeover
ポイズン・ピル，毒薬	poison bill ＊当該企業を魅力のないものにする企業買収防衛策。
バックエンド・ピル	back-end pill ＊敵対的買収に対する対抗措置のひとつ。
クラウン・ジュエル	crown jewel ＊買収標的となった会社の資産の最優良部分。将来高成長が見込まれる事業部など買収をしかける側のいちばん欲しいところ。
大型合併	megamerger
提携	team-up [tíːm ʌp] ／ tie-up ／ link-up

15 仕事をする

★財務など

（資産）

資産，財産	assets [ǽsets]
固定資産	fixed assets
流動資産	current [liquid] assets
流動比率	current ratio
運用資産	working assets
繰延資産	deferred charges
減価償却	depreciation [diprìːʃiéiʃən]
減価償却費	depreciation expense
残余価値	residual value
資産回転率	asset turnover
ポートフォリオ，資産構成	portfolio
資産価値	property value ／ asset value

（資本金）

資本金	capital [kǽpətl]
資本を調達する	raise capital
資金調達	capital raising
運転［経営］資本《略：WC》	working capital
自己資本	equity capital

★主な会計用語

（財務諸表）

財務諸表	financial statements
貸借対照表（B/S）	balance sheet
連結財務諸表	consolidated financial statements
単独財務諸表	non-consolidated financial statements
損益計算書（P/L）	profit and loss statement
損益分岐点	break-even point
キャッシュフロー計算書	cash flow statement《略：CFS》／ statement of cash flow
株主資本等変動計算書	statement of changes in net assets

（主な貸借対照表の項目）

勘定科目	account title
流動資産	current [liquid] assets
現金	cash
小口現金	petty cash
当座預金	checking accounts
普通預金	savings accounts
定期預金	time deposits
受取手形	trade notes receivable
売掛金	trade accounts receivable

貸倒引当金	allowance for doubtful accounts
売買目的有価証券	trading securities
商品	merchandise
原材料	raw materials
仕掛品	work in process
製品（完成品）	finished goods
貸付金	loans receivable
未収利息	interest receivable
未収配当金	dividends receivable
前払費用	prepaid expenses
繰延税金資産	deferred tax assets
固定資産	non-current assets
有形固定資産	property, plant and equipment
建物	buildings
構築物	structures
機械装置	machinery and equipment
運搬具	vehicles
減価償却費累計額	accumulated depreciation
土地	land
建設仮勘定	construction in progress
無形固定資産	intangible assets
のれん	goodwill

特許権	patents
著作権	copyrights
商号商標権	trade marks and trade names
投資その他の資産	investments and other assets
投資有価証券	investment securities
敷金	lease deposits
創立費	organization costs
開業費	start-up costs
流動負債	current liabilities
支払手形	notes
買掛金	accounts payable, trade
短期借入金	short-term loans payable and long-term debt with current maturities
コマーシャル・ペーパー	commercial paper
1年内償還予定の社債	bonds due within one year
未払法人税等	income taxes payable
賞与引当金	allowance for employees' bonuses
役員賞与引当金	allowance for bonuses for directors and company auditors

15 仕事をする

未払費用	accrued expenses
前受金	advances by customers
前受収益	deferred revenues
繰延税金負債	deferred tax liabilities

固定負債	non-current liabilities
社債	bonds
長期借入金	long-term debt
繰延税金負債（固定）	deferred tax liabilities
退職給付引当金	employees' pension and retirement benefits
役員退職慰労引当金	retirement benefits for directors and company auditors
受入保証金	deposits received

株主資本	shareholders' equity
資本金	capital stock
資本剰余金	capital surplus
資本準備金	capital reserve
利益剰余金	retained earnings
利益準備金	legal reserve of retained earnings
自己株式	treasury stock, at cost

★主な損益計算書の項目

（売上高）

売上高	sales [séilz]
売上値引および戻り高	sales returns and allowances
売上割引	sales discount

（売上原価）

売上原価	cost of sales
仕入	purchases
仕入値引・返品	purchases returns and allowances
仕入割引	purchases discounts
売上総利益, 粗利益	gross margin ＊「総売上高」から売上値引などを差し引いた「純売上高」から「売上原価」を控除した額。

（販売費及び一般管理費〔販管費〕）

販売費及び一般管理費	Selling, general and administrative expenses
給料	salaries expense
賃金	wages expense
賞与	seasonal bonuses
退職給与	employee retirement allowance
法定福利費	payroll taxes expense
研修費	training expense
広告宣伝費	advertising expense

旅費交通費	traveling expense
交際費	entertainment expense
郵送費	postage expense
水道光熱費	utilities expense
修繕費	repairs expense
事務用品費	stationery expense
保険料	insurance expense
図書費	library expense
会費	membership expense
減価償却費	depreciation expense
寄附金	donations expense
販売促進費	promotional expense
貸倒損失	bad debt expense
営業利益	operation income ＊本来の営業活動から生じた営業収益から営業費用（売上原価・一般販売管理費）を差し引いた差額。

（営業外収益）

営業外収益	non-operating revenue ／ non-operating expenses ＊有価証券売却益や受取利息など，企業の本来の営業活動以外からもたらされた収益。
受取利息	interest income
受取配当金	dividend income
有価証券売却益	gain on sale of securities
持分法による投資利益	equity in earnings of affiliates

為替差益	net foreign currency translation gain

（営業外費用）

営業外費用	non-operating expenses
支払利息	interest expense
有価証券売却損	loss on sale of securities
持分法による投資損失	equity in losses of affiliates
雑損失	miscellaneous loss
経常利益	ordinary income

（特別利益）

特別利益	special income
固定資産売却益	gain on sale of property, plant and equipment and intangible assets
投資有価証券売却益	gain on sale of investment securities
関係会社株式売却益	gain on sale of shares of subsidiaries and affiliates

15 仕事をする

（特別損失）

特別損失	special expenses
固定資産除却損	loss on disposal of property, plant and equipment and intangible assets
固定資産売却損	loss on sale of property, plant and equipment and intangible assets
減損損失	loss on impairment
投資有価証券評価損	loss on devaluation of investment securities
投資有価証券売却損	loss on sale of investment securities

（キャッシュフロー）

キャッシュフロー，現金収支	cash flow
営業キャッシュフロー《略：OCF》	operating cash flow
投資キャッシュフロー《略：ICF》	investing cash flow
財務キャッシュフロー《略：FCF》	financial cash flow
現金同等物	cash equivalents
割引キャッシュフロー《略：DCF》	discounted cash flow
フリーキャッシュフロー《略：FCF》	free cash flow .

キャッシュフロー・マネージメント	cash flow management ＊会計上の利益ではなく、手元にあるキャッシュ（現金と現金等価物）を重視する経営手法。

（その他～コスト関係）

原価計算	cost accounting ＊ cost-efficient ／ cost-effective（費用効率のよい），costly（費用がかかる）
固定費	fixed cost
変動費	variable cost
機会原価	opportunity cost
営業費用	operating expenses
家賃	rent
出資	capital subscription
出資する	provide capital
準備資金	reserve funds
資本投資	capital investment
設備投資	capital spending
過剰設備，生産能力過剰	overcapacity
間接費，諸経費	overhead

（その他～収益関係）

売上収益	sales revenue
年商	annual sales
（販売達成目標の）ノルマ	sales quota
営業利益率	operating ratio

収益	earnings ／ proceeds ／ returns ／ gains ＊achieve [generate] higher returns（より高い収益を得る［生む］）
利幅	markup ＊売値から仕入れ値を差し引いた差額。
利益率，利益幅	profit margin ＊売上に対する利益の割合。
売上総利益率	gross profit ratio ＊売上高に対する売上総利益（粗利益）の比率。
限界利益，貢献利益《略：CM》	contribution margin ＊売上高から変動費を差し引いた差額。
儲かる《形》	profitable ＊a highly profitable business（非常に収益性の高い事業）
赤字（続き）の，採算の合わない［取れない］	money-losing ＊money-losing division（赤字部門）
（利益の）分配，支払い	disbursement
税引き前利益，経常利益	pretax profit
総資本利益率	return on asset
株主［自己］資本利益率《略：ROE》	return on equity
投資利益率《略：ROI》	return on investment
内部利益率《略：IRR》	internal rate of return
当期純利益	bottom line

税引き前当期純利益	net income before taxes
特別損益	special profits and losses
純損益	net profits and losses
純益，純益率	net profits ＊総収入から総経費を差し引いた利益。

（監査）

監査（する）	audit [ɔ́ːdit]
監査役	auditor
内部監査	internal audit
外部監査	external audit
監査法人	audit corporation
監査報告	audit report

（負債）

負債，借金	debt [dét]
多重債務	multiple debts
多重債務者	multiple debtor
債務者，負債者	debtor [détər]
債権者	creditor [kréditər]
有利子負債	interest-bearing debt
債務，負債	liabilities [làiəbílətiz]
固定負債	fixed liabilities
流動負債	current liabilities
長期借入金	long-term liability
短期借入金	short-term liability
連帯責任	joint liability

15 仕事をする

289

（倒産）

倒産，破産	bankruptcy [bǽŋkrʌptsi]
倒産する	go [become] bankrupt ／ go [become] insolvent ／ go out of business
店じまいする	close down
破綻する	collapse ／ fail
（店・工場などが）休業する	shut down
破産	insolvency
自己破産	personal bankruptcy ＊file for personal bankruptcy（自己破産する）
清算，整理，破産	liquidation [lìkwidéiʃən]
（会社・組織などの）再建	reestablishment

（債権回収）

債権回収	debt collection
債務不履行	default ＊債務者が返済できなくなった状態。
債務救済	debt relief ＊多重債務者に対する救済措置。
債権放棄	debt forgiveness ＊経営が悪化した企業に対して，銀行が融資の返済の一部または全部を免除する制度。

3. 労働，事務用品・文房具など，職業，雇用など

★労働

（労働）

労働，仕事，職業	work [wə́ːrk]《不可算名詞》
仕事，職業	job [dʒáb]《可算名詞》
求職申し込み	job application
人員削減	job cut
転職	job hopping
求職者	job hunter ／ job seeker
就職活動	job hunting
就職口	job offer
職務満足，働きがい	job satisfaction
労働，賃金労働	labor ／ labour《英》
労働力	labor force
職業	occupation
職業病	occupational disease
知的職業，専門的職業	profession
知的職業人，専門家，プロ選手，プロの	professional
職業上の資格	professional qualifications
プロ意識，プロ根性，職人気質（かたぎ）	professionalism
天職	vocation [voukéiʃən]
経歴，履歴	career [kəríər]

労働法	labor law ／ labor legislation
労働基準法	labor standards act
労働契約法	labor contracts act
労働組合法	labor union act
労働関係調整法	labor relations adjustment act
労働安全衛生法	industrial safety and health act
労働者災害補償保険法	industrial accident compensation insurance act

（労働者）

労働者，就労者	worker ／ laborer
従業員	staff ＊集合的な意味で用いることが多く，通例，単複両扱い。
働き者	hard worker
仕事熱心な，勤勉な	hard-working
やり手	go-getter ＊ambitious go-getter（野心を持ったやり手）
非常勤労働者，パート	part-time worker
フリーター	job-hopping part-time worker ／ job-hopping part-timer

15 仕事をする

ニート	NEET（Not in Employment, Education or Training）
ホワイトカラー	white-collar worker
肉体労働者	blue-collar worker
熟練労働者，技能労働者	skilled worker
熟練工	artisan [ά:rtəzən]
専門職従業者	professional
出稼ぎ労働者	migrant worker
外国人労働者	foreign worker
不法就労者	illegal worker

★事務用品・文房具など

（事務用品・文房具など）

ホワイトボード	whiteboard / dry-erase board
ホワイトボードマーカー	dry erase marker
ホワイトボード消し	whiteboard eraser / dry erase eraser
カラーマグネット	whiteboard magnet
マグネットクリップ	magnet clip

ボールペン	ballpoint pen
万年筆	fountain pen
シャーペン	mechanical pencil 〈米〉 / automatic pencil 〈英〉 / propelling pencil 〈英〉

シャーペンの芯	mechanical pencil lead [léd]
鉛筆	pencil
鉛筆削り	pencil sharpener
電動鉛筆削り	electric pencil sharpener
消しゴム	eraser 〈主に米〉 / rubber 〈英〉
筆箱，筆入れ	pen [pencil, brush] case
蛍光ペン	highlighter
マーカー，マジックペン	marker / marker pen 〈英〉
油性マーカーペン	permanent marker
水性マーカーペン	washable marker

修正液	whiteout 〈主に米〉 / correction fluid [flù:id]
修正ペン	correction pen
修正テープ	correction tape

紙，用紙	paper * copier paper（コピー用紙）
画用紙，製図用紙	drawing paper
ノート，メモ帳	notebook
付箋	sticky note / Post-it 〈商標〉 / tag / slip / label * put a tag（付箋を付ける）
はがき	postcard

便箋	writing paper ／ letter paper		（のりなどの）接着剤	adhesive [ədhíːsiv, æd-]
封筒	envelope		糊（のり）	glue [glúː]
ガムテープ	packing tape		ものさし，定規	ruler [rúːlər] ＊use a ruler to draw a (straight) line（定規を使って線を引く）
グリーティングカード	greeting card			
リーガルパッド，法律用箋	legal pad ＊黄色の罫線入りレポート用紙。		分度器	protractor
			三角定規	triangle〈米〉／ set square〈英〉
（はぎ取り式の）メモ用紙[帳]	notepad		コンパス（製図用の）	compasses〈単数扱い〉
			しおり	bookmark
請求書	bill ／ invoice		クリップ	(paper) clip ＊clip documents together（書類をクリップで留める）〈動詞〉
伝票	pay slip			
領収書	receipt [risíːt]			
			クリップ入れ	(paper) clip holder
文房具，事務用品，筆記用具	stationery〈集合的に〉		クリップボード	clipboard
			バインダー	binder
筆記用具	writing materials ／ writing implements		電卓	calculator
			シール	seal
			拡大鏡，虫眼鏡	magnifying glass
ハサミ	scissors [sízərz]〈発音注意〉		輪ゴム	rubber band〈米〉／ elastic band〈英〉
カッターナイフ	cutter ／ utility knife		ファイル	file
セロテープ	Scotch tape〈米〉〈商標〉／ Sellotape〈英〉〈商標〉 ＊scotch-tape two pieces of paper（2枚の紙をセロテープで留める）〈動詞〉		パンチ	punch
			シュレッダー	shredder
			画びょう，押しピン	thumbtack〈米〉／ pushpin〈米〉／ drawing pin〈英〉
ホチキス	stapler			
ホチキスでとめる	staple ＊staple the manuscript（原稿をホチキスでとめる）		コピー機	copy machine ／ photocopier ／ copier
ホチキスの針	staple		プリンター	printer

15 仕事をする

293

プリンターの トナーカート リッジ	printer toner cartridge
複合機のプリ ンター	multifunction printer
ファクス	fax [fǽks] ／ fax machine ／ facsimile [fæksíməli]

書類整理棚	file cabinet
積み重ねトレー	stacking tray
間仕切	partition
棚	shelf
本棚	bookshelf
コートクロゼット	coat closet
机	desk
デスクパッド	desk pad

蛍光灯	fluorescent light
空調	air-conditioner

備品室	supply room
収納室	storage room
会議室	conference room
従業員ラウンジ	employee lounge
自動販売機	vending machine
掲示板	bulletin board （米） ／ notice board （英）

★職業

（主なビジネス・経営・経済関係の職業）

実業家	businessman ／ businesswoman ／ business person
人事部長	human resource manager
営業部長	sales manager
マーケティン グ部長	marketing manager
広告部長	advertising manager
広報部長	public relations manager
（広告・サー ビス業の）顧 客担当部長	account executive
経理部長	accounting manager
経理を担当し ている	be in charge of accounting
総務部長	administrative manager ／ chief of general affairs
セールスマン	salesman ／ salesperson ＊I am a car salesman. （私は車のセールスマンを しています）
在庫管理員	stock clerk
秘書	secretary
税理士	licensed tax accountant
会計士	accountant

公認会計士	certified public accountant 《米》／ chartered accountant 《英》
経営コンサルタント	management consultant
企業アナリスト	corporate analyst
不動産鑑定士	real estate appraiser 《米》／ estate surveyor 《主に英》
宅地建物取引主任者	registered real-estate transaction manager
社会保険労務士	certified social insurance and labor consultant
エコノミスト	economist

（主な法律・政治・外交関係の職業）

判事	judge ／ justice * justice は《米》では「最高裁判事」，《英》では「最高法院判事」を指す。
検察官，検事	(public) prosecutor
弁護士	lawyer [lɔ́:jər, lɔ́iər] ／ jurist [dʒúərist]《米》／ attorney《米》 * lawyer は法律を専門とするすべての人に用いられる一般的な語。「弁護士に相談する」は consult a lawyer。
弁理士	patent lawyer
司法書士	judicial scrivener [dʒu:díʃəl skrívənər]
行政書士	public notary [pʌ́blik nóutəri]

執行官	enforcement officer
司法修習生	paralegal
政治家	politician ／ statesman《男性》／ stateswoman《女性》 * statesman [stateswoman] は《米》《英》ともに「立派な政治家」というよい意味で用いる。politician は米国では「政治屋」と悪い意味で使われることがある。
外交官	diplomat [dípləmæt] 《アクセント注意》

（主な保安関係の職業）

警察官	police officer
海上保安官	coast-guard officer
警備員	security guard
守衛	gatekeeper
救急救命士	paramedic
救急隊員	ambulance attendant
消防士	firefighter
看守	(prison) guard
麻薬捜査官	narcotics agent
自衛官	(Japan) Self-Defense Force official
陸上自衛官	Ground Self-Defense Force personnel
海上自衛官	Maritime Self-Defense Force personnel
航空自衛官	Air Self-Defense Force personnel
交通誘導員	traffic controller

15 仕事をする

軍人	serviceman ／ servicewoman ／ service member

（主な機械・電気・化学関係の職業）

技術者	engineer
機械技術者	mechanical engineer
機械修理技術者	machinist
機械設計技術者	mechanical design engineer
電気技術者	electrician
電気主任技術者	chief electrical power engineer
電気通信技術者	telecommunication technician
配管技術者	piping engineer
化学技術者	chemical engineering technician
高圧ガス作業主任者	chief high pressure gas technician

（主な建築・土木関係の職業）

建築家	architect [ɑ́ːrkitèkt]
一級建築士	first-class architect
建設技術者	architect engineer
建築技師	building engineer
土木設計技士	civil design engineer
土木技師	civil engineer
建築設備士	building equipment engineer

測量士	land surveyor
測量技術者	land survey technician
建設労働者	construction worker
配管工	plumber [plʌ́mər]
大工	carpenter
左官	plasterer

（主なコンピュータ関係の職業）

Web デザイナー	web designer
Web プログラマー	website programmer
コンピュータ・プログラマ	computer programmer
コンピュータ科学者	computer scientist
システムエンジニア《略：SE》	systems engineer
システムアナリスト	systems analyst
情報処理技術者	data processing technician
カスタマーエンジニア《略：CE》	customer service technician
セキュリティエンジニア	security engineer
CG デザイナー	CG designer
ゲームプログラマー	game programmer
CAD オペレーター	CAD operator

（主な運輸・ドライバー関係の職業）

運転手	driver
タクシー運転手	taxi driver

バス運転手	bus driver
トラック運転手	truck driver
(電車・地下鉄などの) 運転士	motorman
(バス・列車などの) 車掌	conductor 《米》／ guard 《英：列車の車掌》
(バスの) 車掌	bus conductor
パイロット, 操縦士	pilot
(飛行機の) 機長	captain
客室乗務員	flight attendant
配達ドライバー	delivery driver
配送員	delivery person
お抱え運転手	chauffeur [ʃóufər]

(主な生産・製造関係の職業)

鋳物工	caster
鍛冶工	smith
石切工	quarrier
旋盤工	turner
溶接工	welder
組立工	assembler
整備士	mechanic
プレス成型工	press mold operator
自動車整備士	automobile mechanic
航空整備士	aircraft mechanic
織工	weaver
洋裁師	dressmaker
農夫	farmer
職人	artisan [ɑ́ːrtəzən]

(主なサービス業・飲食業関係の職業)

接客係, 係員	attendant
メートルディー	maitre d' [mèitrə díː] (=maitre d'hotel) 《仏》＊「レストランの案内係」「ホテルの支配人」
ウェイター	waiter ／ waitperson 《米》
ウェイトレス	waitress
(店・ホテルなどの) 会計係, レジ係	cashier [kæʃíər] 《アクセント注意》
理髪師	barber
美容師	beautician ／ hairdresser
メイクアップアーティスト	makeup artist
ネイルアーティスト	nail artist
調理師	cook
料理長	chef
菓子職人	confectioner [kənfékʃənər]
観光ガイド	tour guide
添乗員	tour conductor
販売員	salesclerk 《米》／ shop assistant 《英》
ホテルスタッフ	hotel staff
家政婦	housekeeper
介護ヘルパー	home care [health] aide ／ personal care worker 《米》／ home help 《英》
ベビーシッター	baby-sitter

15 仕事をする

店員	store clerk [stɔ́ːr klɔ́ːrk]
受付係	receptionist

（主な芸術関係の職業ほか）

芸術家	artist [áːrtist] ＊ほかに「絵のうまい人」の意味があり，I'm not an artist. と言えば「そんなに絵はうまくありませんよ」のニュアンス。
画家	painter
彫刻家	sculptor
木彫家	woodcarver
陶芸家	potter [pá(ː)tər | pɔ́tə] ／ ceramic artist
木工職人	woodcrafter ／ woodworker
ガラス工芸家	glazier
美術品鑑定士	connoisseur [kànəsɔ́ːr]
デザイナー	designer
グラフィックデザイナー	graphic designer
イラストレーター	illustrator
アートディレクター	art director
インテリアデザイナー	interior designer
照明デザイナー	lighting designer
（映画・テレビなど動画の）カメラマン	cameraman
写真家	photographer
漫画家	cartoonist

スタイリスト	stylist
庭師	gardener
ゴミ収集作業員	sanitation worker

（主な介護・福祉関係の職業）

介護士	care worker
介護福祉士	certified care worker
精神保健福祉士	mental health welfare worker
ホームヘルパー，訪問介護員	home caregiver 〈米〉／ home carer 〈英〉＊ home helper は和製語。
ケアマネジャー	care manager
福祉司	welfare worker
生活指導員	welfare counselor
家庭相談員	family counselor
児童福祉司	child welfare worker
身体障害者福祉司	disability social worker
心理カウンセラー	psychology counselor
医療ソーシャルワーカー	medical social worker
ホームヘルパー	home attendant

（主な出版・マスコミ・言語関係の職業）

作家，著者	writer ／ author
編集者	editor
小説家	novelist
随筆家，エッセイスト	essayist
雑誌記者	magazine writer

校正者	proofreader	放送記者	TV reporter ／ network journalist
装丁家	book (cover) designer	新聞記者	newspaper reporter
評論家	critic [krítik]	ジャーナリスト	journalist ＊報道記事の記者・編集者・報道関係者など。
翻訳家	translator [trænsléitər]		
通訳者	interpreter [intə́rprətər]	気象予報士（テレビ・ラジオの）	weather forecaster
コピーライター	copywriter		
コラムニスト（新聞・雑誌の）	columnist [ká(:)ləmnist | kɔ́l-]	（公務員）	
脚本家	scriptwriter	公務員	government employee ／ government worker ／ public servant
劇作家	dramatist ／ playwright		
シナリオ作家	screenwriter	国家公務員	national government employee
アナウンサー	announcer	地方公務員	local government employee
ニュースキャスター	newscaster		
報道記者（新聞・ラジオ・テレビなどの）	reporter	特別公務員,特別職	special government employee

15 仕事をする

★雇用など

（雇用）

雇用	employment [emplɔ́imənt]
就職試験	employment test
再雇用する	re-employ
再雇用制度	re-employment system
雇用者，雇い主	employer
被雇用者	employee
条件付き雇用	conditional employment
雇用期間	period of employment
（採用者の）試用期間	trial period ／ probation period
終身雇用	lifetime employment ／ lifelong employment ／ career-long employment
年功序列	seniority system
採用率，就職率	hiring rate
新規採用	new hiring
人員募集	recruitment [rikrúːtmənt]
社風	corporate culture
雇用安定（化）	employment stabilization
職業能力	employability [emplɔ̀iəbíləti]
人材引き抜き，ヘッドハンティング，スカウト	headhunting

（就職）

就職希望者	job-hunter ／ job seeker
求職，仕事探し，就職活動	job search
就職活動	job hunting
仕事を探す	job-hunt 《動》
就職する	get [find] a job [work] ／ find employment ／ get a position ／ get employed ＊ get a job with ABC Company（ABC 社に就職する）
履歴書	resume [rizʒúːm]《米》／ curriculum vitae [váiti	víːtai]《英》《略：cv》 ＊ resume の両方の e（あるいは最後の e だけ）にアクセントマーク（é）をつけることがある。send [write] one's résumé（履歴書を送る［書く］）。
就職の面接（試験）	job interview
面接官	interviewer
被面接者，面接を受ける人	interviewee
就職難	job shortage

（就労資格）

資格	qualification [kwàləfikéiʃən]
労働ビザ（査証）	working visa
グリーンカード，永住許可証	green card

（勤務形態）

労働条件	work conditions ／ job conditions ／ labor conditions
仕事量	workload
契約条件	terms of contract
労働時間	working hours
週労働時間	workweek ＊a five-day workweek （週5日労働）
残業	overtime [óuvərtàim]
残業する	work overtime
サービス残業	unpaid overtime
シフト，交代勤務時間	shift ＊day shift （昼間勤務）, night shift （夜間勤務）
フレックスタイム	flextime
裁量労働制	free time system
不当労働行為	unfair labor practice
在宅勤務	work from home ／ remote working ／ telework(ing) ／ telecommuting
ソーホー《略：SOHO》	small office home office
ジョブ・シェアリング	job sharing
アルバイト，バイト，パート	part-time job
ワーキング・ホリデー	working holiday ＊働いて生活費を補いながら，通学，奉仕活動，旅行など，海外での生活が体験できるように政府間で取り決められた制度。

勤務評定	job assessment
業績給	performance-based pay
社内研修	on-the-job training ／ on-the-job development ／ on-the-job learning
社外教育	off-the-job learning
欠勤率	absentee rate
（正当な理由のない）常習的な欠勤	absenteeism

（休暇・労災）

有給休暇	paid leave
（母親の）育児休暇	maternity leave [mətə́rnəti lì:v]
（父親の）育児休暇	paternity leave [pətə́rnəti lì:v]
労災	work-related accident
労災認定する	recognize as a work-related accident
過労で倒れる	collapse from overwork
労災死	work-related death
過労死	death from overwork
補償	compensation

（昇進・降格）

昇進	promotion [prəmóuʃən]
昇進する	promote
出世する	get ahead
昇給	pay raise [péi rèiz] ／ pay hike ／ pay increase
定期昇給	regular pay raise
不定期昇給	irregular pay raise
降格	demotion
減給	pay cut
差別待遇	discriminatory treatment

（退職・辞職・解雇）

定年退職（制度）	age limit system
定年退職	retirement
希望退職	voluntary retirement
早期退職制度	early-retirement system ／ early-retirement program
退職金	retirement allowance
雇用延長	expansion of employment
辞職［辞任］する	resign [rizáin] ＊He resigned as president. (彼は社長を辞任した)
辞職，辞任	resignation [rèzignéiʃən]

（離職・失業）

離職（率）	turnover
転職する	change jobs [careers]
転職	job-hopping
レイオフ，一時帰休，一時解雇	layoff

（失業）

失業	unemployment ／ joblessness
失業率	unemployment rate ／ jobless rate
失業給付金，失業手当	unemployment benefits ／ unemployment compensation

（労働運動）

労働組合	labor union ／ trade union ／ worker's union
企業内組合	company union
労働運動	labor movement
団体交渉	collective bargaining [kəlèktiv báːrginiŋ]
ロックアウト，工場閉鎖	lockout [lákàut]
ストライキ，スト	strike [stráik] ／ walkout
和解	settlement

索引

342

つ

386

中村 秀和（Hidekazu Nakamura）

Writer / Director / Educational Content Creator

ART QUEST, Inc. CEO

http://www.artquest.jp

【執筆協力】
Christian Storms

© Hidekazu Nakamura, 2024, Printed in Japan

何から何まで言ってみる
暮らしの英単語9000

2024年1月31日　　初版第1刷発行
2024年10月31日　　　第2刷発行

著　者　中村 秀和
制　作　ツディブックス株式会社
発行者　田中 稔
発行所　株式会社 語研
　　　　〒101-0064
　　　　東京都千代田区神田猿楽町2-7-17
　　　　電　話 03-3291-3986
　　　　ファクス 03-3291-6749
組　版　ツディブックス株式会社
印刷・製本　シナノ書籍印刷株式会社

ISBN978-4-87615-426-5 C0082

書名　クラシノ エイタンゴ キュウセン
著者　ナカムラ ヒデカズ
著作者および発行者の許可なく転載・複製することを禁じます。

定価はカバーに表示してあります。
乱丁本，落丁本はお取り替えいたします。
株式会社語研
語研ホームページ https://www.goken-net.co.jp/

本書の感想は
スマホから↓